Texas Tales

Texas Tales

Stories That Shaped a Landscape and a People

Myra Hargrave McIlvian

SUNSTONE
PRESS

SANTA FE

Sunstone books may be purchased for educational, business, or sales promotional use.
For information please write: Special Markets Department, Sunstone Press,
P.O. Box 2321, Santa Fe, New Mexico 87504-2321.
Body typeface › Chaparral Pro
Printed on acid-free paper
∞
eBook 978-1-61139-493-1

Library of Congress Cataloging-in-Publication Data

Names: McIlvain, Myra Hargrave, author.
Title: Texas tales : stories that shaped a landscape and a people / by Myra Hargrave McIlvain.
Description: Santa Fe : Sunstone Press, 2017. | Description based on print version record and CIP data provided by publisher; resource not viewed.
Identifiers: LCCN 2017003678 (print) | LCCN 2017012082 (ebook) | ISBN 9781611394931 | ISBN 9781632931634 (softcover : alk. paper)
Subjects: LCSH: Texas--Biography--Anecdotes. | Texas--History--Anecdotes.
Classification: LCC F386.6 (ebook) | LCC F386.6 .M397 2017 (print) | DDC 976.4--dc23
LC record available at https://lccn.loc.gov/2017003678

SUNSTONE PRESS IS COMMITTED TO MINIMIZING OUR ENVIRONMENTAL IMPACT ON THE PLANET. THE PAPER USED IN THIS BOOK IS FROM RESPONSIBLY MANAGED FORESTS. OUR PRINTER HAS RECEIVED CHAIN OF CUSTODY (COC) CERTIFICATION FROM: THE FOREST STEWARDSHIP COUNCIL™ (FSC®), PROGRAMME FOR THE ENDORSEMENT OF FOREST CERTIFICATION™ (PEFC™), AND THE SUSTAINABLE FORESTRY INITIATIVE® (SFI®). THE FSC® COUNCIL IS A NON-PROFIT ORGANIZATION, PROMOTING THE ENVIRONMENTALLY APPROPRIATE, SOCIALLY BENEFICIAL AND ECONOMICALLY VIABLE MANAGEMENT OF THE WORLD'S FORESTS. FSC® CERTIFICATION IS RECOGNIZED INTERNATIONALLY AS A RIGOROUS ENVIRONMENTAL AND SOCIAL STANDARD FOR RESPONSIBLE FOREST MANAGEMENT.

WWW.SUNSTONEPRESS.COM
SUNSTONE PRESS / POST OFFICE BOX 2321 / SANTA FE, NM 87504-2321 /USA
(505) 988-4418 / ORDERS ONLY (800) 243-5644 / FAX (505) 988-1025

For Stroud

Glynn Hargrave McIlVain

June 7, 2017

Contents

4
Colliding Cultures / 73

5
Power In A Skirt / 93

6
Newcomers Make Their Mark / 129

Preface

Tales from Texas is a collection of stories that share the character and complexity of a land and a people known for swagger, big hats, and loud mouths. I began writing the tales as a weekly blog in an effort to paint with a broad brush the challenges and the dreams that created a place known, but not always understood, throughout the world.

I became interested in history as a college freshman when my professor revealed the Puritans as people with all the bumps and sores and crazy notions that made their story alive. That class taught me that history is the unpolished story of individuals who move around on the landscape of their time. That is what this book is all about—people who colored Texas bold.

My first taste of telling the little-known stories came as a freelancer writing Texas Historical markers, those signs travelers see along the highways and affixed to special buildings and standing at gravesites. Story-telling expanded into longer articles about those markers and finally into guide books that told the stories and directed lovers of history to little-known sites around the state.

Social media opened a new opportunity in the format of blogging to reach out to readers around the world who nurture a curiosity about Texas and its people. Readers began suggesting that I put all the blog posts into a book that offered a chance to hold the Texas story in a permanent format suited for gifts and personal enjoyment.

I am fortunate that the Texas Historical Commission gave me the opportunity to hone my skills, to discover the unpublished tales of Texas, and to practice my love of story-telling. The University of Texas Press published three of my five guidebooks and faithful readers have encouraged me to write three historical novels—all Texas stories. Finally, my husband Stroud has been my biggest supporter, always at my side, encouraging me to keep writing.

1

Padres, Preachers, Politicians, and Power Brokers

"Example is not the main thing in influencing others. It is the only thing."

—Albert Schweitzer

Padre Island, Hope and Heartbreak

The treasures of Padre Island, playground on the Texas Gulf coast, reveal far more than sandy beaches and sand dunes rippling in the steady breeze. Buried beneath the sand castles lies a legacy of grand visions and broken dreams.

Padre, a textbook example of a barrier reef island, edges the Texas coast for 113 miles from Corpus Christi to the Rio Grande. Its width varies from a few hundred yards to about three miles. South Padre, the town on the southern tip of the island, enjoys a year round tourist industry from spring breakers who hang from the rafters of elegant hotels to families who come at other times in search of a retreat from the summer heat and winter chill.

Stretching toward the southern end of the island, Queen Isabella Causeway rises majestically over Laguna Madre and the Intracoastal Canal offering a panoramic view of high-rise hotels and condominiums, surf and sand, fun and sun of South Padre Island. In anticipation of an exciting holiday, it is easy to overlook the life-size statue of Padre José Nicolás Ballí welcoming visitors with open arms to his island.

A secular Catholic priest, Padre Ballí was born about 1770 in Reynosa, Mexico, the oldest son of a wealthy Spanish colonial family who owned over a million acres in South Texas. Padre Ballí served as a missionary in the villas and haciendas along the lower Rio Grande. In 1800 he made application for a Spanish land grant of 11.5 leagues (about 154,280 acres) on "Corpus Christi Island," one of the many names given to Padre Island.

Padre Ballí took his nephew Juan José Ballí as a partner, had the land surveyed, and established the island's first settlement in 1804 called Rancho Santa Cruz, which lay about twenty-six miles north of the present town of South Padre. The Ballís ran large herds of cattle, horses, and sheep on their land, and the padre established a mission to Christianize the Karankawa Indians who lived on the island.

Although the title did not clear until 1829, eight months after his death, Padre Ballí left one-half of the land to his nephew Juan and the other one-half to Juan's brothers and sisters. Juan left for a time and then returned and lived on the island until his death in 1853.

Meantime, in 1847 a three-masted schooner wrecked during a storm near the south end of the island. Captain John F. Singer, his wife, Johanna, and several sons were the only survivors. The family built a house using material from their ship and wreckage of other vessels they found along the shore.

Mrs. Singer had inherited wealth, and in 1851 she bought the Ballí interest in Rancho Santa Cruz. The family rebuilt the ranch, raised large herds of cattle and grew vegetables, which they took by raft across Laguna Madre to sell in Port Isabel. John Singer became wreck master of Padre Island and made huge profits salvaging material that washed ashore from storm-wrecked ships. In 1861 Singer told the postmaster in Brownsville that he had received a letter from his brother Merritt informing John that the $500 he loaned Merritt enabled him to obtain a patent on a device making the newly invented sewing machine more practical for home use. His invention made Merritt quite wealthy and he was thanking John by authorizing him to draw $150,000 from Merritt's bank.

John Singer planned to establish a steamship line to New Orleans; however, the Civil War halted Singer's dream. The Singers, known as Union sympathizers, fled to the mainland near Corpus Christi. Stories circulated that they buried gold and silver worth $62,000 before they left.

The Union army occupied Padre Island for the duration of the war, used the cattle to feed their forces, and tore the ranch apart to build their military installation. When the Singers returned after the war, they discovered shifting sand destroyed every landmark, every guide to where they hid their treasure. After his wife died, John Singer left the island and never returned.

Over the years, the Ballí family continued selling pieces of their land believing they retained mineral rights. The next man with grand ideas was Sam Robertson, a railroad official who laid the tracks for the St. Louis, Brownsville, and Mexico Railway in the early 1900s. He saw potential in the rich delta land near the Rio Grande and organized investors to develop present San Benito north of Brownsville. Then he turned his creative genius to Padre Island. The stretch of hotels and condominiums visitors see today in South Padre represents the dream Robertson visualized forty-five years too early. He saw Padre and Brazos islands as Texas' biggest resort areas. He confidently began developing the full length of Padre Island—established a ferry across the bay from Corpus Christi in 1927 and built twelve miles of asphalt road to his Twenty-Five Mile Hotel. He completed a toll bridge to Brazos Santiago from Boca Chica at the mouth of the Rio Grande, built a bridge between Padre and Mustang islands (at the north end of Padre), and constructed a two-way causeway across Laguna Madre at the midway point on the island.

The stock market crash in 1929 forced him to abandon his scheme. The 1933 hurricane blew away all the new roads and bridges, bringing a devastating end to Robertson's last big dream. He died in 1938.

Ballí descendants grew to over 300 and continued legal claims over the years to collect royalties from the vast oil and gas mineral deposits. The Ballí heirs won an $11 million award in 2005 claiming they were defrauded out of their mineral rights in 1938. The Texas Supreme Court ruled against the Ballís in 2008, claiming the family filed their suit after the statute of limitation expired.

When vacationers romp in the Gulf water, build sand castles along the beach, and relax in the luxurious hotels, not many know this tiny strip of sand offers a history rich in grandiose plans and devastating disappointments.

Preacher With A Gun

William "Choctaw Bill" Robinson, a Baptist preacher, came to Texas in 1848 and preached with his gun beside his Bible until his death at the age of eighty-nine. By the time Robinson reached Texas, his first wife was dead after giving birth to eight children. He and his second wife had another six children, and all the family accompanied Robinson to Texas where he became licensed as a Baptist minister. The tall, dark, longhaired and bearded preacher believed so strongly in his gospel message that he did not hesitate to exhort those beliefs in four-hour sermons. He became known as "Choctaw Bill" after word spread that a group of Choctaws departed during one of his sermons saying, "White man lie. Him talk too long."

Part of Choctaw Bill's enthusiasm included his certainty that only members of the Baptist faith knew the "true religion." Since Methodists made up the largest number of non-Baptists on the frontier, Choctaw Bill carried a copy of *Methodist Discipline* and used every Bible text at his command to prove his Methodist brothers wrong.

Over the years Robinson organized or served as pastor of at least twenty Baptist Churches. Since ministers of that day did not receive a salary, Robinson supported his wife and large family by farming and raising cattle. Some report that he carried his branding iron regularly and was rather free in its use. On weekends he rode a horse (some say a mule) to preach in settlements that did not have organized congregations. At one village, it is reported that ruffians had broken up earlier attempts to hold services. Robinson leaned his rifle against the pulpit and placed a pistol on each side of his Bible. He looked intently at the congregation for a few minutes and then announced that he was there to preach the gospel by the grace of God and his trusty rifle. There were no disturbances.

In later years Choctaw Bill operated a sawmill and gristmill at Hazel Dell, one of the roughest towns in Texas, located between present-day Waco and Abilene. Some claim that of the first ten settlers in the community, Choctaw Bill is the only one who escaped a violent death. He held services under the shade of an oak tree across the road from a store and saloon and preached to the patrons who came from the saloon. The tree became known as "Choctaw Robinson Oak."

Despite arriving in Texas with considerable wealth, Robinson at the age of eighty wrote to the state Baptist paper, "I have preached on the Texas frontier from the Red River to the Rio Grande. Now I am old and feeble with no finances and no home. Help me what you can." Choctaw Bill died a poor man in 1898.

From Slave to Powerful Politician

Despite being born into slavery in 1846, Norris Wright Cuney did not live an ordinary slave's life. His education and other opportunities led the way to his becoming one of Texas' most powerful black political leaders of the nineteenth century. Cuney's white father, Colonel Philip Cuney, one of the largest landholders in Texas, owned 105 slaves and operated the 2,000-acre Sunnyside Plantation near Hempstead. Cuney's mulatto mother Adeline Stuart was one of the colonel's slaves, but she worked as the colonel's chief housekeeper and bore eight of his children. Cuney's mother made sure that he and his siblings never lived in the slave quarters or worked as plantation field hands. In fact, Cuney learned to play the bass violin and carried it with him when he traveled on business trips with his father.

During the time Cuney was growing up, his powerful father also had a white family. Colonel Cuney embarked on a political career as a member of the House of Representatives of the Republic of Texas in 1843, and at about the same time he married his second wife. He was a delegate to the 1845 Convention that voted for Texas annexation to the United States, and he served as Brigadier General in the Texas Militia. After Texas joined the Union, Cuney's father was elected to both the Texas State Legislature and the State Senate. In 1853, not long after Colonel Cuney married his third wife, he left his plantation in the hands of an overseer and moved all his family with him to Houston, including Adeline Stuart and her children. That same year he began freeing his black children, starting with Cuney's older brother Joseph who was sent to the Wylie Street School for blacks in Pittsburgh, Pennsylvania. Over the years Colonel Cuney freed all his black children and their mother Adeline Stuart.

When Cuney and his sister Jennie were freed in 1859, Cuney was sent to school in Pittsburgh, and Jennie traveled to Europe for her education. Jennie later passed as a member of the white community.

The Civil War disrupted Cuney's studies, and he spent the war years working on steamboats between Cincinnati and New Orleans where he met and was influenced by black leaders such as P.B.S. Pinchback who later served for thirty-five days as Louisiana's first black governor. After the Civil War, Norris Wright Cuney settled in Galveston near the homes of his mother and brothers. He began studying the law and took advantage of being a literate, educated mulatto, and son of a wealthy white man. He worked with the Freedmen's Bureau and the Union League during the Reconstruction-era to push former slaves to the voting booth, which resulted in more than 100,000 blacks voting annually into the 1890s. When the Reconstruction Legislature established a public school system, Cuney worked to ensure that tax money also went to black students within the segregated system.

Cuney married Adelina Dowdie, a schoolteacher who also was the daughter of a mulatto slave mother and a white planter father. The Cuneys had two children, and since both parents were musical—Cuney played the violin and Adelina was a singer—their home was filled with art and music, and they emphasized education. Their son Lloyd Garrison Cuney, named for the abolitionist William Lloyd Garrison, became an official in the Congregational Church. Their daughter Maud Cuney Hare studied at the New England Conservatory of Music in Boston and became an accomplished pianist, folklorist, writer, and community organizer in Boston. She wrote *Norris Wright Cuney: A Tribune of the Black People* (1913), a biography of her father.

Over the years of Cuney negotiating with the white elite and despite serious strikes, unionized blacks finally gained access as workers on Galveston's docks. After being elected Texas national committeeman in the Republican Party in 1886, Cuney became Texas Republican party chairman, which was the most powerful position of any African-American in the South at that time. However his position did not sit well with some Republicans in Texas and throughout the country, which led to some in the party trying to have black leaders expelled. Cuney coined the term "Lily-White Movement" to describe the Republican effort.

In 1889 Cuney was appointed U.S. Collector of Customs in Galveston, the highest-ranking position of any black man in the South in the late nineteenth century, however, Cuney's death that year coincided with efforts across the South to disenfranchise black and poor white voters. Laws were passed to make voter registration difficult, and Texas instituted poll taxes and white primaries that greatly reduced the number of black voters from the high of 100,000 in the 1890s to less than 5,000 by 1906. During the Great Depression, racial strife in the unions dissolved much of the labor cooperation that had been established between blacks and whites.

Despite Cuney's legacy, which inspired other black leaders, and the designation by some historians of the period between 1884 and 1896 as the

"Cuney Era," it would take the passage in the 1960s of the Civil Rights laws before the right to vote was restored to blacks across the South.

An account of Norris Wright Cuney's life is portrayed in Douglas Hale's *A Southern Family in White & Black: The Cuneys of Texas*.

Rabbi Henry Cohen of Galveston and the World

In 1888 Rabbi Henry Cohen, a wiry little man barely five feet tall with a booming British accent, arrived in Galveston to serve Temple B'nai Israel. He wore black, tuxedo-type suits, starched white bow ties, and white shirts with stiff cuffs on which he wrote his appointments and sermon notes. Dressed in this formal getup, he rode about Galveston on a bicycle from jail cell to hospital bed to Galveston's red-light district, ministering to and helping every person in need regardless of his or her faith or lack thereof. He was known for saying "there is no such thing as Episcopalian scarlet fever, Catholic arthritis, or Jewish mumps."

He may have been small but he showed a giant's determination when facing injustice. Upon hearing of a girl being kept in prostitution against her will, he tore across town on his bicycle, barged into a whorehouse, and found the girl half naked. Wrapping her in a blanket and walking with one arm around her and the other guiding his bike, he led her to a clothing store where he told the merchant to "fit her out from head to foot." He took her home to his wife and found her a job. His fearlessness quickly created a name for himself in the back streets of Galveston. When a prostitute on her deathbed asked to be given a "Christian burial," Rabbi Cohen received a request to conduct the service. Not bothering to ask what kept a Protestant minister from showing up, Rabbi Cohen marched to the cemetery where he found a large crowd from the brothels. He led the service reading passages from the New Testament.

Rabbi Cohen played a major role in providing jobs and homes for immigrants throughout the South and Midwest. Beginning in the 1880s, millions of European Jews had arrived on the East Coast without the means to survive in the strange new world. They settled with fellow emigrants in the slums of New York's Lower East Side where several families crowded into tiny rooms, even sleeping in hallways. Unable to speak English or find work, they huddled in congested, impoverished conditions that led to child labor and crime. Wealthy Jewish philanthropists who had come to America and prospered were embarrassed that members of their community lived in such squalor. They devised a plan that allowed immigrant ships to bypass Ellis Island and go instead to Galveston where Rabbi Cohen set up an immigration office and personally met most every ship.

Since he traveled extensively preaching in cities and towns that did not have a rabbi, he had developed a network of contacts in communities that let him know what occupations they needed. It might be cobblers, hat makers, tailors, carpenters or clerks. El Paso, for example, asked to have trunk, harness and saddle makers, whereas Corsicana needed weavers, spinners, and doffers for its new textile industry. Between 1907 and 1914 Rabbi Cohen and the organization that became known as the Galveston Movement placed 10,000 immigrants in jobs and homes west of the Mississippi.

After World War I the Ku Klux Klan began making inroads in towns across the South and Midwest. When the Klan came to Galveston and tried to get a parade permit, Rabbi Cohen and his friend Father James Kirwin used their considerable influence with the city commissioners to block the parade. The Klan never got a foothold in Galveston.

Rabbi Cohen worked for prison reform, often having prisoners paroled into his care. He found them jobs, loaned them money, and remained in touch with them after they began new lives. After he heard of a man raping a twelve-year-old girl and being set free, Rabbi Cohen worked for years to get legislation to raise the age of consent in Texas from ten years old to eighteen.

Rabbi Cohen heard that a Russian had arrived illegally and faced immediate deportation. He responded in his usual dramatic fashion; he boarded a train for Washington D.C. and secured a meeting with President William Howard Taft. Explaining to the president that the immigrant faced a firing squad if he returned to his own country, Rabbi Cohen added that he could find the man a job in Texas.

President Taft listened courteously, and then said he could do nothing for the gentlemen. The president added, "I certainly admire the way you have gone to so much trouble and expense for a member of your faith."

"Member of my faith!" Rabbi Cohen bellowed. "This man is a Greek Catholic. A human life is at stake." President Taft picked up the phone and arranged for the man to be released to the custody of the fiery little rabbi.

Rabbi Cohen was fluent in eleven languages; he held the respect of presidents, governors, and cardinals; he wielded influence in state and national legislatures; but the legacy that he would claim with pride was that he made life more bearable for thousands of his fellow human beings.

Ma Ferguson, Housewife Governor

Society in 1924 expected women to stay at home, run the household, raise the children, and follow the lead of their husbands. In that atmosphere Miriam A. Ferguson became the first female governor of Texas. She ran her campaign while maintaining that she was just a little homemaker, and that when she was elected, her husband would be running the show. She used a two-pronged approach that appealed to newly franchised women and to men who expected their wives to remain in the background. She told women's groups that she was running for governor to do what any wife and mother would do to restore her family's good name. "Enemies," she said had conspired against her husband, James Edward Ferguson, the first governor in Texas to be impeached, convicted, and removed from office. Before male audiences she played the retiring wife, deferring to her husband who winked and nodded at the farmers and small business people who were reveling in the idea of turning the tables on the politicians that had declared Jim Ferguson ineligible to ever again serve as governor. When a man asked Jim what he thought of women's suffrage, Miriam kept a straight face when her husband delighted the male audience by saying, "If those women want to suffer, I say let them suffer!"

Miriam played down her background as the daughter of a wealthy Bell County family, a well-educated woman who had attended Baylor Female College before she married Jim Ferguson. A cultured and reserved woman, she felt the campaign slogan "Me for Ma and I Ain't Got a Durned Thing Against Pa," didn't suit her dignity, but she did not complain because it fit the role she was playing. Calling her "Ma" got started after a reporter for the Houston *Press* wrote campaign stories in which he referred to Miriam as M.A. Ferguson. Before long, "M.A." became "Ma." The campaign song "Put on Your Old Gray Bonnet," was another part of the image that Miriam endured because she and her husband understood how to make her more appealing to an electorate. She told voters that, if elected, she would follow the advice of her husband and Texas would get "two governors for the price of one."

She often delighted audiences by announcing that Jim would make the speech, and then she would sit down. Those who knew her, especially her two daughters, claimed that she was anything but retiring. They said she was the strong one in the family, enforcing the rules, and Jim was the quiet pushover. The couple met after Miriam's father died and her mother employed a young lawyer, James Edward Ferguson, to settle the estate. Jim Ferguson, the son of a Methodist preacher, was from the other side of the tracks, and he felt fortunate after a long pursuit to have finally won the reluctant Miriam.

When James Ferguson ran for governor as an anti-prohibitionist Democrat in 1914, Miriam remained silent despite her strong disapproval of drinking. (No alcohol was ever served in the governor's mansion, and she did not allow swearing or card playing.) During his second term, when he was impeached and convicted of ten charges, including misapplication of public funds and receiving $156,000 from an unnamed source, she continued to keep her silence.

Although Miriam was a teetotaler, she followed her husband's policies and supported the "wets" in the fight against prohibition. She campaigned against the Ku Klux Klan that was gaining influence across the country. After her election she got an anti-mask bill passed, which was aimed at the KKK, only to have it thrown out as unconstitutional. Despite trouncing her Republican rival, or perhaps because of it, the rumors of wrongdoing plagued her two-year term as governor. The Fergusons were obsessed with the plight of prisoners, even going as a family to visit jails. Miriam Ferguson pardoned an average of 100 convicts a month (over 4,000 during her two non-consecutive terms), claiming many of them had only violated prohibition laws. Her fiscal conservatism led many to believe that her liberal acts of freeing prisoners were meant to relieve the cost of housing them in the penitentiary. Critics claimed that prisoners paid Jim Ferguson for their pardons and paroles and that Miriam should be impeached. No proof was ever presented. The accusations that she and "Pa" were accepting bribes from prisoners and that the Fergusons received lucrative kickbacks in exchange for state highway contracts allowed Attorney General Daniel Moody to beat Miriam Ferguson in the election of 1926.

When the Texas Supreme Court refused to allow Jim Ferguson to run for governor in 1930, Miriam Ferguson stepped forward, only to be defeated. Again in 1932, after voters had experienced the full impact of the Great Depression, Miriam Ferguson won her second term by blaming then Governor Ross Sterling for the state's woes. She promised to lower taxes and cut state expenditures, condemning Sterling for waste, graft, and political favoritism—many of the vices for which she was blamed in her first term.

The second time around, Governor Miriam Ferguson tried unsuccessfully to get a state sales tax and corporate income tax. She continued her liberal policy of pardons and paroles and did not suffer the attacks of her first term. She made one last run for governor in 1940, polling more than 100,000 votes, only to lose to W. Lee O'Daniel.

Miriam Ferguson listed the accomplishments of her administration as taxing gasoline for highway improvements and taxing tobacco for school financing. She signed a law establishing the University of Houston as a four-year institution and was most proud of a more strenuous bootlegging law. In her bias against alcohol, she had even demanded that Amon C. Carter, nationally known civic booster and founder/publisher of the Fort Worth *Star Telegram*, resign as chair of the Board of Directors of Texas Tech because he was seen drinking liquor ("drunk as a biled owl") at the Texas-Texas A&M football game. He did not resign.

After all the years of being accused of getting rich at the public trough, financial troubles in 1935 caused the Fergusons to lose their Bell County ranch.

Governor James Ferguson suffered a stroke and died in 1944. Governor Miriam Ferguson, who remained a controversial member of the brand of populism known as "Fergusonism," died of heart failure on June 25, 1961.

Dan Moody Beats the KKK

Daniel James Moody, Jr. set a record number of firsts: the youngest, at age twenty-seven, elected as Williamson County Attorney; the youngest district attorney at twenty-nine; the youngest attorney general of Texas at thirty-two; and the youngest governor of Texas at thirty-four.

Dan Moody was a tall, redheaded young man in a hurry. He entered the University of Texas at seventeen and began taking law courses two years later. He started practicing law before he finished school and then served in the National Guard and the U.S. Army during World War I. The year he returned to his home in Taylor after World War I, his political career got underway. The circumstances that propelled him into state and national attention occurred while he served as district attorney of Williamson and Travis counties at the peak of the Ku Klux Klan's resurgence in 1923.

The national KKK preached white supremacy and hatred of blacks, Jews, Catholics, immigrants, gamblers, and people who broke the law. In Williamson County, the Klan targeted a young salesman, R. W. Burleson, who stayed on business trips at the home of a young widow. A Baptist preacher and anti-Catholic lecturer sent a note to Burleson that bore the seal of the Georgetown KKK No. 178 in which the preacher warned Burleson to end his relationship with the young widow. Burleson burned the note and threatened to kill any Klan member who bothered him. On Easter Sunday in 1923, Burleson, the widow, and another couple were stopped on a country road by two cars bearing eight or ten men wearing robes and hoods. The men dragged Burleson from his car, hit him with a pistol, threw him in one of the cars, and took off with his feet still hanging out the door. They placed a heavy trace chain around his neck and tied it to a tree. Holding a pistol to his head as a warning not to cry out, the KKK members removed his clothing, and used a four-foot-long, three-inch-wide leather strap to lash Burleson's naked back with about fifty licks. Throughout the beating, Burleson was questioned and threatened. Finally, he was loaded into a pickup, driven to the lawn of the Taylor City Hall and fastened by the chain to a tree. They poured tar or creosote over his head and body and left him there in the darkness of early evening.

Burleson freed himself, and with the chain still around his neck, he walked toward the light at a nearby boarding house. The law officers who were called testified that Burleson had cuts and bruises all over his body, that his back was raw. He had creosote or tar on his hair, ears, face, shoulders, and body. A machinist cut the chain from Burleson's neck and a doctor used oil to remove the tar. The constable testified that blood soaked through the mattress on which Burleson was placed—the worst beating the constable had ever seen. It was "as raw as a piece of beef from the small of his back to the knees; and in many places the skin had been split and the flesh was gaping open."

Five men were arrested, and the local Klan collected funds to retain the best legal team, including a state senator and his brother. Enormous crowds and media from all over the United States came to hear the trial of each defendant. By the time the last man was sentenced to prison, District

Attorney Dan Moody—the first prosecuting attorney in the United States to win a legal battle against the Ku Klux Klan—had launched his political career.

Despite the Klan's opposition, Dan Moody was elected Attorney General in 1925 at the same time Miriam "Ma" Ferguson won her first election as governor. Within a few months, scandals began developing over highway contracts. Moody took the case to court and proved that $32 million in contracts—three times their actual value—had been awarded to Ferguson friends. He sealed his political future by traveling to Kansas City and Dallas to retrieve about $1 million of the state's cash and securities that had been paid for the contracts. Armed with claims of Ferguson fraud, Dan Moody challenged the sitting governor in one of Texas' nastiest political campaigns.

Moody married Mildred Paxton, a newspaperwoman, just as the campaign got underway, and the press labeled it the "Honeymoon Campaign." While Dan Moody focused his charges against the Fergusons' corruption, Jim Ferguson made speeches for his wife's reelection in which he called Mildred a "lipstick" that would chase Moody around the Governor's Mansion with a rolling pin. On a platform supporting prohibition, women's suffrage, and other positions that the Fergusons opposed, Daniel Moody handily beat Governor Miriam Ferguson.

In addition to becoming Texas' youngest governor, Moody's inauguration was the first to be held outdoors; it was the first to be broadcast on the radio and received national coverage because of Moody's fame; and it was the first Texas election that denied a sitting governor a second term. As a reform governor, Moody served two terms, ending the Ferguson's convict-pardon policies; reorganizing the state highway department, including a program for a connected network of roads; and cutting the cost of highway construction by almost half. He also created an office to audit state accounts.

At the end of Moody's second term, he returned to a private law practice, and after coming in third in the 1942 primary for the U.S. Senate, his only political defeat, he never again ran for public office. He became known as an opposition leader to the New Deal and to the renomination for a fourth term of President Franklin Roosevelt. He supported Lyndon Johnson's rival in his election to the U.S. Senate in 1948. As a Democrat, Moody supported Republican Dwight D. Eisenhower for both his presidential victories and Richard M. Nixon for president in 1960. Dan Moody represented the conservative faction in the Democratic Party that eventually led, with the Nixon campaign, to the wholesale movement in Texas of Democrats to the Republican Party.

Politics and Salt Did Not Mix

Travelers driving east from El Paso may find it difficult to imagine the longtime controversies that took place in the shadow of the majestic Guadalupe Peak rising from the desert floor. The tallest mountain in Texas soars 8,751 feet above its western flank where an ancient salt flat sprawled across 2,000 acres. The salt and gypsum formed dunes that flowed from three to sixty feet above the desert landscape. This treasure, lying about 100 miles east of present-day El Paso, was so important for the region's Native Americans that for centuries they viewed it as a sacred place where they secured salt for tanning hides, for use as a condiment, and as a preservative. Things began to change when the Spanish discovered the site in 1692. The villages, such as San Elizario that developed along the Rio Grande near present-day El Paso, viewed the Salt Flats as common land to be used by all the peoples of the region. The Indians, especially the Apaches, did not welcome the intruders who defied Indian attack to gather the precious resource. Even after the 1848 Treaty of Guadalupe Hidalgo that ended the Mexican-American War and drew Mexico's boundary with Texas at the Rio Grande, the Tejano farmers and ranchers supplemented their meager incomes by selling the salt as far away as the rich mining regions in Northern Mexico where it was used in smelting the silver.

More problems arose after the Civil War when El Paso came under the control of prominent Republicans who tried to claim the Salt Flat and charge a fee for Mexican-Americans to gather the salt that had been free for many generations. Meantime, Charles H. Howard, a Democrat, arrived in El Paso in 1872 with the intention of turning the Republican stronghold into a Democratic electorate. Howard was successful for a time, got appointed district attorney and worked against the Republicans and the "Anti-Salt Ring." Then, Howard changed course, filed on the salt deposits in the name of his new father-in-law, which infuriated the area Hispanics who felt besieged by the Republicans and the Democrats. When Howard had the sheriff arrest local Tejano men to keep them from collecting the salt, a group of enraged local citizens held Howard prisoner until he agreed to relinquish all rights to the salt deposits.

Eventually, in frustration over the attempted control of their community and their economic future, the Tejano people of San Elizario closed the entire county government and replaced it with committees (community juntas). The Anglos, who numbered less than 100 out of a population of 5,000, called on the governor who sent a detachment of Texas Rangers. When Howard arrived with the Rangers, a two-day siege ended with the surrender of the Texas Rangers, the first time in its history that a company of Rangers surrendered to a mob. Howard and the ranger sergeant and two others were executed. The disarmed Rangers were sent out of town, the Tejano leaders fled to Mexico, and residents looted the buildings. Twelve people were killed and fifty were wounded. No one was ever charged with a crime.

San Elizario paid a hefty price for its demands: the county seat was removed to El Paso; the 9th Cavalry of Buffalo Soldiers re-established Fort Bliss to patrol the border and watch the local Mexican population; the railroad bypassed San Elizario; its population declined; and the Mexican Americans lost their political influence in the area.

By the 1930s, floods had deposited silt across much of the flats, and salt gathering came to a halt. Today the ghost town of Salt Flats, which consists of a scattering of mostly deserted buildings, edges the highway. Scattered vegetation grows out of the silt covering the old salt beds. Spotted among the weeds, barren white stretches still offer a glimpse of the precious early-day resource.

Galveston Rising

The 1900 storm that struck Galveston still carries the designation as the worst natural disaster in U.S. history. Periodically, storms flooded the marshy bayou-creased island on the Gulf of Mexico, but experts believed that the lay of the land somehow protected the thriving seaport from the vicious storms that had destroyed the port city of Indianola (1886) on down the southern coast and that often ravaged Louisiana to the east.

Galveston had grown into Texas' most prosperous city with a population of 38,000. Known as the Wall Street of the Southwest, it served forcefully as the business capital of Texas where all the state's major insurance companies, banks, cotton brokers, and mercantile businesses maintained headquarters.

Then on the morning of September 8, heavy winds and rain began and by 4:00 P.M. the city lay under four feet of water. At 8:00 P.M. the wind reached an estimated 120 miles an hour, driving a four-to-six-foot tidal wave across the island. Houses splintered into debris that moved across the city like a battering ram destroying everything in its path. Finally, it crashed against the massive Gresham mansion and created a breakwater that protected the remainder of the city. At midnight the wind ceased and then the water rushing back out to sea sucked away many unsuspecting victims. As dawn came on September 9, the shattered city stared in horror at the devastation—over 6,000 dead and $40 million in property damage.

But Galveston refused to die. An esprit de corps developed among the populace, especially the business community that literally worked miracles to bring Galveston back to life. A board of three engineers headed by retired Brigadier General Henry M. Robert (author of *Robert's Rules of Order*) recommended building a seawall and raising the level of the city behind the wall.

The Galveston seawall is one of the great engineering feats of its time. The solid concrete wall rises seventeen feet, spreads sixteen to twenty feet at the base, and is three to five feet wide at the top. In July 1904 at the completion of the first phase, the wall protected 3.3 miles of waterfront. Over the years it has stretched further along the coast.

To raise the level of the city, dikes of sand were built to enclose quarter-mile square sections of town. Dredges scooped up the sand from the ship channel and moved along canals dug from the port side of the island. Owners paid to have their houses within each cordoned-off section raised on stilts, making it possible for huge pipes to funnel the sand under the raised buildings and in this fashion to lift streets, streetcar lines, alleys, gas and water lines, and even the privies.

The three-ton St. Patrick's Church was the heaviest structure raised. Workers placed 700 jackscrews under the building. The workmen sang songs to synchronize the operation, and on designated words, they cranked the jacks one-quarter turn. In this fashion, they lifted the 3,000-ton structure five feet without causing a single crack, even in the bell tower. Church services continued without interruption. Other structures of almost equal weight were also lifted.

Because of frequent flooding, many buildings already sat on piers or were built with a first level used only for a carriage house and storage. Those structures simply had the first level filled in as the area around them grew higher. The first floor of some two-story buildings disappeared under the sand and the second floor became ground level.

Catwalks crisscrossed the city to allow residents to get about above the stinking, muddy silt hauled in from the bottom of the ship channel.

A drawbridge across one of the canals allowed movement about the city. Tourists came to see the activity. When two dredges collided and had to be pulled from the canal, residents brought picnic baskets and sat on the bank to watch the operation. It became fashionable for ladies to carry their nice slippers in a little bag and upon arrival at an event, they simply changed their shoes.

By the time the grade raising was complete in 1910, over 2,300 buildings—large and small—had been lifted from five to eight feet.

Before the storm, Galveston reigned as the business center of the Southwest, but with the completion of the seawall and grade raising, and the construction of a new causeway that handled five rail lines a day, an electric interurban track, a highway for automobile traffic, and a thirty-inch water line from the mainland, the business community asked: Why not have a first class beachfront hotel and add holiday destinations to Galveston's allure? In 1911 the Galvez, a one million dollar hotel of the finest order opened overlooking the Gulf. Galveston was ready for its next chapter.

2

Texas in the Beginning

Cabeza de Vaca, Texas' First Historian

*I*n 1527, six years after the Spanish conquest of Mexico, Alvar Núñez Cabeza de Vaca had not planned to become a historian when he set sail as the second in command of the Pánfilo de Narváez 600-man expedition to the New World. Following desertions in Santo Domingo and a terrible hurricane in Cuba, the Spaniards spent the winter re-outfitting the expedition. About 500 Spaniards and five ships struck out again in April 1528. Available maps of the Gulf of Mexico were so inaccurate that when they reached Florida's west coast, Narváez, believing they were near the River of Palms in Panuco Province (present Tampico, Mexico)—a miscalculation of about 1,500 miles—ignored Cabeza de Vaca's protests and put ashore an exploring party of 300 men and forty horses.

After slogging along the Florida Gulf coast for a month, suffering from Indian attack and food shortage, they realized that they must return to the sea for their travel. The Spaniards' lone carpenter guided the construction of five rafts using deerskin and hollow pieces of wood as bellows. They melted stirrups and bridle bits to cast primitive saws and axes for felling trees and shaping crude planks that they caulked with pine resins and palmetto fibers. They fashioned sails out of their shirts and trousers and wove rigging from the hair of horse manes and tails. They tanned the skin from the legs of horses to form bags for carrying fresh water. They fed themselves by killing a horse every third day. On September 22, 1528, they loaded fifty men on each raft and set out along the Gulf, remaining within sight of the shore.

Soon after passing the mouth of the Mississippi River, strong winds separated the rafts, eventually driving all ashore between Galveston Island

and Matagorda Peninsula. About ninety Spaniards and at least one African slave named Estevanico landed two rafts west of Galveston Island on a beach Cabeza de Vaca soon named la Isla de Malhado (the Isle of Misfortune). The exhausted and starving men were terrified to see six-foot giants towering over them. Using sign language the Karankawas, who occupied the islands along the coast, indicated that they would return the following day with food. Cabeza de Vaca wrote that the next morning, after taking their fill of food and water, the Spaniards tried launching their rafts only to have them capsize and drown three men before tossing the others back onto the shore. When the Karankawas saw the terrific loss of men and all their possessions, Cabeza de Vaca said the Spaniards were stunned when these "crude and untutored people, who were like brutes," sat down with the survivors and cried, weeping and wailing for half an hour.

Still believing they were close to the province of Panuco, four strong swimmers were sent ahead with an Indian guide. Over the winter Cabeza de Vaca observed the Karankawas, noting that when a child died the entire village mourned the loss for a full year. He observed this same sensitivity to everyone in their society except for the elderly, whom they viewed as useless, occupying space and eating food that the children needed. He also wrote that during the first winter, five Spaniards became stranded on the mainland. As they reached starvation they began eating one another until only one man was left. The Karankawas were revolted by the cannibalism and horrified that the Spaniards were so disrespectful of their dead that the survivors feared the Indians were going to kill them all. By spring 1529, exposure, dysentery, and starvation had decimated the wayfarers. Only Cabaza de Vaca and fourteen others had survived.

Cabeza de Vaca set out alone to explore inland, and became seriously ill. When he did not return as expected, he was given up for dead, and twelve of the survivors decided to move on down the coast toward Mexico. Two men refused to go because they could not swim and feared having to cross rivers they might encounter.

Meantime, Cabeza de Vaca recovered from his illness, and for almost four years he traded with the Indians, carrying seashells and sea snails to interior tribes, which they used to cut mesquite beans, in exchange for bison skins and red ochre, a dye prized for body paint by the coastal Indians. The natives gave him food in exchange for what they believed were his healing powers. He blew his breath on the injured or afflicted parts of the body and incorporated prayers and the Catholic practice of crossing himself, which he reported almost always made those receiving the treatment feel better. Each winter he returned to Malhado to check on the two survivors who steadfastly refused to leave.

In 1532, when one of the men on Malhado died, the survivor, Lope de Oviedo, agreed to journey down the coast after Cabeza de Vaca promised to carry him on his back if they had to swim across streams. At Matagorda Bay a tribe Cabeza de Vaca called Quevenes threatened to kill them, frightening Oviedo into turning back with a group of native women and disappearing into history. Despite their threats, the Quevenes told Cabeza de Vaca the names of "three Christians like him" and agreed to take him across the bay. Upon reaching the other side, he traveled to the "River of Nuts," present-day Guadalupe and found three of his former companions being held as slaves, the other nine having died as they made their way along the coast.

For the next eighteen months the four endured slavery under the Coahuiltecans, always planning to escape at their first opportunity. During their captivity they heard stories of the fate of their expedition. Some had died of exposure and hunger; others succumbed to violence among themselves or from natives, and some of the survivors resorted to eating the flesh of their companions. In late summer 1534, the four men slipped away separately and headed toward the Rio Grande. Despite the odds, they soon met again and joined friendly Indians southwest of Corpus Christi Bay, where they remained for the next eight months.

They crossed the Rio Grande into Mexico near present Falcon Dam Reservoir, but upon hearing of hostile Indians along the Gulf coast, turned back across northern Mexico to the Gulf of California and the Pacific Ocean. Four men out of the original 300 reached Mexico City in July 1536, almost eight years after setting foot on the Florida Gulf coast.

Cabeza de Vaca had not completed his service to the crown. He was assigned the governorship of present-day Paraguay in Central South America. His experience in Texas, despite mistreatment and slavery, had made him a champion of the native people. When he tried to initiate policies that would help the local tribes—removing Indian slaves from cruel masters and placing them with kinder owners, instituting restrictions against holding Indian women as concubines, and adding modest taxes, settlers determined to exploit the native population removed him from office and sent him back to Spain in chains.

During his six-year trial, conviction, and his subsequent pardon, Cabeza de Vaca wrote *Relación* ("Account"), his detailed description of his Texas experiences as merchant, doctor, ethnologist, historian, and observer of plants and animals. He recorded Native American's incest taboos, dietary habits—spiders, ant eggs, worms, lizards, and poisonous vipers—when nothing else was available, and methods used for insect repellent. He even recorded his profound distaste for sodomy among the hunting and gathering culture. His description of the buffalo was the first written account of those wild creatures.

Cabeza de Vaca died about 1559 and his burial site is unknown, but his extraordinary adventures and his detailed documentation have earned him the title of Texas' First Historian. He performed one other amazing task as he and the other castaways walked barefoot across Mexico. His description of removing an arrowhead lodged in the chest just above an Indian's heart earned Cabeza de Vaca fame as the "Patron Saint" of the Texas Surgical Society.

LaSalle Legacy

Two years after his murder in 1687, explorer, fur trader, Frenchman, and visionary René Robert Cavelier, Sieur de La Salle changed the history of Texas. He began his adventures in 1666 at age twenty-two when, with a small allowance from his family, he sailed from his home in Rouen, France to Canada to join his brother Jean, a Sulpician priest. La Salle worked in the lucrative fur trade, which led to his exploring the river systems connected to the Great Lakes and his dream of establishing trading posts along the Illinois River and down the Mississippi.

Believing the Mississippi, flowing into the Gulf of Mexico, offered a western passage to China, he canoed in 1682 to its mouth, claiming along the way all the lands that drained into the river and naming the territory La Louisiane in honor of Louis XIV.

Upon his return to France, La Salle obtained the king's blessing for a voyage to the mouth of the Mississippi to establish a colony, to secure French Canada's access to a warm water port for its fur trade, and to challenge the Spanish Empire's claim to all the land from the coast of Florida to Mexico.

La Salle departed France on July 24, 1684, with four ships and 300 colonists. Pirates captured one ship in the West Indies. Recent discoveries of early documents indicate La Salle's "lack of geographical understanding" caused him to miss the mouth of the Mississippi and sail another 400 miles to Matagorda Bay on the mid-Texas coast.

As the expedition entered the mouth of the bay on February 20, 1685, the rough waters of Pass Cavallo sank the store ship *Aimable*. Her crew and several disenchanted colonists returned to France on the *Joly*, leaving only the vessel *La Belle*. Before La Salle's colony left Matagorda Island, their numbers dwindled to 180. Malnutrition, Indian attack, and overwork reduced their numbers even more after they moved inland and constructed Fort St. Louis on Garcitas Creek in present-day Victoria County.

The following October, La Salle left Fort St. Louis to explore the region and determine his exact location. Upon his return in March 1686, he learned a winter storm had wrecked *La Belle*, the colonists' last hope of escape. Finally realizing the bay they entered lay west of the Mississippi, La Salle made two marches back toward East Texas into Hasinai, or Tejas Indian territory hoping to find the Mississippi and reach the fort he had established on the Illinois River. On March 19, 1687, a dispute in a hunting camp resulted in the death of seven of his followers. Then one of La Salle's own men assassinated him. Six of the survivors finally reached Canada and eventually returned to France to tell their story.

About twenty women, children, handicapped, and those out of favor with La Salle remained at Fort St. Louis. One of the children later recounted the story of all the adults being killed in a Karankawa attack around Christmas 1688. Karankawa women saved the children whom the Spanish eventually rescued and sent as servants to Mexico.

When Spaniards learned of La Salle's intrusion into Texas, they began the search—five sea voyages and six land marches—in pursuit of the French intruders. They found parts of *Aimable* on April 4, 1687, but it took another two years before Alonso De León discovered the destroyed fort.

The accidental landing of La Salle on the Gulf coast changed the course of Texas history. Fear that the French in Louisiana might move into East Texas prompted the development of six Spanish missions in East Texas. The goal was to Christianize the Indians, turn them into good Spanish citizens, and establish the region as a buffer against French Louisiana. The first, Mission San Francisco de los Tejas opened in 1690 and lasted only three years before the padres fled from the irate Indians. Subsequent efforts to establish mission footholds proved little better, resulting by 1772 in the closure and relocating of the missions to San Antonio. The development of missions, however, began the process of opening Texas to settlement. When Mexico won independence from Spain in 1821, it expanded into empresarial contracts that brought Anglos by the thousands into the untamed land. In only fifteen years, the new Texans took the land for themselves and established the Republic of Texas.

Today a statue of La Salle looks out into Matagorda Bay near the ghost town of Indianola and streets, cities, counties, hotels, causeways, and schools bear the explorer's name from Texas to the Canadian provinces.

In 1995 the Texas Historical Commission led an archeological excavation in the muck of Matagorda Bay to raise *La Belle*. Her timbers have been preserved and experts began in October 2014 reconstructing the 600-piece vessel at the Bullock Texas State History Museum in Austin. The wreckage of *Aimable* has not been found.

Escandón, Spanish Colonizer

Each time European colonial governments showed interest in the New World, Spain moved into action. Its war with England, coupled with the English occupying Georgia in 1733, spurred new worries about invasion along the Gulf coast from Tampico in Mexico to Matagorda Bay on the Central Texas coast. The answer seemed to lie in establishing villas and missions along the Rio Grande. The viceroy of New Spain appointed José de Escandón as military commander and governor of the new province of Nuevo Santander, which spread from modern-day Tamaulipas, Mexico into Southern Texas.

Charged with establishing settlements and missions between Tampico and the San Antonio River, Escandón sent seven divisions in search of the most favorable locales for future villas. His lieutenants nixed colonizing the area around present-day Brownsville and Matamoros because the land appeared too low, subject to flooding. Moving up the Rio Grande, Escandón found eighty-five families waiting at its confluence with the San Juan River. On March 5, 1749, the colonizer named Camargo (across the Rio Grande from present-day Rio Grande City) as his first villa. A nearby mission opened to convert the Indians who occupied jacales circling the home of the missionary priests. Nine days later Villa de Reynosa became the second settlement.

Finally, in 1755 Escandón established his last villa where Tomás

Sánchez de la Barrera y Gallardo, one of Escandón's captains, convinced him an old Indian ford on the Rio Grande offered a good locale for a villa. Sánchez brought three families to make up the original settlement on his 66,000-acre land grant. Present-day Laredo grew from that original ranch to become the largest and most successful of Escandón's permanent Spanish settlements in Southwest Texas.

In 1767 a Spanish royal commission began granting land to individual colonists within the villas bordering the Rio Grande. Due to the need for access to the river for transportation and irrigation in this near-desert region, the commissioners surveyed 170 *porciones*, rectangular strips of land about one mile wide fronting the Rio Grande and sixteen miles long, extending north away from the river for grazing cattle. Over the years, larger, cattle-grazing grants, which spread north of the *porciones* and along the Gulf Coast, went to influential residents of Camargo and Reynosa.

Escandón, who is known today as the "Father of the Lower Rio Grande Valley" and his lieutenants founded twenty-four towns and fifteen missions on both sides of the Rio Grande.

Canary Islanders, Texas' First Settlers

After years of little success in Christianizing the Texas Indians and turning them into good Spanish citizens, the colonial authorities realized that securing control of the vast area required more than missions and a military presence—civilians were needed to populate the province of Texas. By 1718 Mission San Antonio de Valero (present-day Alamo) and its presidio still lacked a civilian presence.

Originally the Spanish crown planned to move 400 families from the economically distressed Canary Islands, which lay off the northwest coast of Africa, to establish a civilian community near the Mission San Antonio de Valero and its presidio. The King of Spain intended to completely fund the move through Havana and on to Vera Cruz, including all the necessities for the journey. However, after six years of planning, the original numbers were deemed too large and the transportation too expensive. By the time the Islanders actually sailed for America in 1730, there were only twenty-five families, fifteen of whom stopped in Cuba and only ten traveled all the way to Vera Cruz on the Mexican Gulf coast. As they followed the route laid out for them by the Spanish government up through the center of Mexico, they stopped at places like San Luis Potosi and Saltillo where they received food and clothing. At Presidio San Juan Bautista on the Rio Grande they left their worn-out horses and continued their trek on foot to the banks of the San Antonio River. The journey of almost a year brought heartache, including deaths that left two widows as heads of large households and the three Cabrera children--Ana, José, and Marcos—whose parents died on the trip. Marriages along the way increased the entourage to fifteen families—fifty-six people—reaching their new home on March 9, 1731.

Each family received generous land grants, including the three Cabrera orphans. They named their town "Villa de San Fernando" in honor of the prince, Don Fernando, who became King Ferdinand in 1746. By August the Islanders, "Isleños," had finished plowing and planting and had elected civilian officials to legally establish the first chartered civil government in Texas. Because of their position as the first civilian settlers, the Isleños had permission from the crown to carry the title of "hidalgo," or son of noble lineage. For years they represented the political and socioeconomic elite of the community.

Tensions arose between the three communities—the Isleños, the military in the presidio, and the Franciscans in the nearby missions—over access to water, which had to be delivered by acequias or irrigation canals, the use of the land, and the management of livestock.

Indian attacks—Comanche, Apache, and other roving tribes—caused the lines of differences between the groups to begin blurring and a cohesive community emerged as they were forced to band together against the outside threat that made it difficult for farmers to work in their fields and sometimes even cut off communication with authorities in New Spain.

The Isleños laid the cornerstone in 1738 for the Church of San Fernando, the first parish church in Texas and completed its construction in 1750. Over the years the church was enlarged and in 1874 Pope Pius IX named San Antonio a diocese with San Fernando as its cathedral.

The first formal census, dated December 31, 1788, refers to the "Villa of San Fernando" and the mission and its presidio as "San Antonio de Béxar." After Mexico won independence from Spain, San Antonio de Béxar served as the capital of the province and when Texas finally won independence from Mexico in 1836, the city became known as San Antonio.

The dome of the original San Fernando Church served as the geographic center of the city and the point from which all mileage was measured to San

Antonio. When Mission San Antonio de Valero (the Alamo) was secularized in 1793, its congregation became members of San Fernando. Finally in 1824, after missions Concepcíon, San José, and Espada were all secularized, their members joined the San Fernando parish. Jim Bowie married Ursula de Veramendi, daughter of the Governor of the State of Coahuila y Tejas at San Fernando in 1831. The Battle of the Alamo began when General Santa Anna raised the flag of "no quarter" from the tower of the San Fernando church. It is claimed that a sarcophagus or marble coffin at the back of the sanctuary holds the ashes of Davy Crockett, William B. Travis, and Jim Bowie who died at the Alamo. Today, the cathedral plays a major role in San Antonio as it continues to function as a religious institution while hosting symphonies, concerts, television specials, and the constant arrival of tour buses carrying visitors eager to see one of the oldest cathedrals in the United States that began as a parish church for Canary Islanders.

Wreck of the 300

Three Spanish galleons, caught in a storm in the Gulf of Mexico, wrecked on the sandbars just off Padre Island on April 29, 1554. As the flotilla sailed from Veracruz, a Dominican missionary on his way for an audience with the Pope shared his sinister forebodings: "Woe be to those who are going to Spain. Neither we nor the fleet will ever arrive there. Most of us will perish before then, and those who survive will endure intolerable hardships, which will cause the deaths of most of them."

Four vessels began the journey loaded with about 400 people—old conquistadores and Spanish families heading for home, merchants whose wealth was stored in the ships' holds, and soldiers eager to see their homeland—plus bars of gold and silver bullion, and chests of freshly minted coins. Twenty days into the voyage, a vicious storm hit with such force that the ships fought to stay afloat. The severely damaged San Andrés limped into port at Havana. The other three, the San Esteban, the Espíritu Santo, and the Santa María Yciar carrying about 300 passengers, tossed without control until all three ships sank within two and a half miles of each other about a half-mile from the coast. Over half of the passengers, grabbing anything they could find to save themselves, drowned before reaching shore. Only the San Esteban remained visible above the waves and its master and a group, probably the most skilled sailors, managed to save one of the ship's small boats and sailed immediately for Veracruz to seek help. The survivors, huddled together on shore, managed to save a large quantity of food and supplies. Believing they were within a few days march of a Spanish outpost, they began walking. Actually, they were 300 miles from Tampico. Only one man, Francisco Vasquez, elected to remain with the wreckage and wait for rescue.

The group met local Karankawa Indians and accepted the natives' offer of food, only to be attacked when they reached the Karankawa campsite. As the Spaniards fled, some of them stripped off their clothing thinking that's what the Indians wanted. The Indians continued the chase, killing the terrified survivors as they ran and inflicting others with arrows including Fray Marcos de Mena who took seven arrows. His companions, thinking he would soon die, buried him with only his head exposed hoping to protect his body from wild animals. The warmth of the sand apparently revived Fray Marcos, and he dug his way out. As he continued walking, he came upon the ultimate horror—all his companions lay dead. Fighting mosquitos, hunger, and thirst, he pushed on, finally coming to a river only to discover that it was salty. Two Indians found him, gave him food and water, and as they carried him on a bed of hay, they kept saying only one word, "Tampico." The village lay only a short distance away.

When Fray Marcos' report of the wreckage verified the account of the survivors who had returned earlier on the boat, the viceroy ordered a salvage expedition to retrieve some of the most valuable cargoes ever to leave the New World. When six salvage ships reached the site in July 1554, they found the emaciated and joyful Francisco Vasquez and the partially exposed *San Esteban*. Divers uncovered and hauled almost 36,000 pounds of treasure back to Veracruz, about 41 percent of the original cargo.

Four hundred years later, in 1967 the Texas General Land Office received information that an out-of-state salvage crew was recovering artifacts off Padre Island near Port Mansfield inside the 10.35-mile coastal boundary the Supreme Court had ruled belonged to the state of Texas. The company doing the recovering was not licensed to operate in Texas, and after several years of lawsuits Texas recovered all the artifacts and the salvage company was awarded over $300,000. The thousands of treasures, encrusted with centuries of hard calcium carbonate deposits, included a small solid-gold crucifix, a gold bar, several silver discs, cannons, and crossbows. The most valuable find were three astrolabes, extremely rare navigational instruments used in the sixteenth century. The Texas Legislature passed an Antiquities Bill in

1969, which protects and preserves archeological landmarks and resources and sets strict limits on salvaging and excavation by individuals and companies. Although the *Santa María* had been destroyed in the 1950s during the dredging of the Port Mansfield Channel, excavations in the 1973–74 season used more advanced techniques to probe the layers of sand and shell to reach the treasures lying in a thick deposit of clay. Over 26,000 pounds of encrusted artifacts were recovered, including a large enough fragment of one ship to estimate the length of the vessel between seventy and ninety-seven feet. After the materials were processed and catalogued, the Corpus Christi Museum of Science and History was named repository of the collection.

San Sabá Mission Massacre

The Santa Cruz de San Sabá Mission, built in 1757, is the only Spanish mission in Texas destroyed by Indians. So thorough was the destruction that it took another 235 years for archeologists to finally confirm the site on the banks of the San Sabá River about 120 miles northwest of San Antonio.

Construction of the mission was a dream of Franciscan padres in San Antonio who believed a mission in Apache territory would put an end to almost perpetual warfare with the tribes. Encouraged by a peace ceremony with the Apaches in 1749 and the Indians' request to have a mission and a presidio to protect them from the Comanches, Spanish officials sent three expeditions into Apache territory in search of a suitable site. Several factors influenced the choice of the San Sabá River valley, including its potential for irrigated farming and the concern that rumors of rich veins of minerals in the area might attract the French if the Spanish failed to establish a presence. Officials, always concerned about the cost of every endeavor in its Texas province, finally authorized the new mission when religious ornaments and furnishings became available after the closing of three missions on the San Gabriel River. And, a wealthy mine owner agreed to fund the cost of up to twenty missionaries for three years providing that his cousin Fray Alonso Giraldo de Terreros be placed in charge of the new mission.

With Colonel Diego Ortiz Parrilla appointed commander of the San Sabá presidio, the march to the new site began on April 5, 1757. A total of about 300, including six missionaries, arrived on April 17 with 1,400 cattle and 700 sheep. To their dismay they found no Apaches waiting to join the mission. To satisfy concerns of the padres who feared the soldiers would corrupt their Indian neophytes, Parrilla selected a site for the presidio on the opposite side of the river and about two miles from the mission.

By mid-June not a single Indian had come to the mission. Then, to the padres' delight 3,000 Apaches who were heading north to hunt buffalo and fight Comanches, camped nearby. After ignoring the missionaries' overtures, the Indians left behind two of their group who were sick and promised to join the mission upon their return. By this time, three of the original six missionaries had given up and returned to San Antonio.

Winter brought rumors of northern tribes gathering to fight the Apaches and destroy the mission. The padres seemed unaware that despite Apaches never one time coming to the mission, it looked to the Comanches like the Spanish were siding with their bitter enemies. On February 25, 1758, after Indians stole fifty-nine horses, Parrilla led soldiers in pursuit, only to find hostile Indians all over the countryside. Returning to the mission, he tried unsuccessfully to convince Father Terreros to move the remaining three missionaries and thirty-three other inhabitants to refuge in the presidio.

On March 16 as the mission went about its morning routine, 2,000 Comanches and other tribes that were enemies of the Apaches attacked the log stockade with some of the warriors using European guns at a time when most Indians fought with bows and arrows or hatchets. Father Terreros and seven residents were killed, while one missionary and about twenty other residents escaped to the presidio. The attackers killed almost all the animals, including the cattle, and set fire to the stockade.

The Indians moved on to the presidio and when they could not lure the soldiers outside the fortress, they departed on March 18. After less than one year, the Santa Cruz de San Sabá Mission had come to an end.

The Spanish government, determined not to appear weak to the Co-manches, refused to close the presidio. In September 1759, Parrilla was sent with 500 soldiers and Apache braves into Comanche country to punish the warriors for the attack on the mission. After several brief encounters, Parrilla found Comanches and other tribes on the Red River in a village surrounded by a stockade and a moat and flying a French flag. The Comanches had been warned of the Spanish approach. Parrilla suffered fifty-two dead, wounded, or deserted before he finally relented and ordered a retreat.

The Spanish government insisted that the San Sabá Presidio remain open despite the superior power of the Comanche and other northern tribes who had firepower similar to the Spanish. Many soldiers asked to be transferred and despite the presidio being rebuilt in limestone and surrounded by a moat, the soldiers were killed if they ventured out of the compound.

In 1769, Presidio San Sabá was finally closed, over ten years after the fall of the mission it had been built to protect.

The Pirate Jean Lafitte on Galveston Island

The mention of Jean Lafitte stirs romantic images of a daring, adventurous fellow who charmed his way into New Orleans society by 1804 and flirted with the young women while he and his older brother Pierre ran a smuggling operation out of their blacksmith shop in the city's French Quarter.

In the early nineteenth century, countries lacking their own navy issued letters of marque, contracts with privateers who attacked enemy ships, robbed them, and returned a portion of the valuable cargo to the sponsoring country—the balance remained with the privateer and his crew. The Lafitte brothers mastered the privateers' tactics and expanded their smuggling empire to a barrier island near the mouth of the Mississippi River, a vantage allowing them to skirt the high tariffs on imported goods at customhouses in New Orleans.

Local residents appreciated the charming, well-educated young man who spoke four languages (French, English, Spanish, and Italian), swaggered through the New Orleans streets, and operated a black-market business providing locals with furniture, clothing, utensils, jewelry, laces, silks, calicos, and fine spices at discount prices.

The United States did not have a navy large enough to stand up to Britain's powerful force when it declared war on Britain in 1812, which prompted the U.S. to issue letters of marque to private owners of armed ships—privateers. Under this arrangement, New Orleans issued six letters of marque to privateers who worked primarily for Lafitte. The men readily shared booty they seized from British ships with New Orleans customs officials, but they kept the goods captured from ships flying other national flags. With the loss of customs revenue from Lafitte's privateering, coupled with insufficient U.S. ships to act against Lafitte's island empire, the government went to court. A series of arrests and releases followed.

With the British poised to attack New Orleans in early 1815, Lafitte tried to redeem himself with authorities by offering his services to General Andrew Jackson. At first Jackson refused Lafitte's overture calling him "that hellish banditti," but as it became clear the Americans stood to lose control of the mouth of the Mississippi River, Jackson welcomed the militia, the sailors, and the artillerymen under Lafitte's command. Lafitte's men fought like pirates, and after Jackson's decisive defeat of the British, he praised Lafitte's men for having "exhibited courage and fidelity."

As their reputation grew, Spanish colonial officials recruited the Lafitte brothers to move their base of operation to San Louis (present-day Galveston Island) to spy on filibusterers working to secure Mexican independence from Spain. Pierre Lafitte kept Spanish officials abreast of plans in New Orleans to overthrow the colonial government while Jean Lafitte went to San Louis in 1817 and immediately took control of the island from the revolutionaries.

Spying for Spain quickly took second fiddle to Jean Lafitte's plans for a new smuggling base on the island, which he named *Campeche*. Within a year the colony grew to nearly 200 and soon reached 1,000 men and a few women who took a loyalty oath to Jean Lafitte. They constructed a two-story headquarters on the bayside docks, surrounded it by a moat, painted it red, and named it *Maison Rouge*.

Lafitte ruled with an iron hand, lived on his ship, *The Pride*, and issued letters of marque from his non-existent country, which authorized ships sailing from Campeche as privateers to attack vessels from all nations. The booty rolled in, and Lafitte's men quickly sold it on the black market in New Orleans.

Although the United States passed a law in 1808 prohibiting the importation of slaves into any U.S. port, a giant loophole in the law allowed for slaves captured on slave ships to be turned over to customs officials who auctioned off the chattel with half the profits given to whomever turned in the slaves. Lafitte and his men took full advantage of the law, captured slave ships, and sold their valuable human cargo for one dollar a pound (average weight of 150 pounds). James Bowie and his brothers were among the buyers who came to the island. They marched their newly purchased chattel to customs officials in New Orleans who sold the slaves at auction. The Bowies bought the slaves at the auction and then received the reward for turning them in to the customs officials. Then they resold their new purchases legally all over the South. Between 1818 and 1820 the Bowie brothers earned $65,000 in the slave trade.

During Lafitte's occupation of the island, filibusterers such as Dr. James Long continued to make stops on Campeche seeking Lafitte's support in their efforts to win Texas independence from Spain. Each visitor received a gracious welcome, enjoyed the finest of foods and wines at the *Maison Rouge* lavishly furnished with elegant linens and silver—all privateering booty. But, Lafitte did not commit himself to anything beyond his privateering business.

By 1821 the United States reached the end of its patience with Lafitte whose men continued attacking U.S. ships. The *U.S.S. Enterprise* sailed to Campeche to evict the inhabitants. Given three months to evacuate, Lafitte burned all the structures on the island and without offering resistance sailed away on the *Pride* on May 7, 1821, and disappeared into the mists of legend.

Some say he buried his vast wealth all along the Texas coast, which prompted treasure hunters to shovel through every square inch of the barrier islands in search of booty. Some say his men, overhearing him pacing the floor and muttering, "I buried my treasure under the three trees," rushed to the site of the three trees, and quickly exposed a long wooden box. Raising the lid, they stared into the face of Lafitte's dead wife. The most recent tale surfaced in 1948 when John Laflin, claiming to be Lafitte's great-grandson (historians know of only one child, a son who died of yellow fever at age twelve in New Orleans in 1832), produced a journal Laflin said had been written by Lafitte between 1845 and 1850. Eventually, paper and ink analysis confirmed its mid-19th century origin. Although most historians believe the journal is a forgery, it is displayed in the Sam Houston Regional Library and Research Center near Liberty, Texas. A Texas Historical Marker notes the spot where Lafitte's *Maison Rouge* flourished on Galveston Island.

Texas in the American Revolution

Texas' inclusion in the American Revolution began on June 21, 1779, when Spain declared war on Great Britain. Over 10,000 head of Texas cattle were rounded up on the vast rancheros operated by the Spanish missions that spread along the San Antonio River. Presidio La Bahía at Goliad served as the gathering point from which its soldiers escorted the vaqueros trailing the cattle and several hundred horses up through Nacogdoches in East Texas to Natchitoches and on to Opelousas in Louisiana. To help finance Spain's involvement in the war, King Carlos III asked for donations of one peso "from all men, whether free or of other status" and two pesos from Spaniards and nobles. An accounting dated January 20, 1784, lists a total of 1,659 pesos from presidios all over Texas where the cavalry had two pesos each taken from their pay. At that time two pesos represented the price of a cow.

King Carlos III commissioned Bernardo de Gálvez, the governor of Louisiana, to raise an army and lead a campaign against the British along the Mississippi River and the Gulf of Mexico. Governor Gálvez had been in contact with Patrick Henry, Thomas Jefferson, and Charles Henry Lee who sent emissaries requesting that Gálvez secure the port of New Orleans and permit only American, Spanish, and French ships to travel the Mississippi River. The Mississippi served as the doorway through which vast amounts of arms, ammunition, and military supplies could be moved to the troops fighting in Kentucky, Illinois, and along the northwestern frontier.

The cattle grazing the mission rancheros in Texas offered the best hope for Gálvez to feed his Spanish troops and the governor of Spanish Texas eagerly answered the request. The Texas beef helped feed from 1,400 men to over 7,000 as the campaigns under Gálvez moved from defeat of the British at Manchac and Baton Rouge in Louisiana and on to a victory at Natchez, Mississippi. After a month-long siege using land and sea forces in 1780, Gálvez captured Fort Charlotte at Mobile. The final push to secure the Gulf Coast began in 1781 when Spanish troops captured Pensacola, the British capital of West Florida. The next year, a two-month siege finally overwhelmed Fort George in Pensacola, leaving the British with no bases in the Gulf of Mexico. Finally, the Spanish force under Gálvez captured the British naval base in the Bahamas. The war ended before General Gálvez could initiate plans to take Jamaica. The campaigns under Gálvez kept the British from encircling the American revolutionaries from the south and kept the supply lines open from the western flank.

Gálvez helped draft the terms of the 1783 Treaty of Paris, which officially ended the American Revolutionary War and returned Florida to Spain from British control. George Washington honored Gálvez by placing him to his right in the July 4 parade and the American Congress recognized Gálvez for his service during the revolution. Gálvez capped his career in 1785 when the Spanish crown appointed him viceroy of New Spain.

While Gálvez served as governor of Louisiana, he ordered a cartographer to survey the Gulf Coast. The mapmaker named the largest bay on the Texas coast "Bahía de Galvezton," later becoming Galveston. Galveston County and St. Bernard Parish in Louisiana are among several places that bear his name. The famous Hotel Galvez, built in 1911 on Galveston Island overlooking the Gulf of Mexico, also bears the name of the Spanish hero of the American Revolution.

Moses Austin Plans a Colony

History takes little note of Moses Austin (1761–1821). The man known for his grand plans, bold schemes, and really big failures initiated Anglo settlement in Texas, which led to Texas' independence from Mexico, which led to Texas' annexation to the United States, which led to the Mexican War, which resulted in the United States expansion all the way to the Pacific Ocean. He died before seeing the history he set in motion, which makes it necessary to ask: Who was Moses Austin?

Born in Durham, Connecticut, the fifth generation in a long line of Austins in the United States, Moses Austin at age twenty-one didn't look much like a mover and shaker as he began a career in the dry-goods business with his brother Stephen. Over the next seven years the Austin brothers' dry-goods business prospered, but for some reason they moved in 1789 in a completely different direction—taking over lead mines in southwestern Virginia. By agreeing to use only Virginia lead on the roof of the new Virginia capitol in Richmond, the brothers gained control of the state's richest lead deposit.

They did not enjoy smooth sailing. The new lead roof leaked and had to be replaced with slate; however, by 1791 Moses Austin moved his family, which now included two-year-old Stephen Fuller Austin, to the mines and named the new community Austinville. During this period of gigantic land speculation, the Austin brothers' business thrived and then failed rather suddenly. It is thought that the young men, not known for conservative business moves, over-extended themselves. The scant records indicate Moses Austin was impetuous, lending credence to the story of a rift that never completely healed after Moses left his brother Stephen to salvage the business in Virginia.

Moses Austin struck out west on his own to the rich lead deposits in Spanish Upper Louisiana (present southeastern Missouri). He found rich lead deposits forty miles west of St. Genevieve. Despite the site being in Osage Indian country, he obtained a Spanish land grant of one league (4,428 acres) under an agreement to swear allegiance to the Spanish crown and settle families in the area. In 1798 Moses led his family and forty whites and a few blacks to a primitive site where he established a settlement named Potosi. In the next few years, despite his personal short-comings—lack of patience, tact, and diplomacy—Moses Austin used a furnace design he learned from the English to gain control of most of the smelting in the region, allowing the family to live very well in Durham Hall, their southern-style mansion.

This second period in the history of the American lead industry became known as the "Moses Austin Period." The Louisiana Purchase of 1803 and the transfer of government to the United States stimulated emigration to Missouri and increased business for Moses Austin.

Fortunes changed during the War of 1812, however, paralyzing trade and the lead mining industry in Missouri. Moses Austin tried unsuccessfully to use leased slave labor to expand the mining operation. Then, in an effort to increase the money supply in circulation, he helped organize the first bank west of the Mississippi in St. Louis. It failed in the Panic of 1819. Stretched beyond his capacity, Austin suffered complete financial ruin.

The following year, his eldest son Stephen F. Austin took charge of the mines and the other businesses in Potosi hoping to "free the family of every embarrassment," but the financial collapse proved more than he could salvage.

As Moses searched for ways to recover from his losses, he kept mulling the possibility of another daring scheme, acquiring a land grant from the Spanish government in Texas, an opportunity to make another fortune by settling families on the Texas frontier.

Sometime in November 1820, after visiting with his son Stephen F. Austin in Little Rock, Moses set out for a meeting with Spanish officials in San Antonio. He traveled with a gray horse, a mule, a slave named Richmond, and fifty dollars—a borrowed cache valued today at $850 for which he agreed to repay Stephen F. Austin.

He reached San Antonio on December 23, claimed to be fifty-three years old (he was actually fifty-nine), a Catholic, a former subject of the King of Spain, and a representative of 300 families who wished to settle with his family in Texas.

The Spanish governor turned him down without looking at his papers. Fortunately, as a dejected Moses crossed the plaza on the way back to his quarters, he met Baron de Bastrop, a man he knew from earlier years in Louisiana. The baron intervened for Austin with the governor and in three days Moses received a Spanish grant to settle 300 families in Texas.

Stories differ as to what caused Moses Austin to suffer exposure and exhaustion on his return trip to begin preparations for Texas settlement, but his body grew weak from the journey and despite ill health, he continued feverish preparations for establishing his new colony. In late May 1821 he developed pneumonia and despite his young doctor blistering and bleeding him "most copiously," he died on June 10.

With his dying breath he begged his wife to tell their son Stephen to fulfill the dream of settling Texas for the benefit of the family.

Next, we'll look at the mirror image of Moses Austin in the life and legacy of Stephen F. Austin, "Father of Texas."

Stephen F. Austin, "Father of Texas"

Stephen F. Austin came to Spanish Texas in response to his own father Moses Austin's deathbed wish for Stephen to continue with Moses' dream of settling 300 families in Texas. Like many apprehensive fathers, Stephen F. Austin reluctantly embraced his responsibilities and spent the remainder of his life lovingly guiding his colony and all of Texas toward its best opportunity for success.

Austin understood and admired the adventurous, hard-working settlers willing to move to a wilderness and carve out a new life. Unlike Moses Austin who had a quick temper and a need to challenge those with whom he disagreed, Stephen embraced patience, tact, willingness to compromise, and the diplomacy necessary to work with the independent-minded settlers and the tangles of Spanish and Mexican government bureaucracy.

Stephen reached San Antonio in August 1821, soon after Mexico won its independence from Spain. The change in government required Stephen to renegotiate the land grant with the new Mexican authorities. Again, with the help of the Baron de Bastrop, Stephen received a Mexican empresarial colonization grant with the same land allocations his father had received—640 acres for each man, plus 320 acres for a wife, 160 acres for each child, and eighty acres for each slave at a cost of twelve and a half cents per acre to be paid to Austin for administering the surveys and expenses of establishing the colony.

Settlers eagerly grabbed the land offer as Austin scrambled to find financial partners. From the beginning of his colony, Austin insisted all land grants be carefully recorded in bound volumes to preserve a permanent record. His first test of diplomatic prowess came in December 1821—the first settlers were already arriving—when Mexican authorities refused to approve the terms of Austin's land grant.

He left immediately for Mexico City, and after patient negotiation, the Mexican government established a new empresarial policy offering each married man a free league of land (4,428 acres) and opened colonization to several more empresarios, agents like Austin who received permission to bring settlers into Texas. The law denied empresarios the right to charge administrative fees, providing instead 67,000 acres to each empresario only after he settled 200 families. Selling that acreage when settlers were receiving free land proved very difficult.

Despite mounting personal debt as he bore more and more of the unforeseen costs of establishing the colony, by late 1825, Austin's colony had grown to 300 families—known today as the "Old Three Hundred." Between 1825 and 1829, Austin settled an additional 900 families.

Dealing with the Mexican government required constant compromise. The slavery issue presented a continuing challenge since most settlers came from slave-holding states and the original colonization law allowed them to bring their chattel into Texas. When the new constitution of the state of Coahuila and Texas prohibited slave importation, an uproar spread through the colony. Austin's personal beliefs (he owned a slave woman he described as old and not worth anything) seemed to shift. As with other issues that he felt represented the best interest of the colonists, he negotiated a scheme allowing settlers to free their slaves at the Texas border and make them indentured servants for an indefinite time.

Recognizing the plight of many colonists who came to Texas without paying their debts in the United States, Austin secured a law closing the courts for twelve years to debt collectors and permanently exempting land, tools, and implements used in business and farming from creditors—an early version of the homestead exemption law.

Austin located his colony in fertile farmlands with access to transportation along the Colorado and Brazos rivers, and then lobbied the Mexican congress to legalize the port of Galveston and to allow trade through ports at the mouth of the Brazos and other rivers.

Despite Austin's efforts to ease tensions between the differing cultures and remain aloof from Mexican government intrigues by encouraging the colonists to "play the turtle, head and feet within our own shells," outside forces kept Mexican officials on the defensive. Several offers from President Andrew Jackson for the United States to buy Texas resulted in Mexico passing an 1830 law halting further colonization by settlers from the United States. Austin wrangled an exemption for his and for Green DeWitt's colony, and by the next year succeeded in getting the law repealed.

However, when Haden Edwards, in an effort to win Texas independence from Mexico tried to drag Austin's beloved colonists into the Fredonian Rebellion, Austin sent a militia to Nacogdoches to put down the revolt to save his settlers from the wrath of the Mexican government.

The colonists' dissatisfaction with Mexican President Anastacio Bustamente's heavy-handed immigration controls and introduction of tariffs finally led to Austin joining the colonists in supporting Antonio López de Santa Anna in the Mexican presidential elections. Santa Anna soon proved not to be the liberal leader of his campaign, but a dictator who clamped down on the increasingly independent-minded colonists.

Austin did not favor the conventions held in 1832 and 1833 to express Texan grievances, and believed they would not serve the colonists' best interests, but he attended each event hoping to moderate the actions of the increasingly dissatisfied settlers. Despite his efforts to temper the resolutions, the delegates, even those who disagreed with Austin, recognized his influence with the Mexican authorities, and elected him to carry their petitions to the government in Mexico City.

Austin's negotiations resulted in important reforms, but as he headed back to Texas, Santa Anna ordered him arrested and held until July 1835—an absence from Texas of twenty-eight months. Without Austin's calming presence, the war clouds in Texas grew beyond his control; strong factions organized a consultation to begin the process of declaring independence.

Upon his return to Texas, he recognized that war for independence was inevitable. The consultation delegates selected Austin and two other men as emissaries to the United States to solicit loans and volunteers and arrange credit for munitions and other equipment, including warships. The men were also charged with getting a commitment of recognition of Texas independence and eventual annexation to the United States.

By the time Austin returned to Texas in June 1836, the celebrated Battle of San Jacinto on April 21 had decisively won the Texas war for independence from Mexico.

Austin "offered his services" as president of the new republic in the

September election, but it was not to be. Sam Houston, the man who marched across Texas with the army, the flamboyant general who led the troops in the winning eighteen-minute Battle of San Jacinto, won the contest. President Houston appointed the quiet and unassuming Austin to the office for which he was well suited—Secretary of State. Despite failing health and no money to heat his tiny office and living quarters, Austin worked diligently to set up the state department of the new Republic of Texas.

As he lay near death with pneumonia on December 27, 1836, he roused from a dream with these last words: "The independence of Texas is recognized. Didn't you see it in the papers?"

Austin died at age 43 without knowing his beloved Texas, which he nurtured and guided with such patience, would become the twenty-eighth state to enter the Union in 1845, and that annexation would trigger the Mexican War (1846–48). Like dominoes falling across the historic landscape, the Treaty of Guadalupe Hidalgo ending that conflict stretched the United States borders to the Pacific Ocean, adding nearly a million square miles and increasing the size of the nation by almost one third.

Baron de Bastrop, Fraud or Patriot?

Felipe Enrique Neri (1759–1827), a charming gentleman hailed as the Baron de Bastrop, paved the way for the first Anglo-American colony in Texas. No one knew he had left his wife and five children in Holland or that he fled his country with a bounty of 1,000 gold ducats on his head for embezzling taxes from the province of Friesland.

Neri arrived in Spanish Louisiana in 1795, claiming to be the Baron de Bastrop, a Dutch nobleman forced to leave Holland after the French invasion. After ten years of various business dealings, including settling ninety-nine colonists under a Spanish land grant, Neri appeared in San Antonio in 1806 assuming an air of gentility and posing as a loyal Spanish subject, adamantly opposed to the United States' 1803 Louisiana Purchase. As the Baron de Bastrop, Neri opened a freighting business in San Antonio, and soon gained enough respect to be appointed alcalde (mayor) in the ayuntemiento (local government).

In an odd twist of fate, the baron met his friend Moses Austin on the plaza in San Antonio after the Spanish Governor flatly refused to even consider Moses Austin's request to establish a colony in Texas. The baron intervened on Austin's behalf, securing permission for Austin to settle 300 families by arguing that Spain needed settlers occupying the country between San Antonio and the Sabine River as a cushion against the Indian threat; that Spaniards and Mexicans were not coming into Texas, rather they were leaving; and that Anglo colonization had already proven successful in Spanish Louisiana. Within three days the Spanish governor granted Austin permission to establish his colony in Texas.

After Moses Austin died and his son Stephen F. Austin applied for his father's grant, Baron de Bastrop again used his influence to secure permission for Stephen to continue with Moses Austin's grant to settle 300 families in Spanish Texas.

By 1823 Bastrop won appointment as Stephen F. Austin's commissioner of colonization with authority to issue land titles. From all accounts, the baron faithfully handled his duties even after he was chosen in 1824 as a legislator representing the new state of Coahuila and Texas. He served as an ideal intermediary for Austin to enact laws that were in the best interest of the colonists such as an act establishing a port at Galveston.

Mexican law required the salary of legislators be paid by contributions from their constituents, resulting in such sparse payment that when Bastrop died on February 23, 1827, he lacked enough money for his burial. Despite the state of poverty in which he died, the Baron de Bastrop, still claiming to be of noble birth in his last will and testament, left land to his wife and children.

Although many people in his day viewed his origins as suspect—some believed him to be an American adventurer—he held respect for his diplomatic and legislative work on behalf of Texas. Within the past fifty years, records from the Netherlands revealed the true story of his mysterious past.

Don Martín De León Colony

Soon after winning independence from Spain in 1821, Mexico began issuing empresarial grants, contracts allowing men to bring settlers into Mexico's northernmost state of Texas. Of approximately thirty empresarial grants issued between 1821 and 1832, only one went to a Mexican. Don Martín De León and his wife Doña Patricia De León were wealthy descendants of aristocratic Spanish families who had immigrated to New Spain in 1750. De León received his empresarial grant in April 1824 to settle forty-one

Mexican families "of good moral character" on the lower Guadalupe River. He had been in Texas since 1805, operating ranches along and south of the Nueces River and driving huge herds of cattle to market in New Orleans.

De León's grant lay southwest of Stephen F. Austin's, the first and most successful of the colonies. De León named his settlement Guadalupe Victoria, after the first president of the Republic of Mexico. Each family received a town lot, one league (4,228 acres) of land for grazing, and a labor (177 acres) for farming. Upon completion of the colonization contract, the empresario was to receive five leagues.

One of De León's sons-in-law platted the town and the empresario designated the main street "La Calle de los Diez Amigos" (The Street of Ten Friends) for the ten homes of citizens who were charged with the welfare of the town from 1824 to 1828. Three of the ten friends were his sons-in-law and two were his sons. Not all the settlers were Mexicans; sixteen families, primarily Irish immigrants, joined the colony. A devout Catholic, De León brought priests from La Bahía (present Goliad), Nacogdoches, and San Antonio until the founding in late 1824 of St. Mary's Catholic Church. The colonists built a school and a fort, organized a militia, and started a courier service with the neighboring Austin colony.

Victoria quickly became a cultural center as the family maintained contact with friends who were kings, emperors, and both military and political leaders in the United States. The children and grandchildren were sent to schools in the major cities of Europe and the business of the colony was considered among the most substantial. Cattle, horses, and mules were the primary business. The family corralled wild Longhorns and mustangs by the thousands.

De León's five-league ranch, which spread along Garcitas Creek in present-day southeastern Victoria County, probably included the land where the Frenchman La Salle had built Fort St. Louis in 1685. Many claim De León's cattle brand, which he had registered in 1807, was the first in Texas. It consisted of a connected E and J meaning "Espiritu de Jesús," the brand used by Jesuits for hundreds of years and adopted by the De León family in Spain.

From the beginning of his colony, De León, a wealthy and cultured man, looked with disdain at the Americans in surrounding colonies. His attitude and the preferential treatment he received from the government as a Mexican citizen added to tensions among the neighboring settlements. The boundaries of his colony were not clearly drawn and in disputes with other colonies, the Mexican courts usually sided with De León. The ensuing squabbles led to hatred and mistrust between De León and Green DeWitt whose colony at Gonzales lay just to the north. De León tried unsuccessfully to have the government annul the grant for an Irish colony that lay to the south.

De León died at age 68 in the 1833 cholera epidemic, leaving his wife and ten children an estate of about a half million dollars. His sons completed the settlement, which made the De León and the Austin colonies the only two in Texas to fulfill their empresarial agreement.

The family members were strong Federalists and as troubles brewed with the Centralists government under the Mexican Dictator Antonio López de Santa Anna, the De Leóns sided with the Texans who supported independence. The De Leóns took part in all the plans for the Texas revolution; they served in the army or helped in other ways to aid the Texas cause. They contributed so substantially to the war that when General José de Urrea occupied Victoria after the massacre at Goliad, the De Leóns were arrested as traitors.

Despite their contributions, after Texas won independence, Anglo-Americans began coming into Texas looking for land and charging the De Leóns as Mexican sympathizers. After the murder of one son and the severe injury of another, the family, one of the wealthiest in Texas, left all behind and fled to safety in New Orleans. Three years later, the oldest son Don Fernando De León, returned to Victoria and spent the remainder of his life in unsuccessful litigation for the return of the family's property.

In 1972 a Texas historical marker was placed in Victoria's Evergreen Cemetery honoring the De León family. Attendees at the dedication included Patricia De León, great-granddaughter of the empresario, and Dr. Ricardo Victoria, great-grandson of President Guadalupe Victoria for whom the town is named.

La Réunion, Dallas Commune

On June 16, 1855, residents of the area around the village of Dallas (population 400) declared a holiday in anticipation of greeting about 200 very foreign-looking immigrants from France, Belgium, and Switzerland. The newcomers, who spoke French and wore odd-looking clothing and sabots (wooden shoes) arrived after a twenty-six-day trip from Houston—some walking, others on horseback. They were accompanied by ox-drawn wagons on which they carried household goods necessary to begin a utopian community. Unlike most frontier settlers, La Réunion colonists were brewers, watchmakers, weavers, and shopkeepers—unsuited to the rigors of farm life. Over several months more settlers arrived, bringing supplies such as an organ, piano, flutes, and violins. One wave of newcomers brought thirteen trunks and had to pay ox-cart drivers three cents a pound to haul the heavy load. An elderly man had broken his leg on shipboard and had to pay the freight rate to ride in a cart.

The groups' founder Victor Prosper Considerant planned a loosely structured experimental utopian community on the banks of the Trinity River in which members shared in the profits based on the amount of capital each one invested in the cooperative and the quantity and quality of work contributed by each participant. Unlike communism, Considerant advocated voting by both men and women and individuals owning private property. He had been a leader in the democratic socialist movement in France and had been forced to flee to Belgium in 1851 after taking part in a failed insurrection against Louis Napoleon Bonaparte. His travels with a follower of the French philosopher Charles Fourier had led Considerant to North Texas where he found the people, climate, and land perfectly suited for establishing a cooperative utopian society. Upon his return to Paris he established the European Society for the Colonization of Texas and published *Au Texas* (In Texas) in which he praised the ideal climate and claimed the fertile soil well suited for growing tropical fruit.

Considerant sent advance agents who purchased about 2,500 acres on the chalky, limestone bluff near the forks of the Trinity River, three miles west of Dallas. The land was not suitable for farming, even if the colonists had known how. They did plant a large garden, bought 500 head of cattle, sheep, pigs and some fowls. They purchased equipment for mowing, reaping and thrashing wheat and by the following year they had laid out a town site, built offices, buildings suitable for making soap and candles and operating a laundry. They prepared their meals in a cooperative kitchen and built two dormitories for individual families.

Their Saturday night parties, which included music, singing, and dancing, shocked some of their Dallas neighbors whose Protestant faith led them to believe that violins were instruments of the devil and singing should be limited to sacred songs. La Réunion residents vigorously defended their entertainment by insisting that keeping the Sabbath meant worship and pleasure. The locals claimed that a half day on Saturday should also be set aside. It wasn't long before a few of the younger, more independent Dallas residents began attending the parties and romances soon followed.

Although groups continued to arrive, the population never grew beyond 350. After putting 430 acres into cultivation, a blizzard in May 1856 damaged the crops and froze the Trinity River. The heat of summer brought drought and grasshoppers descended to feast on the remaining crops.

Settlers began leaving as tensions developed over Considerant's poor financial management, unclear land deeds, impractical distribution of work, and disagreements over how meals should be served to provide equal sharing. Some headed back to Europe while others moved into Dallas and surrounding communities.

In 1860 Dallas incorporated La Réunion land and the colonists offered their considerable skills to the growing city. M. Monduel opened the first brewery in 1857; Emil Remond experimented with the white rock on the banks of the Trinity and eventually established a cement plant; Julien Reverchon became an internationally known botany professor at Baylor University College of Medicine and Pharmacy in Dallas and Jacob Boll, who had been Julien Reverchon's Texas teacher, discovered and classified many Texas plants and flowers. Jacob Nussbaumer opened the city's first butcher shop. Benjamin Long served two terms as Dallas mayor, John B Louckx created the public school system, and Maxime Guillot's carriage factory operated for fifty years, leading to Dallas becoming a world center for the carriage and harness-making industry.

Today, the 561-foot Reunion Tower completed in 1978 in downtown Dallas is about three miles east of the old colony and serves as a handsome reminder of the contributions made by the little band of visionaries.

3
A Country All Its Own

Mystery of the Twin Sisters

*I*n November 1835, three months before Texas declared its independence from Mexico, war clouds were growing into a full rebellion and the citizens of Cincinnati, Ohio, eager to lend support, began raising money to purchase two cannon for the looming battle. Since the United States remained neutral throughout the war, the two iron six-pound cannon were secretly shipped down the Mississippi River labeled as "hollow ware." Stories abound about how they actually reached Sam Houston's volunteer army camped about seventy-five miles up the Brazos River from its mouth at the Gulf of Mexico.

Most accounts say the cannon traveled from New Orleans aboard the schooner *Pennsylvania* to Galveston where Dr. Charles Rice's nine-year-old twin daughters Elizabeth and Eleanor were invited to be part of the official handing over of the cannon to Texas. Since the ceremony consisted of twins presenting the two cannon, the six-pounders became known as the "Twin Sisters." The *Pennsylvania* continued to the mouth of the Brazos River and traveled inland about eighteen miles to Brazoria. It was still nearly sixty miles upriver to Houston's camp and according to an account taken from General Houston's correspondence and orders, worry over the terrible condition of the roads and concern that Santa Anna's army might intercept the Twin Sisters, led to the cannon being shipped back to Galveston. Over the next eleven days the cannon moved through Galveston Bay and up Buffalo Bayou to Harrisburg (in present-day Houston) Ox-carts, pulled by horses, slogged through the rain, mud and fiercely cold weather to General Houston's campsite on the Brazos River.

As soon as the Twin Sisters arrived, nine men drew assignment to each cannon and the drilling and firing began as the Texan Army moved east along the very route the Twin Sisters had just covered. Sam Houston's army of about nine hundred men set up camp on April 20 in a thick growth of timber where Buffalo Bayou flowed into the San Jacinto River. The Twin Sisters spent the afternoon in their first combat dueling with Santa Anna's Mexican cannon.

The following afternoon, the Twin Sisters led the charge across the rise in the prairie toward Mexicans who, convinced the Texans would not dare attack, were enjoying their usual siesta. At 200 yards the two little cannon, loaded with the Texans' only ammunition—musket balls, broken glass, and horseshoes—began firing. The battle cry of the Texans split the air with "Remember the Alamo, Remember Goliad." In eighteen minutes the startled forces of Mexico's superior army had been defeated. The carnage did not stop, however, as the Texans in a furious retaliation for the brutal deaths of almost 200 Texans at the Alamo on March 6 and 350 massacred at Goliad on March 27, continued to use rifle butts and bayonets to kill the enemy.

Although the Twin Sisters had secured their place in history, their travels did not end at San Jacinto. After being moved to Austin, probably to help protect the frontier capital from Indian attack, the two cannon appeared again on April 21, 1841, when they were fired to celebrate the fifth anniversary of the Battle of San Jacinto. Later that year as Sam Houston kissed the Bible at the conclusion of his inauguration for the second time as president of the Republic of Texas, the cannon roared to life in a salute to the new president and hero of the Battle of San Jacinto.

The Twin Sisters made no further public appearances and became part of the property—fortifications, barracks, ports, harbors, navy and navy yards, docks, magazines, and armaments—ceded to the United States in 1845 when Texas joined the union. All Texas' military stores were moved to the federal arsenal at Baton Rouge, Louisiana.

When secession talk reached full tilt with the election in 1860 of Abraham Lincoln, Benjamin McCulloch who as a young man had served on the crew manning the Twin Sisters and was destined to become a general in the Confederate Army, sent a letter to then Governor Sam Houston asking him to bring the Twin Sisters back to their home in Texas. In the years after the cannon arrived in Louisiana, the Twin Sisters had been sold as scrap iron to a foundry. An investigation found that one cannon remained at the foundry in poor condition and the other had been sold to a private individual. The Louisiana legislature purchased and repaired the cannon at a cost of $700 and returned them to Texas on April 20, 1861, the twenty-fifth anniversary of their first skirmish with the Mexicans at San Jacinto.

The Twin Sisters performed again at the January 1, 1863, Battle of Galveston in which Confederate forces regained control of Galveston Island. Lieutenant Sidney A. Sherman, whose father had fought at the Battle of San Jacinto, was killed while serving as commander of one of the Twin Sisters.

Stories abound about what happened to the Twin Sisters after the Battle of Galveston. One account says they were sent to Colonel John "Rip" Ford in San Antonio as he prepared to march to the Rio Grande to take it from federal troops; however, no record exists of the cannon reaching San Antonio. Some veterans claim to have seen the Twin Sisters at various locations around the Harrisburg area of Houston. Another tale claims that several Confederate veterans, concerned the Twin Sisters would fall into the hands of the federal troops during Reconstruction, buried the cannon in an area hugging Buffalo Bayou. For years history buffs and the curious have searched without success for the burial site.

In 1985 two graduates of the University of Houston's College of Technology supervised the making of replicas of the Twin Sisters, which stand today on the San Jacinto Battlegrounds waiting for the discovery that will return the original Twin Sisters to the site where they made Texas and world history.

Sam Houston's Problems With the Ladies

Before he became the hero of the Battle of San Jacinto and the first president of the Republic of Texas, Sam Houston was the darling of all the ladies, except for one, Anna Raguet. The well-educated Miss Raguet was fourteen in 1833 when she moved with her father from Cincinnati to Nacogdoches, which was still part of the Mexican state of Coahuila y Tejas. Marquis James, Houston's biographer says in *The Raven* that Anna's father Henry Raguet was a merchant and landowner, and provided the best house in Nacogdoches for his family where they entertained extensively. Anna, the apple of her father's eye, played the French harp in the parlor and translated Spanish, especially for the young men in the area who claimed they needed to improve their correspondence with the Mexican government. And, like the forty-year-old Sam Houston, enjoyed the company of the charming young Anna.

When Houston met Anna Raguet he was a Texas newcomer with plenty of personal baggage. Under circumstances that were never made public, his bride Eliza Allen had left him in 1829, and he had resigned as governor of Tennessee. On top of that mystery, he had returned to his former life with the Cherokees and married a Cherokee woman who had refused to come with him to Texas. In addition to his lady problems, Houston was known, even among his beloved Cherokees, as "the Big Drunk."

To clear the way for a serious courtship, Houston hired a divorce lawyer who failed to get the decree because divorce was against the law in Mexico. Even as Houston began his law practice, hobnobbed with Nacogdoches society, and became deeply involved with the political faction seeking Texas independence from Mexico, he pursued his courtship of Anna through letters and his gentlemanly manners.

Although she did not always encourage his entreaties, she snipped a lock of his hair and tied his sword sash, which required wrapping the sash around the man's waist and tucking it in—a rather friendly gesture—before he left Nacogdoches to serve as commander in the Texas War for Independence. He kept up a one-sided correspondence with Anna during the war and after the Battle of San Jacinto, as his surgeon probed his badly injured ankle for fragments of bone and mangled flesh, Houston propped himself against a tree, weaving a garland of leaves. He addressed a card "To Miss Anna Raguet, Nacogdoches, Texas: These are laurels I send you from the battle field of San Jacinto. Thine. Houston."

Houston was the hero of the day after San Jacinto and easily won election as the first president of the Republic of Texas. In the midst of the challenges of organizing a new government, he did not return to Nacogdoches for several months. Instead, he worked out of a shack on the banks of the Brazos River in the temporary capital of Columbia and tried to continue his courtship of Anna Raguet by mail. She had ignored the laurel of leaves and card sent from the battlefield of San Jacinto. To avoid gossip that would surely reach her in Nacogdoches, Houston refrained from socials engagements as much as possible and stayed away from alcohol.

Houston's biographer claims that Dr. Richard Irion, a gentlemanly young physician who had practiced medicine in Nacogdoches and had been elected to the First Congress of the Republic, accepted Houston's appointment as his Secretary of State after the death of Stephen F. Austin, the first Secretary of State. Dr. Irion worked closely with the president and had even listened to Houston's worries about the scarcity of mail from Miss Anna. When Irion went home to Nacogdoches on a short leave, he carried Houston's letters to Anna.

In early 1837 Houston wrote Irion: "Salute all my friends and don't forget the Fairest of the Fair!!!" Again Houston wrote: "Write...and tell me how matters move on and how the Peerless Miss Anna is and does! I have written her so often that I fear she has found me troublesome, and...I pray you to make my apology and...salute her with my...very sincere respects." While Houston waited for letters that did not come, he received regular reports of Miss Anna nearing the steps of the altar, although no one seemed to know who the fortunate fellow might be.

Ignoring the laws under the Republic of Texas that required an Act of Congress to secure a divorce, President Houston empowered a judge to quietly hear the case in his chambers and issue the decree. News of the divorce that Anna Raguet received was apparently all it took to settle any doubts she may have harbored. The one-sided romance came to an end.

Dr. Robert Irion, upon hearing the news, promptly persuaded Miss Anna Raguet to marry him. The nuptials took place in March or April of 1840. The couple had five children, and they named their first son Sam Houston Irion.

Houston's Cherokee wife died in 1838 and two years later Sam Houston married his third wife, twenty-one-year-old Margaret Moffett Lea. A beautiful and very religious young woman, Margaret eventually convinced Houston to give up alcohol. It took longer to get him baptized, but even that finally took place in a creek near Independence. The Houstons had eight children, the youngest born just two years before Houston's death in 1863.

Texas' Bloodless War

A larger-than-life bronze of barefoot Angelina Eberly lighting an equally gigantic cannon dominates the corner of Congress Avenue and 7th Street in Austin. The story requires a little explanation.

After Texas gained independence from Mexico in 1836, Sam Houston won the election as the new Republic's first president. The capital was moved to Sam Houston's namesake village on Buffalo Bayou; however, the constitution allowed the president only one two-year term at a time. Houston's successor and nemesis, Mirabeau B. Lamar, envisioned the capital of the Republic farther west in anticipation of settlement moving beyond the swampy coastal region. A selection committee agreed with Lamar's choice of Waterloo, a hamlet on the Colorado River in Central Texas. The new site was named for Stephen F. Austin, the empresario who brought the first group of Anglo settlers into Texas.

Many, especially Sam Houston, regarded Austin as a poor choice because it sat in the wilderness and suffered constant danger from Indian and Mexican attacks. After Houston was reelected president in 1841, the Mexican army made forays into San Antonio, which frightened away some of the Austin settlers and offered Houston an excuse to move the congress, the courts, even the foreign embassies to what he claimed as safer territory in Washington, a tiny community on the Brazos River. The determined residents in Austin refused to allow the archives—consisting of all the Republic's land titles, treaties, military records, and other documents—to be removed because they knew the loss of those vital papers would spell the end of Austin's claim as the capital city.

Finally, a determined Sam Houston secretly dispatched about twenty-two men and three wagons with instructions to haul the archives to Washington. Before dawn on December 30, 1842, Angelina Eberly, an Austin innkeeper, and one of the few women left in the village, happened to be outside. Who knows why? She saw the men in an alley loading the archives into their wagon. Mrs. Eberly rushed to the cannon that had been given to Austin for Indian protection and began firing to alert the townspeople. Sixty-eight Austin citizens gave chase.

The little band of men with the archives headed north to Kenney's Fort, near present-day Round Rock, and camped for the night inside the fort's picket enclosure. The following morning, Houston's men discovered the Austinites surrounding the fort, backed by their cannon, demanding the return of the archives.

Sam Houston's men complied, ending what became known as the Archives War or the Bloodless War. The standoff with Houston did not end. The government of the Republic remained in Washington during the inauguration of Anson Jones, Houston's successor. Even the session of congress that approved Texas' annexation as the 28th state in the Union took place in Washington. In the late summer of 1845 Austin again became the official capital of Texas.

The Texas Historical Marker telling the story of the Archives War is located at the State Archives and Library Building at 1201 Brazos, Austin, Texas.

The Black Bean Episode

Despite the glorious story of Texas winning its independence from Mexico in that eighteen-minute battle at San Jacinto on April 21, 1836, the new republic remained embroiled in a series of political, economic, and military struggles. The Black Bean Episode reveals the culmination of all those forces coming together for a grand failure.

Despite having lost the war for Texas Independence, Santa Anna regained favor with the Mexican people in 1838 and won the presidency. Mexico remained in a constant civil war between the forces that wanted a centralized government under the likes of Santa Anna and the Federalists who longed for more freedom within the various Mexican states. The disruption of constant war in Mexico kept the government from launching a full scale attack to recapture Texas. However, Mexican troops continued to harass Texas towns. When the army invaded Goliad, Refugio, and Victoria and continued on to San Antonio, the frightened populace abandoned the city. The Mexicans withdrew, but they left the settlements along the western edge of Texas in panic, demanding that President Sam Houston send an army into Mexico to halt the attacks.

Sam Houston, anxious to avoid another war that the republic had no way of financing and eager to work toward building a strong republic, reluctantly made appeals to the United States for money and volunteers in preparation for an invasion of Mexico. The needed assistance from the United States never arrived. On September 11, 1842, General Adrián Woll, with 1,200 Mexican troops, captured San Antonio. Texans gathered at nearby Salado Creek to drive out the raiders, and while they were making headway in a pitched battle, less than two miles away a disaster was taking place. When word had spread of the need for Texan support at San Antonio, Captain Nicholas M. Dawson had raised a company of fifty-three men from the La Grange area. On September 18, Dawson's men rushed headlong into battle with Mexican cavalry patrols only to be overpowered by a column of

500, reinforced by two cannons. When the cavalry pulled back and opened fire with the cannons, Dawson's men were completely overpowered. Despite trying to surrender, survivors claimed the Mexicans continued firing. By the time the fight ended in late afternoon, thirty-six Texans were dead, fifteen were taken prisoner, and two escaped. The dead were buried where they fell among the mesquite trees. The prisoners were marched to Perote Prison near Vera Cruz and only nine finally returned to Texas.

After what became known as the Dawson Massacre, Sam Houston finally called on Alexander Somervell, a customs officer from Matagorda Island, to organize a volunteer militia to punish the Mexican Army for the attacks. Somerville raised a force of 700 young men who were eager for revenge, for adventure, and for plunder. The expedition left San Antonio at the end of November 1842 and captured Laredo on December 7. Finding a town with little wealth to plunder, the men ransacked Laredo. Somerville, who had not been especially eager for the expedition, realized he was losing control of his command, and that they would be facing a much better trained and stronger Mexican army as they marched south. On December 19, he ordered his men to disband and head home. A group of 308 Texans, including five captains, ignored Somerville's command and under the leadership of William S. Fisher, continued their march down the Rio Grande.

Crossing the river to Ciudad Mier, the Texans battled all Christmas Day and into the night against a much larger Mexican force before finally surrendering. As captives, the Texans began the long march south toward Perote Prison. On February 11, 1843, the Texans overpowered their guards and in an effort to avoid capture fled into the arid mountains of Mexico, only to suffer for six days without food and water. When the Mexican troops rounded up the starving Texans, orders came from an infuriated Santa Anna to execute each of the 176 captives. It is unclear how Santa Anna was convinced to change his mind and decree instead that one in every ten should be executed.

Seventeen black beans were placed in a pot of white beans. Some accounts say that the black beans were added last, and that the officers were required to be the first to draw, then the selection proceeded in alphabetical order. The seventeen men who held black beans were executed before a firing squad. The other prisoners eventually reached Perote Prison. Over time, some escaped, others had family and friends who arranged their release, and some died of illness and starvation. Finally, on September 16, 1844, Santa Anna ordered the release of the remaining 104 Texas prisoners.

In 1847, while the United States Army occupied northeastern Mexico during the Mexican-American War, Captain John E. Dusenbury who had drawn a white bean, returned to the burial site of his comrades who had drawn black beans. He exhumed the remains and carried them by ship to Indianola and then by wagon to LaGrange. The citizens of LaGrange retrieved the remains of those who had died in the Dawson Massacre. All the fallen were reinterred in a common vault on a 200-foot bluff overlooking the Colorado River and the city of LaGrange. Today, the gravesite is part of the Monument Hill and Kreische Brewery State Historic Sites.

The Texas Navy

The Republic of Texas existed from March 2, 1836 until February 19, 1846. During most of that time it boasted its own navy with a history as colorful as its government. As Texas settlers, unhappy with the Mexican government, prepared to go to war for independence, officials of the interim government realized ships would be needed to keep Mexico from blockading the Texas coast and to maintain the flow of military supplies from New Orleans. Historians estimate that three-fourths of the troops, supplies, and money needed for the rebellion came via shipboard from the port at New Orleans.

The provisional government in November 1835 passed a bill providing for the purchase of four schooners. It issued letters of marque to privateers authorizing them to defend the Texas coast until the navy ships could be put into service. In January, the Texas Navy became a reality with the purchase of a former privateer rechristened the *Liberty*. The *Invincible*, a schooner built originally for the slave trade, was commissioned a few days later and the *Independence*, a former United States revenue cutter, which had been used to enforce customs regulations and catch smugglers, became the third purchase. Finally, the *Brutus* completed the Texas naval fleet. Immediately, the little band of vessels halted Mexican ships ferrying supplies to General Santa Anna's army, forcing it to forage for food as it marched across Texas. The ships also captured Mexican fishing vessels, sending their cargoes to the volunteer Texas army.

After Texas won independence from Mexico in the Battle of San

Jacinto on April 21, 1836, the *Liberty* escorted the ship carrying the injured General Sam Houston to New Orleans for medical treatment. That's when the navy experienced its first setback—the *Liberty* remained in New Orleans for repairs and when the new Republic of Texas could not pay its bill, the *Liberty* was sold. Financial worries continued the following September when the *Brutus* and the *Invincible* were in New York for repairs. When the city's customs collector realized the Republic of Texas could not pay the bill, the gentleman paid the tab himself.

Meantime, Mexico refused to ratify the treaty that General Santa Anna signed after his army's defeat at San Jacinto. Unable to launch a full attack on Texas because it was embroiled in its own civil war, Mexico continued making threatening forays along the Texas coast. The schooner *Independence* underwent repairs in New Orleans in April 1837. On its way back to Galveston it was lost in a four-hour gun battle with two Mexican ships.

With the fleet reduced to two vessels, President Houston believed the ships needed to patrol the Texas coast; however, the secretary of the navy and its commodore decided to boost the overall morale by sending both ships on a cruise raiding Mexican coastal towns. On August 26, 1837, both ships returned triumphant to Galveston. *Brutus* entered the harbor towing a prize Mexican ship. But, the *Invincible* drew such a deep draft that it could not cross the bar into the harbor. As it sat at anchor waiting for high tide to allow it to proceed, two Mexican ships attacked. The *Brutus* sailed out to help in the fight and ran aground on a sandbar. After a daylong battle, the *Invincible* attempted to enter the harbor, went aground and was destroyed. The *Brutus*, last of the ships of the Texas Navy, was lost the following October in a storm at sea.

Although the Republic of Texas had no active navy from September 1837 until March 1839, Mexico was too preoccupied with problems at home to take advantage of the unprotected coastline, which gave Texas time to purchase six more ships at a cost of $280,000. In March 1839 a steam packet was purchased and renamed the *Zavala*, the first ship in the second Texas Navy, followed by the *San Jacinto*, the *San Antonio*, the *San Bernard*, the brig *Wharton*, the sloop-of-war *Austin*, and the *Archer*.

Political differences existed from the beginning of the republic between President Houston and Vice President Mirabeau B. Lamar and came dramatically to the surface in December 1838 when Lamar became the second president of the Republic of Texas. Whereas Sam Houston wanted Texas to use its ships to protect the coast and insure the republic's increased industry and commerce, Mirabeau Lamar encouraged the navy to pursue an aggressive policy of raids to keep Mexico busy defending its coastline.

During Lamar's presidency, he initiated a friendly relationship with the Yucatán after it declared independence from Mexico. In December 1841, just as Sam Houston was returning for a second term as president, Lamar sent the *Austin,* the *San Bernard,* and the *San Antonio* to the Yucatán for defense against Mexico. Immediately after Houston's inauguration, he ordered the fleet to return.

In the meantime, the only mutiny in the Texas Navy occurred in New Orleans on February 11, 1842. The schooner *San Antonio* was in port to be refitted. Apparently concerned the sailors and marines would desert, the officers confined the men to the ship while the officers went ashore. The men got drunk on liquor that was smuggled aboard and Sergeant Seymour Oswalt led a mutiny in which a lieutenant was killed. Eventually the men were brought to trial; three were flogged, four were hanged from the yardarm of the *Austin*, and Oswalt escaped from jail.

Mirabeau Lamar had appointed Edwin Ward Moore, a ten-year veteran of the United States Navy, commodore of the second Texas Navy, and Moore was determined to defend the Yucatán. Moore had constant problems financing the repair of his ships and because paydays did not come regularly, he had trouble recruiting. The *Zavala* had been allowed to rot and was eventually sold for scrap. Houston recognized that the republic was financially destitute. Determned to reduce spending in his second term, he withheld funds allocated by Congress for the navy. Moore raised almost $35,000 to repair his ships and when it became clear he could not raise enough money in New Orleans to refit the ships, Houston ordered him back to Galveston. Hearing of renewed Mexican troubles on the Yucatán, Moore arranged to supply the Yucatán with Texas ships for $8,000 a month. He sent the *San Antonio* to the Yucatán but it was lost at sea. Just when the *Austin* and the *Wharton* were ready to sail from New Orleans, commissioners arrived with orders from Houston instructing Moore to sell the fleet immediately for whatever price he could get. Further, Houston suspended Moore from command and told him to return immediately to Texas. Moore convinced the commissioners to allow him to sail the vessel back to Texas but when he heard that Yucatán was about to surrender to Santa Anna, Moore headed instead for the Yucatán. The resulting battle against the much larger Mexican vessels did not produce a victory, but it broke the blockade of Campeche and allowed Texas ships to get supplies to the forces fighting the Yucatán land battle. After a week, the Mexican force sailed away, Yucatán was not retaken, and Moore believed Texas was spared the invasion that would have followed if Mexico had captured the Yucatán.

A very angry President Sam Houston claimed Moore's cruise was illegal and charged him as a pirate, a murderer, a mutineer and an embezzler. When Moore returned to Galveston on July 14, 1843, he was welcomed by a harbor full of boats loaded with cheering people. Houston discharged Moore dishonorably from the Texas Navy for disobedience of orders, fraud, piracy, desertion, and murder. Moore insisted on a court martial and was acquitted of all the charges except disobedience. The following year he was cleared of the charge of disobedience.

The political battle had not ended. Texas had attracted volunteers to fight in its war for independence by passing a bounty act on November 24, 1835, promising 640 acres for two years of military service. Almost ten million acres were distributed as bounties, but veterans of the Texas Navy did not get a single acre. Houston, claiming they were an "unnecessary extravagance," vetoed a resolution on January 6, 1842 that would have allowed navy veterans to receive a bounty. He added, "Generally, the seaman has no interest (except a transitory one) on shore." An effort to reintroduce the bill and pass it over Houston's veto met no success.

The Texas Navy had come to an end. The Republic of Texas was negotiating with the United States to join the Union. As part of annexation, the *Austin, Wharton, Archer,* and *San Bernard* became part of the United States fleet. Their officers hoped to be included in the transfer, but US naval officers were against the plan, and the Texas ships were declared unfit for service.

The Texas Navy was forgotten until 1958 when Governor Price Daniel established a Third Texas Navy. In October 1970 Governor Preston Smith reestablished the headquarters for the Third Texas Navy at its original base in Galveston. The new organization serves as a commemorative nonprofit, chartered by the State of Texas to assure the survival of Texas naval history.

Santa Anna: A Paradox

Some call his era the "Age of Santa Anna." He was known as a brave soldier and a cunning politician. Over his forty-year career, he served multiple times as a general and eleven times as president of Mexico. He thought of himself as "the Napoleon of the West," yet historians say he was among the many leaders of Mexico that failed the nation. His political endeavors and his military failures resulted in Mexico losing over half its territory in the American west, first to Texas after its revolution and finally to the United States after the Mexican-American War.

Antonio López de Santa Anna was born in 1794, the son of middle class *criollos* (persons of European descent born in the Americas) in the Spanish province of Veracruz. His family had enough money to send him to school for a time, but at sixteen, he became a cadet in the Fijo de Veracruz infantry regiment. For five years his regiment policed Indian tribes and fought against insurgents, including filibusterers from the United States who were trying to free Texas from Spain. Many historians believe that this early period of Santa Anna's military career shaped his ideas of how to put down rebellions through the use of a fierce policy of mass executions, which he later used during the Texas War for Independence.

As a member of the Royalist army, the dashing young man, who used his charisma to charm acquaintances, fought for a while on the Spanish side as Mexico began its eleven-year war for independence from Spain. However, as he did throughout his military and political career, he realized his best interest lay in switching sides to join the rebel forces fighting for independence. All during the turbulent 1820s as coups ushered in first one and then another president, Santa Anna changed his allegiance to whomever was clawing his way to the top, quickly rising through the ranks while gaining the reputation as a valuable if treacherous ally.

In 1829 Santa Anna achieved what some claim was his greatest (and perhaps only) military victory when Spain made its last attempt to regain control of Mexico by invading Tampico. Santa Anna, who was good at stirring up emotions and quickly rounding up an army, led an expedition that defeated the Spanish force. The invading army was suffering from yellow fever, but the defeat was real and Santa Anna emerged as a national hero. Without hesitation he branded himself "The Victor of Tampico" and "The Savior of the Motherland." More coups followed, accompanied by presidential exiles and executions, until the new congress of Mexico elected Santa Anna as president on April 1, 1833. Despite having run as a liberal, within a year Santa Anna claimed that the country was not ready for democracy. He dissolved the congress and centralized power, turning his regime into a military dictatorship.

Liberals all over Mexico felt betrayed and several states began to defy the new authority including citizens in Texas and Coahuila, which was the northernmost state in Mexico. The Texas settlers, who were mostly from the United States, had received generous land grants from the Mexican government and were demanding more fair treatment and the return to the original liberal terms they had received during colonization. Several open rebellions occurred along the Texas coast, at Nacogdoches, and finally at Goliad. When citizens in Zacatecas also rose up in December 1835 in defiance of Santa Anna's new authority, he moved quickly to crush the resistance and allowed his army to loot the town for forty-eight hours. Then, he marched his army at top speed through winter cold to San Antonio where he raised the red flag of no quarter and demanded surrender of the Texans, whom he called "land thieves." The thirteen-day siege ended on March 6, 1836, with the killing of all the inhabitants of the Alamo fortress except for some women, children, and slaves. The next demonstration of his intent to dominate the rebellious citizens occurred at Goliad when he ordered the execution of over 300 captives who had surrendered on the battlefield to General Urrea. Despite Urrea's letter requesting that the honorable surrender be recognized, Santa Anna sent word that they should be executed as pirates. On the morning of March 27, the prisoners who could walk were marched away from the Goliad fort and shot. Those who had been injured in the battle were shot inside the compound. When word spread of the massacre at Goliad, people who had thought of Santa Anna as cunning and crafty, realized that he was indeed cruel and the realization fueled an infusion of volunteers from the United States to help the Texans fight for independence.

Santa Anna continued to march eastward intending to kill or drive across the Sabine River all the Texas land thieves whom he held in such disdain. His amazing ability to hastily round up an army had never been tested at such long distances from the center of Mexican supplies or in the bitter cold and rain of that Texas spring. He did not have ample food or supplies for his men, and as he chased the rebels across Texas, his nemesis, General Sam Houston, had the towns burned and supplies destroyed as Texas settlers fled in terror before the advancing Mexican Army. Still confident of his superior force and determined that his military skill would win the day, Santa Anna left half his force on the banks of the Brazos River as he raced eastward to catch the officials of the interim Texas government and then defeat the ragtag army of Texas volunteer farmers and merchants.

When the two armies finally met on the banks of Buffalo Bayou on April 21, 1836, Santa Anna grossly underestimated the fury and determination of the Texans to repay the Mexican Army for the slaughter at the Alamo and at Goliad. In fact, as the Mexican Army enjoyed its afternoon siesta, the Texans using two cannons that had only recently arrived from citizens of Cincinnati, Ohio, raced across less than two miles separating the two camps and in an eighteen-minute battle defeated the startled Mexicans. Despite their victory, the furious Texans continued killing the Mexicans until 630 lay dead and 730 were taken prisoner. The Texans lost nine.

Santa Anna was found the next day, dressed in peasant clothing and hiding in a marsh. When he was taken before General Houston and realized his life was to be spared, he boldly announced his willingness to treat with Houston regarding the boundaries of the two countries, a complete about face from the day before when he planned to exterminate the land pirates. Santa Anna signed the Treaty of Velasco agreeing to Texas independence, but the Mexican government, upon hearing of his loss of Texas, deposed him in absentia and refused to ratify the treaty.

Santa Anna was not finished. After a time of exile in the United States, he eventually made his way back to his estate in Veracruz. In December 1838 the French landed in Veracruz after the Mexican government refused to reimburse French citizens for their financial losses in Mexico. Ironically, the government gave Santa Anna command of an army with instructions to defend Mexico by any means necessary. In typical Santa Anna fashion, the assault failed, and Mexico was forced to meet French demands, but Santa Anna managed to turn the disaster to his advantage. He had been hit by cannon fire in his leg and hand, and his leg had to be amputated. He returned to politics as a hero of the war, touting his sacrifice for the fatherland. He even had his amputated leg buried with full military honors.

He served again as acting president the following year and helped over-throw the government in 1841 to become dictator for the next four years. During his reign he sent military expeditions into the Republic of Texas, which convinced many Texans that annexation to the United States would give them powerful support. His autocratic rule fomented so much resistance that he was forced to step down and was exiled to Cuba.

Santa Anna found another chance to return to Mexico with the beginning of the Mexican-American War in 1846. He made a deal with President James Polk to allow him to enter Mexico through the United States naval blockade in exchange for getting a negotiated settlement of land for the United States. At the same time he was making that deal, he was arranging with Mexico's president to lead an army against the northern invaders. Reneging on both agreements, as head of the army, he marched to Mexico City and declared himself president. Again, his military prowess failed and when the United States captured Mexico City, Santa Anna retired to exile in Jamaica. The war ended with the United States gaining all or part of ten western states that stretched its borders all the way to the Pacific Coast.

It is hard to believe that even the conservatives, who wanted a central government under the control of the army and the Catholic Church, would invite Santa Anna back in April 1853. This time his administration was no more successful than before. He declared himself dictator for life, funneled government funds to himself, and sold more Mexican territory to the United States in the Gadsden Purchase. His "Most Serene Highness," as he called himself, finally became too powerful even for his conservative friends. A group of liberals, led by Benito Juárez, overthrew him and he fled again to Cuba. When the new government discovered the extent of Santa Anna's corruption, he was tried in absentia for treason, and all his property was confiscated.

Santa Anna roamed from Cuba to Colombia, to St. Thomas and to Staten Island, New York, where he came up with the idea of selling chicle, the sap from the Mexican sapodilla tree, to the Americans as an additive to expensive natural rubber. He planned to use his new wealth to raise another army to take over Mexico City. Apparently Thomas Adams, a photographer, glassmaker, and inventor, was assigned to oversee Santa Anna. Adams bought one ton of chicle from Santa Anna and tried unsuccessfully for a year to make rubber for carriage tires. After Adams remembered seeing Santa Anna chewing on the chicle, Adams experimented with adding sugar, and began what became known as "Chiclets" chewing gum. That was one windfall that Santa Anna failed to capture.

In 1874, after Mexico issued a general amnesty, Santa Anna returned, a crippled old man who was almost blind from cataracts. He had written his memoirs while in exile and spent the last two years virtually ignored by the Mexican government. "The Napoleon of the West" died in Mexico City on June 21, 1876.

4

Colliding Cultures

The Tragedy of Cynthia Ann Parker

*I*t is probably legitimate to say she died of a broken heart, a heart that started breaking when she was about nine years old. Cynthia Ann Parker's family and several members of the Parker clan moved from Illinois to North Central Texas in the spring of 1835 and built a log fortress they called Fort Parker.

On May 19, 1836, several of the men in the Parker family were out working in the field a mile from the fort when a large force of Comanche, Kiowa, and Kichai attacked the fort. Cynthia Ann's horror began as she watched the slaughter of her father, uncle, and grandfather. As was the custom among Southern Plains Indians, the women were raped. Some were killed or died later from their wounds.

Her uncle James Parker arrived from the field in time to help seventeen family members escape into the nearby forest, but he was too late to help Cynthia Ann. She was carried away as were her brother John, James' own daughter and grandson, and his sister-in-law—five family members—stolen by the Indians who soon divided their captives among different bands.

Over the next several years, the Parker family began recovering first one and then another of its lost members through various ransom arrangements. Stories surfaced of Cynthia Ann being spotted with various Comanche bands, even of her refusing, on one occasion, her brother's plea for her to return with him. An Indian agent claimed that offers to buy her release were rebuffed by Comanches who vowed that only force would induce her captors to release her.

Cynthia Ann married Peta Nocona, war chief of the Nocone band of the Comanche who was so devoted to his white wife that despite Comanche custom, he never took another. She bore two sons Quanah and Pecos and a daughter Topsanna (known as Prairie Flower).

On December 18, 1860, Sul Ross led his Texas Rangers on a surprise attack of a Comanche hunting camp, killing many including women and children. Peta Nocona was shot and scalped, a practice employed by both sides. The Rangers were surprised that one of their captives who carried an infant daughter had blue eyes and spoke broken English.

Some of the Rangers tried to convince Ross to leave her with the Comanches, but he believed so many families across the country had lost children in Indian raids that it would stir terrible unrest to keep her from her white family. When her uncle, Isaac Parker, arrived and said her name, Cynthia Ann patted her chest and said "Me Cincee Ann."

After her "rescue" Cynthia Ann and Prairie Flower were displayed like sideshow characters as crowds rushed to see the strange woman who had become a savage and given up her Christian ways. Throughout the ordeal of returning with her uncle to his home, she stared back at the gawking crowds, tears pouring down her cheeks. She had seen her scalped husband and did not know about the fate of her two sons.

The following April, the Texas Legislature granted Cynthia Ann $100 a year for the next five years, a league of land (about 4,400 acres), and placed her under her uncles' guardianship. Her white family, unable to force her to accept her new life, moved her from one member's home to the next. She refused to give up Comanche grief rituals of cutting her breasts and her arms and wailing for hours. She tried and failed several times to return to her Comanche family. The final blow came in 1864 when Prairie Flower died of influenza. Cynthia Ann never recovered and grieved until her death in 1870.

Rachel Parker Shares Her Story

While Cynthia Ann's story was sensationalized, followed by people all over this country, a less well-known tragedy was taking place—the recounting of which played a significant role in understanding the culture and psyche of the Comanche. On that May morning in 1836, when the Comanche raiding party swooped down on Fort Parker, Rachel Parker Plummer was seventeen, expecting her second child, and caring for her fourteen-month-old son James Pratt Plummer. Her husband Luther, her father James Parker, and eight other family members were working in the field about a mile from the fort. In her book, *Rachel Plummer's Narrative of Twenty One Months' Servitude as a Prisoner Among the Comanche Indians*, Rachel wrote that "one minute the fields (in front of the fort) were clear, and the next moment, more Indians than I dreamed possible were in front of the fort." Her Uncle Benjamin Parker, not believing the white flag carried by the Indians was to be trusted, walked out to meet the Indians, hoping to give the women and children in the fort time to run out through the back entrance. Rachel had delayed leaving with the others because she feared she could not carry her son and keep up with them.

It only took the sound of their whooping to realize the Indians were coming into the fort. As she ran carrying her son, she saw her Uncle Benjamin being stabbed with lances. Rachel said, "A large sulky Indian picked up a hoe and knocked me down." He dragged her by her long red hair until she finally managed to get up on her feet. A Comanche squaw on a horse had taken little James Pratt. She saw her grandfather tortured and killed and her grandmother raped, speared, and left for dead. The Comanches rode away from Fort Parker with three children—Cynthia Ann, her brother John, and Rachel's son—and two women, Rachel and Elizabeth Kellogg (who was returned three months later when Sam Houston paid the $150 ransom).

Rachel wrote that four Indians found a bottle of her father's pulverized arsenic and thinking it was white paint, dissolved the powder with their saliva and smeared it all over their faces and bodies. All four died, probably in agony.

That first night, the war party held a ritual dance dangling the scalps of the slain men before the captives. They beat and kicked the women and children. When the children cried, Rachel wrote that they "were soon hushed by blows I had no idea they could survive." The women were stripped naked and bound so tightly that their arms bled. Then they were repeatedly raped while the children watched. Rachel wrote, "To undertake to narrate their barbarous treatment would only add to my present distress, for it is with feelings of the deepest mortification that I think of it, much less to speak or write of it."

The next morning, all the captives were strapped to their horses and for the next five days the Comanches rode hard, denying them food and allowing only small amounts of water. On the sixth day, the Indians divided them, with Rachel and baby James going with a separate group of Comanches. However, as soon as the Indians realized James had been weaned, they ripped him from Rachel's arms, and she never saw him again.

They rode for weeks into the high plains above the timberline. She described a journey through the snows of the Rocky Mountains where she rarely had anything on her feet and very little covering her body. Her job as a slave was to tend the horses, and to prepare buffalo skins. If she failed to meet her quota, she was beaten. The work entailed scraping the flesh off the skin, applying lime to absorb the grease, and rubbing buffalo brains on the skin until it was softened.

At the time of the raid Rachel was four months pregnant and gave birth the following October to a second son. Her master thought the baby kept Rachel from her work and when he was seven weeks old, several men held Rachel while another man strangled the baby. When he still showed signs of life, they tied a rope around his neck and dragged him behind a horse until he was "literally torn to pieces."

Rachel continued to write about the country and the animals and plants that she saw as the tribe traveled. She noted Comanche folkways, the nightly dances, the worship of pet crows, and taboos. She learned the language and listened to plans for attacks. Eventually she lost all hope of being rescued, and finding that she was unable to kill herself, she decided to provoke the Indians to do it for her. When her young mistress ordered her to get a tool from the lodge, Rachel refused. The mistress ran screaming at Rachel, and instead of cowering in fear, she fought back, threw the girl on the ground, and beat her on the head with a buffalo bone. All the time she fought, Rachel expected a spear to be driven into her body. Instead, a crowd gathered and began screaming, but making no effort to stop Rachel from beating the girl. When it was clear Rachel had won the fight, she picked up the girl, carried her back to camp, and washed the blood from her face. The girl's mother was furious and threatened to burn Rachel, which she had done in the past. But this time Rachel fought back. The two struggled so furiously around the fire that both were badly burned. They continued to fight until they burst through the side of the tipi. Again, the men watched and did not interfere even as Rachel won. When the council met to discuss the fight, all three women gave their account. Rachel was told she must replace the lodge pole she had broken. Sensing a new place in the community, Rachel refused unless the younger woman helped her. The council agreed. Rachel discovered that the Comanches respected those who fought back, who defended them-selves, who did not cower in the face of danger.

Once Rachel realized she would not be killed, she decided her only hope lay in finding someone to buy her. Eventually she met Comancheros, Mexicans who traded with the Comanches. To her surprise, when the Comanchero asked to buy Rachel, her master agreed. The Comancheros who ransomed Rachel were working for William and Mary Donoho, a wealthy couple in Santa Fe who had given them instructions to pay any price to ransom white women. The Donohos and the citizens of Santa Fe warmly welcomed Rachel, however, a Pueblo Indian uprising caused the Donohos, in fear for their lives, to take Rachel with them as they fled Santa Fe. They traveled to their home in Independence, Missouri—a two-month journey of 800 miles across the heart of Comanche territory. Upon her arrival, Rachel was reunited with a family member who immediately set out in the cold winter weather on the 1,000-mile trip to her father James Parker's home. They arrived in Huntsville on February 19, 1838.

Rachel was reunited with her husband who, unlike many men whose wives had been abused by the Indians, welcomed her home. She soon was pregnant with her third child. Near the end of her pregnancy, the family was forced to flee to Houston to escape vigilantes who were threatening her father. The trip in the dead of winter must have been more than Rachel Plummer's body could tolerate. Soon after reaching Houston, her son, Wilson P. Plummer, was born on January 4, 1839. Rachel died the following March 19 and her son died two days later.

Rachel's book has served historians well. It was among the vast resources used by S.C. Gwynne in *Empire of the Summer Moon*, which was a finalist for the Pulitzer Prize. Gwynne's account is a must-read for anyone wishing to understand the culture of the powerful Comanches. Gwynne deftly employs the raid on Parker's Fort and the subsequent events to weave the fascinating tale of the power and decline of the great Comanche Warriors.

Scalped and Lived to Tell About It

When an old story comes from many sources, it is difficult to glean the exact details. In this case, we know a man was scalped and lived to tell about it.

Farmers like Josiah Wilbarger and his wife who moved to the west accepted the ever-present danger of Indians hostile to encroachment of the new arrivals. Surveyors mapping land grants for the early colonists faced an even greater threat because the Indians feared and hated surveyors, calling their compass "the thing that steals the land."

In addition to farming his land, granted in 1832 a few miles east of the present city of Austin, Josiah Wilbarger worked as a surveyor. Stories vary as to what Wilbarger and his four friends were doing out in the country in August 1833. Most accounts say they were on a surveying trip and stopped near Pecan Springs to have lunch.

The attack came suddenly as a large band of Indians swooped down with rifles and bows, killing one man, shooting another in the hip, and hitting Wilbarger in the calf of his leg.

As the men scrambled to mount their horses, they saw Wilbarger take another blow. Some accounts say a bullet, others say an arrow struck Wilbarger in the neck as the Indians descended on him. Whatever they saw, it convinced Wilbarger's friends that he was dead.

The survivors raced several miles to the protection of the Reuben Hornsby home, planning to return the next morning for the bodies after the Indians finished their scalping ritual. That night Mrs. Hornsby dreamed of Wilbarger sitting under a tree seriously injured. She woke her husband who dismissed her as overreacting to all the excitement. Mrs. Hornsby dreamed a second time, even recognizing the site where Hornsby lay naked.

It's not clear when the men returned for Wilbarger. Some say Mrs. Hornsby insisted they leave immediately; other versions claim the men waited until morning. Either way, Mrs. Hornsby provided a blanket saying, "Take this to make a stretcher. He's not dead but he can't ride."

They found him as Mrs. Hornsby claimed, scalped and near death. Placing his naked body on the blanket, they carried him back to the Hornsby's where Mrs. Hornsby applied poultices of wheat bread and bear grease.

As Wilbarger grew stronger he told of how the arrow in his neck paralyzed him, making him unable to feel as the Indians hovered around obviously believing he was dead. One man carved around Wilbarger's scalp and then snatched his hair so hard it sounded like a mighty clap of thunder as the flesh ripped from his head.

Continuing to feign death, Wilbarger waited until the Indians finished the other scalping rituals and left. Some stories say Wilbarger pulled the arrow from his neck and passed out. When he awoke, he was blazing with fever and crawled to the nearby spring to cool his pain-racked body. He started to crawl toward the Hornsby house, but made it as far as the tree where he passed out again. Upon waking he saw his sister who lived in Missouri come toward him saying for him not to worry, help was on the way. Then, she walked away toward the Hornsby house.

Several months later, word came that his sister died the day before the Indian attack. She was buried on the day her image appeared to Wilbarger.

The hole about the size of a large silver dollar in Wilbarger's scalp never healed. He wore silk bandages cut from his wife's wedding dress to protect his head for the next eleven years. He died at his home on April 11, 1844, after striking his head on a low beam in his cotton gin.

Wild Man of the Navidad

A story, circulated since the 1830s in South Central Texas, contains enough truth to merit a Texas Historical marker. Residents along the Navidad River bottom in Lavaca and Jackson counties started seeing strange footprints along the riverbank, and at the same time they missed small amounts of sweet potatoes and corn. On moonlit nights, food in their cabins disappeared even though an intruder had to step over sleeping dogs. At the same time, tools would vanish, only to be returned later, brilliantly polished and sharpened. In fall around hog-killing time families stopped fattening hogs because a fat hog was invariably replaced with a scrawny substitute. Valuables such as gold or watches were never taken although they were plainly visible when the food disappeared.

Everyone speculated about "it." Slaves called it "The Thing That Comes," thinking it was a ghost. Settlers, finding two sets of footprints, believed one of the intruders to be a man and the other a smaller companion, perhaps a woman or child.

Many people organized search parties trying to capture the "Wild Man of the Navidad." Sometimes they found his camp among the thick growth of trees, but he never returned to the site while the pursuers waited.

Texas folk author J. Frank Dobie in his book *Tales of Old-Time Texas* concluded that the phantom figure had to be a woman because several well-documented sightings reported that "it" had long, flowing hair and facial features more similar to a woman. Dobie writes of a near capture in 1846 during an intense search when a rider heard rustling of the brush just before "it" ran in the light of the moon onto the open prairie. "She ran directly across the prairie in the direction of the main forest. The man nearest her rode a fleet horse and it needed all the speed it had to keep up with the object in pursuit. As the figure neared the dark woods, the rider was able to throw his lasso. But, as the rope neared the woman, the horse shied away and the lasso fell short. The figure darted into the woods never to be seen again."

Dobie said the rider claimed that the creature had long, flowing hair that trailed down almost to her feet, she wore no clothing, and her body seemed to be covered with short, brown hair. "As she fled to the woods, she dropped a club to the ground that was about 5 feet long and polished to a wonder," Dobie said.

Finally, in 1851, with the help of dogs trained to hunt down runaway slaves, local residents following their baying hounds found a black man in a tree. He wore no clothes and spoke no English. Some accounts say he was put in jail where he remained for about six months until a sailor wandered through who was familiar with the native dialect of the captive's African tribe.

The captive said his father, a chief of their tribe, sold his son into slavery for the price of a knife and tobacco. The new slave and a companion escaped after their transport ship reached Texas. They settled in the Navidad River bottom because of the abundance of wildlife and fruit. His companion died from exposure.

The captured man, whom they called Jimbo, was sold back into slavery and lived in Victoria and Refugio counties. Freed after the Civil War, he reportedly died in 1884.

J. Frank Dobie writes, "Of course all of this happened many years ago and in the telling you can always guarantee some buildup in the information will take place. If these things did happen, I cannot explain how."

Battle of Plum Creek

In January 1840, three Comanche chiefs entered San Antonio seeking a peace agreement that would recognize the borders of Comancheria—their ancient homeland. The Penateka, the southernmost band of Comanches, were feeling intense pressure as white settlement moved steadily westward. Smallpox, the white man's disease, swept through the Indian camps. And Cheyenne and Arapaho from the north pushed into Penateka buffalo ranges.

Although they had no intention of halting westward expansion, Texas officials agreed to a council the following March 19, providing the Penateka return with all the white captives held by Comanches. Few Texans understood that Comanches were many separate bands without authority over hostages held by other groups.

On the appointed day, thirty-three chiefs and warriors accompanied by over thirty women and children—painted for the occasion and dressed in their finest feathers—came to the Council House in San Antonio. They brought only one captive, Matilda Lockhart, a sixteen-year-old girl whose body was covered in bruises, burns so horrible that her nose was melted away, and she had been raped. During the eighteen months of captivity, she had learned the Comanche dialects, and she reported that she had seen at least fifteen hostages.

As previously arranged, Texas soldiers entered the Council House and the authorities informed the Indians that they were being held until all white captives were returned. Believing they had been tricked, the Comanches shouted for help to those waiting in the outer courtyard and tried to fight their way to freedom. Thirty of the chiefs and warriors were killed as well as about five women and children. Seven Texans were killed, ten wounded. One woman was released to deliver the message that all Comanche captives would be held for twelve days and then killed if the white captives were not returned. A young man who later was freed from captivity recounted that when the Comanches heard the news of the Council House fight, they grieved violently for days and then turned their revenge on thirteen captives—"roasted and butchered them," including Matilda Lockhart's six-year-old sister.

In early August under the leadership of Buffalo Hump, estimates of 1,000 Comanche and Kiowa, including women and children, swept down across Central Texas in the "Great Comanche Raid." At Victoria, they killed several people and stole about 1,500 horses that were corralled outside town. They raced on to Linnville, a seaport village on Lavaca Bay. Residents clambered into boats anchored in the shallow water and watched in horror for an entire day as the warehouses, businesses, and homes burned while the Indians—warriors, women and children—shrieked in glee, gathering all the loot they could carry from the burning structures. Three people were killed and three taken hostage. The plunder valued at $300,000 consisted of goods just in from New Orleans waiting to be sent to San Antonio and Austin. By the time the Indians retreated, only one structure remained. Joyous in their triumph, the Comanche began the long trek back across Central Texas as word of the raid spread among white settlements.

On August 12, volunteer militias and a company of Texas Rangers gathered at a crossing on Plum Creek, 120 miles inland from the coast. The whites watched the approach of the great army of Indians and horses stretching for miles across the prairie, singing, gyrating, and adorned in the booty from Linnville. Brightly colored ribbons waved from the horses' tails. One chief wore a silk top hat and a morning coat turned backward with shiny brass buttons glistening down his back.

Stories vary as to the outcome of the ensuing battle. Some accounts claim that Texans discovered silver bullion on the pack animals and stopped pursuing the Indians to gather the loot. Others say that eighty Comanches died (twelve bodies were recovered). One Texan was killed, seven injured. The Battle of Plum Creek ended the Comanche presence in settled regions of Central Texas.

Plains Indians Bow to White Supremacy

After the Civil War, views differed about what should be done about the Southern Plains Indians' often-vicious determination to keep their hunting grounds free of white settlement. The Texas government wanted to see the Indians exterminated, while the federal government planned to move them to two reservations established in Indian Territory (present-day Oklahoma).

Two turbulent chapters in history came together in the 1870s to subdue and contain what the white man called the "Indian threat." The first transition followed the completion in 1869 of the Transcontinental Railroad, which opened the east coast and European markets to commercial shipment of buffalo hides from the Great Plains. An avalanche of professional buffalo hunters swarmed onto the Southern Plains where tens of millions of buffalo grazed on the rich grassland. The second upheaval, the Red River War, began in 1874 as a campaign of the United States Army to forcibly move the Comanche, Kiowa, Southern Cheyenne, and Arapaho tribes to the reservations in Indian Territory.

Bison sustained the life of the nomadic tribes who used every part of the buffalo for survival. Hides provided housing and clothing; brains soften the buffalo skin; bones could be scraped into brushes and awls; hair made excellent ropes, stuffing, and yarn; sinew served as thread and bowstrings;

and dung became fuel. Every part of the animal, even the nose gristle, fetus, and hump, contributed to the Indian diet.

Indians hunted with bows and spears, killing only the number of bison they needed for survival, whereas a good buffalo hunter made a stand downwind from a herd and could shoot as many as 100 in a morning and 1,000 to 2,000 in a three-month season. The teams varied in size from one hunter and two skinners to large organizations of hunters, skinners, gun cleaners, cartridge reloaders, cooks, wranglers, and wagons for transporting equipment and supplies. After skinning a beast, which weighed up to 2,500 pounds and stood six feet tall at its shaggy shoulders, the men ate the delicacies—hump and tongue—sold what they could, and left the remaining carcass to rot on the prairie. This careless slaughter almost completely exterminated the buffalo, and observing the demise of their livelihood infuriated the Indians.

While the buffalo hunters destroyed the Indian lifeline, several army columns crisscrossed the Texas Panhandle charged with harassing the agile bands of Indians until they gave up and moved to the reservations. When army units discovered a group of Indians, few casualties resulted, but the army methodically destroyed the supplies and horses, slowly squeezing the size and strength of the roaming Indian population.

In this climate of search and destroy by the army, coupled with Indian anger over destruction of the buffalo, Comanche Chief Quanah Parker (son of Cynthia Ann Parker) and a spiritual leader named Isa-tai led 250 warriors in June 1874, in an attack on Adobe Walls, a small outpost of buffalo hunters in the Texas Panhandle. The hunters, using large caliber buffalo guns, held off their attackers, but the violence surprised government officials. As the warriors continued raiding along the frontier, President Grant's administration authorized the Army to use whatever means necessary to subdue the Southern Plains Indians.

With firm directions from Washington, the Red River War began with a fury as five army columns swarmed across the Texas Panhandle from different directions. Colonel Ranald S. Mackenzie's scouts found a large village of Comanche, Kiowa and Cheyenne hidden in their winter quarters on the floor of Palo Duro Canyon, a 6,000-foot-deep gorge stretching almost 100 miles across the Texas Panhandle.

At dawn on September 28, 1874, Mackenzie's troops hurtled down the steep cliff wall, surprising the Indians who tried to protect their squaws

83

and pack animals as they fled from the persistent army fire. Nightfall found four Indians dead, 450 lodges burned to the ground, and the winter supply of buffalo meat destroyed. The army rounded up 1,400 horses, kept all they could use, and shot the remaining. Out of food and housing, without their horses, and facing the coming winter, the Indians had no choice but to walk to the Fort Sill reservation.

The Red River War ended the following June when Quanah Parker and his band of Comanches—the last of the southwestern Indians—surrendered at Fort Sill. The almost complete devastation of the buffalo and the persistent military attacks successfully ended the Indian presence on the High Plains and opened settlement to white farmers and ranchers.

Bose Ikard, Black Cowboy

More than a quarter of the cowboys in the 19th century were black and Bose Ikard became one of the most famous frontiersmen and trail drivers in Texas. Born on a Mississippi slave plantation in 1843, Bose Ikard moved to Texas when he was nine years old with his master Dr. Milton Ikard. The family settled in Parker County, just west of Fort Worth, where Bose learned to farm, ranch, and fight the ever-present Indians. Even after becoming a freedman at the end of the Civil War, Bose stayed with his master's family until 1866 when Dr. Ikard wrote a letter of recommendation for Bose to work as a trail driver for Oliver Loving and his partner Charles Goodnight. Bose joined the already famous Goodnight-Loving Cattle Trail over which about eighteen men drove cattle more than 2,000 miles from Texas through New Mexico to Colorado.

After Loving's death from injuries in an Indian fight in 1867, Bose continued to work for Goodnight and earned his employer's respect and abiding friendship. Goodnight is quoted as saying: "Bose surpassed any man I had in endurance and stamina. There was a dignity, cleanliness and reliability about him that was wonderful. His behavior was very good in a fight and he was probably the most devoted man to me that I ever knew. I have trusted him farther than any man. He was my banker, my detective, and everything else in Colorado, New Mexico, and the other wild country. The nearest and only bank was in Denver, and when we carried money, I gave it to Bose, for a thief would never think of robbing him. Bose could be trusted farther than any living man I know."

Larry McMurtry patterned *Lonesome Dove* after the adventures of the Goodnight-Loving Trail, modeling the character Deets (played by Danny Glover) after Bose Ikard.

J. Evetts Haley in *Charles Goodnight, Cowman and Plainsman* relates Goodnight's account of Bose Ikard's rugged endurance, ability as a nightrider, and skill at turning a stampeding herd.

When Bose decided to leave the trail and marry in 1868, Charles Goodnight advised him to settle on a farm near Weatherford, an area west of Fort Worth that continued to be plagued by Indian attacks. In 1869 Bose rode with his former master Dr. Milton Ikard in a running battle against Quanah Parker, leader of the aloof and warlike Quahada Comanches who for a decade had refused to move to a reservation.

Bose and his wife Angelina had six children and continued over the years welcoming Goodnight to their home. After Bose died on January 4, 1929, Charles Goodnight had a granite marker placed at his friend's grave in Greenwood Cemetery. It reads: "Bose Ikard served with me four years on the Goodnight-Loving Trail, never shirked a duty or disobeyed an order, rode with me in many stampedes, participated in three engagements with Comanches, splendid behavior." A Texas Historical marker also stands beside Bose Ikard's gravesite.

Texas Slave Stories

It was common for slave families to be broken up as different members were often sold separately, but not all slave families suffered permanent separation. Elizabeth Ramsey was a mulatto slave in South Carolina who gave birth in 1828 to her master's child whom she named Louisa. One account claims that because Louisa looked like the master's white child, Elizabeth and Louisa were sold to a planter in Mobile, Alabama. When Louisa was about thirteen, she and her mother were separated in a sale to different slaveholders. Despite being sold to a man named Williams and taken to New Orleans, Louisa remained determined to find her mother. Williams made Louisa his concubine, and she gave birth to four of his seven children. Upon his death, she was set free and given enough money to move to Cincinnati where she married a mulatto named Henry Picquet who encouraged her continued search for her mother.

When they were separated, Louisa knew that her mother was sold to

Colonel Albert C. Horton. He served as Texas' first lieutenant governor and as acting governor during the Mexican American War. By the opening of the Civil War, Horton was one of the wealthiest men in the state and owned 150 slaves on plantations in Wharton and Matagorda counties.

A friend of Louisa's, who had traveled to Texas, brought back descriptions of Horton that matched Louisa's memory of the man who had purchased her mother. Around 1858 Louisa began writing letters to Horton and to her mother, pleading to buy Elizabeth's freedom. Horton wanted $1,000 to give up Elizabeth. Finally, Louisa convinced Horton to accept $900.

Raising $900 was no easy task. Louisa borrowed against her husband Henry's salary, and she asked for help in May 1860 from Hiram Mattison, a Methodist minister and abolitionist. Mattison tried without success to present her case to a meeting of Methodist bishops. Finally, he published an interview with Louisa centering most of his account on the whiteness of her skin and how shocking it was for white women to be held in slavery. That ploy garnered enough public contributions that combined with Louisa's savings, she was able to purchase her mother and be reunited after a twenty-year separation.

Free Colonists of Color

During the years that Texas was part of Mexico, the government offered free blacks the same rights of citizenship and opportunities for land ownership as were provided to white settlers. And just like the white colonists, the free Negroes worked to establish successful lives in the new country. William Goyens (sometimes spelled Goings) settled in Nacogdoches in the early 1820s and became an Indian Agent, working as a mediator and interpreter between the settlers and Cherokees of Northeast Texas. Born in North Carolina in 1794, the son of a white mother and mulatto father (with Cherokee ancestry), Goyens' fair complexion may have helped him establish a successful blacksmith business in Nacogdoches and begin land speculation. His work as an Indian Agent earned the trust of the Indians, the Mexican government, and the settlers in East Texas. He opened a freight hauling business, manufactured and repaired wagons, traded with the Indians, began lending money, and developed successful sawmill and gristmill operations. He married a white widow and adopted her son. Despite barely escaping being sold back into slavery on two business trips to Louisiana, Goyens owned as many as nine slaves and added to his wealth by entering the slave trade as a buyer and seller of human chattel.

During the buildup to the Texas Revolution, Goyens served as Sam Houston's interpreter as Houston negotiated a treaty with the Cherokees that kept them from siding with the Mexican Army during the war.

After Texas won independence from Mexico in 1836, laws under the new Republic changed the status of freedmen. Many slaveholders feared that the prosperity of freedmen would encourage rebellion among their slaves. The constitution of the Republic of Texas took away the citizenship of free blacks, restricted their property rights, and forbade permanent residence in Texas without the approval of the congress. The laws became even more restrictive for free blacks after Texas' annexation as the twenty-eighth state.

Despite living the rest of his life in the mansion he built west of Nacogdoches and continuing to amass considerable wealth, William Goyens was forced to hire some of the best lawyers in Nacogdoches to defend against white neighbors who constantly attempted to take the property he accumulated. Goyens died in 1856 and is buried next to his wife on the property they acquired near Nacogdoches.

Texas Slavery Laws

After Texas won independence from Mexico in 1836, allowing free persons of color to remain in Texas went against the basic principles of those who supported what was often called the "peculiar institution." Among the many reasons used to hold blacks in bondage was the claim that slaves and free Negroes were incapable of self-government. Consequently the constitution of the new Republic of Texas stated that free blacks could not remain in Texas without permission from Congress. Various resolutions resulted in freedmen being allowed to remain in Texas until January 1, 1842, at which time they would be sold back into slavery. The Digital Library on American Slavery lists 2,894 petitions of former slaves asking to be allowed to remain as free people in Texas.

In 1840 Fanny McFarland's petition stated that William McFarland brought her "to this country" in 1827 and that he freed her in 1835 because of "long and faithfull [sic] services to him and his family." The petition goes on to say that "at the time of the Mexican invasion," by which she meant the 1836 Texas Revolution, she was living in San Felipe de Austin as a free person, and as a result of the war she was driven from her home and lost all her possessions. After Texas won independence from Mexico, she moved to Houston in 1837 and "acquired a little property." Accounts of her early time in Houston indicate that she was a laundress, saved her money, and began buying small pieces of property, eventually operating one of Houston's first successful real estate ventures. Her petition states that she "would beg leave to urge upon your Honors the hardships of being obliged in her old age to leave her children to sacrifice her hard earned property to be obliged to part from friends of years standing to be obliged to leave her only home and be turned loose upon the wide world." The petition continued, "She has four children held as slaves in this Republic so that all her hopes and prospects in this life lie here." She asked, "to spend the few reminding [sic] days of her life as a resident and Citizen of this republic." Despite more than seventy people signing a petition dated October 30, 1840, stating that Fanny McFarland was a good and useful citizen of Houston, the Congress of the Republic of Texas denied her request. Undeterred, Fanny McFarland remained in Houston until her death in 1866. There is no record of whether her children, freed in 1865 at the end of the Civil War, were able to be with their mother in her last year.

Lulu Belle Madison White

Black Women in Texas History chronicles the lives of amazing black females from the days when they first arrived in Texas as both free and slave—during the Spanish Colonial Period—up to their present influence on Texas' politics and education. One of those women was Lulu Belle Madison White who graduated in 1928 from Prairie View College (present Prairie View A&M University) with a degree in English. Before beginning a ten-year teaching career in Houston, White joined the National Association for the Advancement of Colored People (NAACP) where her husband had been active for several years. She resigned from teaching after nine years and devoted the rest of her life to bringing justice to the black community. She was an amazing fund-raiser and organized new chapters of the NAACP throughout Texas. Even before the Supreme Court in 1944 found that the white primary was unconstitutional, White had started organizing a "pay your poll tax and go out to vote" campaign. She was the strongest advocate in Texas for using the black vote to force social change. She argued, "We cannot sit idly by and expect things to come to us. We must go out and get them."

She sought to educate the black community by leading voter registration seminars, and she urged black churches to speak up about public issues without endorsing specific candidates. She pressed white businesses to hire blacks, using boycotts, protest demonstrations, and letter-writing campaigns to influence the change.

In 1946 when the NAACP began its push for integrating the University of Texas, there was only one state-supported black college in Texas, Prairie View A&M, and it did not offer training for professional degrees. White not only persuaded Herman Marion Sweatt, a black mail carrier, to act as the plaintiff against the university, she raised money to pay his legal expenses. Years later Sweatt claimed that it was White's encouragement that helped him maintain his resolve. When the state offered to open a separate black university with its own law school in Houston instead of integrating the University of Texas, White supported Sweatt's rejection of the proposal on the basis that separate was not equal and only continued the status of Jim Crow.

The victory of *Sweatt v. Painter* before the Supreme Court in June 1951 opened the door for *Brown v. Board of Education* and the march toward dissolving the color line in education. A week before Lulu White's unexpected death in 1957, the national NAACP established the Lulu White Freedom Fund in her honor.

Rebecca Fisher, Indian Captive

Rebecca Jane Gilleland was seven when Comanches swooped down on her family, killed both parents, and took as captives Rebecca and her six-year-old brother William. Born in Philadelphia in 1831, Rebecca settled with her family near present-day Refugio about 1837. Rebecca recounted her experiences to the *Galveston Daily News* in 1913, remembering that it was late afternoon when the Comanches surprised the family as they walked not far from their home. Rebecca said that as the Indians bore down on them her father was struck down as he ran to the house for his gun. Her mother grabbed the two children by their arms and was praying loudly that they would be saved as they "were baptized in her blood."

The chief's wife scooped Rebecca onto her horse and at first threatened to cut off their hands and feet if she and William didn't stop crying. However, Rebecca believed the woman kept the other Indians from harming her and soon began to stroke Rebecca's blonde hair. The following morning when they stopped to rest, a company of Texas Rangers led by Albert Sidney Johnston surprised the Indians. In the melee—hand to hand combat—William's body was pierced with a lance and Rebecca took a sharp blow to her temple. The Rangers chased after the Indians, leaving the terrified children behind. Rebecca said William roused from unconsciousness as she carried him to hide in nearby brush. It was only after the Rangers returned, and Rebecca heard them calling her name that she and William emerged from their hiding place.

They stayed with William C. Blair, a Presbyterian minister in Victoria, until an aunt from Galveston came to get them. Rebecca attended school in Galveston and then was sent to Rutersville, a Methodist school between La Grange and Round Top. She met Orceneth Fisher, a minister almost thirty years her senior, who was working at the time as an editor of the *Texas Wesleyan Banner.*

After their marriage in 1848, Rebecca and Dr. Fisher served several churches in East Texas before taking a rugged stagecoach trip to California. They found a reign of lawlessness. When the crusading San Francisco newspaper editor, James King, was murdered, Dr. Fisher was asked to preach the funeral sermon. In the middle of his sermon, word arrived that a gang had hanged the men accused of King's murder.

The Fishers moved––under the protection of army troops––to Oregon where he organized the Methodist Episcopal Church South. On the eve of the Civil War, a mob of 300 stormed a camp meeting and threatened to hang Dr. Fisher, apparently for his perceived southern sympathies. Rebecca said of the experience that she grabbed the leader "by the collar and held him fast. He looked into my eyes and tuned away without speaking. I will never forget the vicious expression of his countenance." She also claimed that her husband quieted the mob with his calm demeanor and assurances that he came with a message of peace and love. During those tumultuous years, while the Fishers raised their six children and expanded the work of Methodism, Rebecca became known as the "woman who quelled the mob."

After returning to Texas in 1870 and settling in Austin, Dr. Fisher served two terms as chaplain for the Texas legislature before his death in 1880. Rebecca's brother William was a highly regarded poet whose work appeared in numerous magazines and newspapers before his death in 1894.

Rebecca Fisher was the only woman elected to the Texas Veterans Association, and after its members who had served from the time of the Texas

Revolution to annexation, all passed away, the work of the organization was taken over by the Daughters of the Republic of Texas (DRT) of which Rebecca Fisher was a charter member. She worked with Clara Driscoll and others to save the Alamo from destruction, and for several years she offered the opening prayer for the Texas legislature. Her portrait was the first of a woman to be hung in the Senate chamber at the Texas capitol. At her death in 1926 at the age of ninety-four, the body of the woman known by many as "the Mother of Texas" lay in state in the Senate chamber, the locale of her funeral service.

Sarah Ridge, Cherokee Texan

Sarah Ridge survived a lifetime of tragedy before she arrived in Texas. Born in 1814 in the Cherokee Nation near present Rome, Georgia, she enjoyed a privileged life as the daughter of Major Ridge, a Cherokee leader, friend of Sam Houston, and plantation owner of black and Native American slaves. Sarah attended mission schools and a girls' seminary in Winston-Salem North Carolina—an excellent education for a woman of her time.

Sarah's father and her brother John were among the Cherokee leaders who signed a treaty in 1835 with the United States that promised to compensate the Cherokees for their rich farmland in Georgia in exchange for land in present Oklahoma and Arkansas. Major Ridge and other Cherokee leaders believed the continued encroachment of white settlers and the failure of the state of Georgia and the federal government to protect the Cherokees' land made it wise for the Cherokees to accept the U.S. offer of financial arrangements for their peaceful removal to Indian Territory.

Soon after signing the treaty, Ridge and his family were among the first group of Cherokees to head west. Another group of about 16,000 refused to leave and continued a legal battle to retain their land. Finally, in 1838 President Martin Van Buren ordered the U.S. Army to round up the Cherokees, place them in temporary stockades, and march them to Indian Territory. The 800-mile journey became known as "The Trail of Tears," because approximately 4,000 Cherokees died from abuse, starvation, and lack of proper clothing in the frigid winter. Anger and a sense of betrayal led a group of Cherokees to assassinate Major Ridge, his son John, and Sarah's cousin Elias Boudinot.

Sarah married George Washington Paschal, an attorney who represented the Cherokees before the U.S. Supreme Court as they fought to retain their land. Finally, he helped move the Cherokees west and eventually served on the Arkansas Supreme Court. Sarah bore six children before the family moved to Galveston in 1848. During the 1850 yellow fever outbreak, Sarah turned their home into a hospital and used her knowledge of Cherokee herbs and medicinal remedies to relieve the suffering of many victims.

After Paschal made an unsuccessful run for Attorney General, the couple divorced. Reasons were never clear, but some people believed Paschal decided that having a Cherokee wife was a political liability. Unlike most women after a divorce, Sarah retained their home and a dozen slaves. Paschal moved on to a prominent legal career and Sarah married Charles Session Pix in 1856 in the home of Mirabeau B. Lamar, the former President of the Republic of Texas known for his anti-Indian policies.

After Pix––twenty-two years Sarah's junior––decided he could make a lot of money with a sugar cane plantation, Sarah traded her Galveston home for 500 acres across Galveston Bay. The dream faded quickly in the heat and humidity and it became clear that Sarah's slaves were unfamiliar with farming. The property was converted to a cattle ranch and Sarah employed a lizard-shaped branding iron that had belonged to her father.

The family divided during the Civil War. When Sarah's sons tried to explain to their mother the loyalty they had been taught to the U.S. flag, she countered that she had not found the U.S. government to be an advocate. Under the cover of darkness, her sons slipped through the coastal blockade and made their way to a Union ship. Charles Pix did not favor secession, but chose to serve in the Confederacy. Sarah continued to run the ranch and became regarded as a medicine woman to all who knew of her.

During their celebrated divorce trial in 1880, that revealed years of infidelities, Pix attempted to take the ranch from Sarah. With her daughter's prompting, Sarah's lawyer forced Pix to admit that when he married the wealthy Sarah Paschal he had only nineteen dollars. Sarah retained her ranch and continued as a mainstay of the community, living with her widowed daughter and two grandsons until her death in 1891. Her heirs still own the land.

5

Power In A Skirt

Jane Long, Pioneer Texan

School children often read that Jane Long was the "Mother of Texas." She was a courageous woman who followed her husband as he led a group of filibusterers intent on freeing Texas from Spanish rule. However, many Native American, Mexican, and several English-speaking women came to Texas before Jane Long arrived in 1819. Born in 1798, the youngest of ten children, Jane Herbert Wilkinson lost both her parents by the time she was thirteen. She lived with her sister on a plantation near Natchez, Mississippi, where she met the dashing James Long after he returned from the battle of New Orleans. They married before her sixteenth birthday, and for several years James Long practiced medicine, operated a plantation, and worked as a merchant in Natchez.

Long and many of the residents in the Natchez area were unhappy over the Adams-Onís Treaty, in which Spain gave Florida to the United States in exchange for the boundary of the Louisiana Purchase being drawn at the Sabine River. Originally they expected, and even Thomas Jefferson stated, that the boundary should be the Rio Grande, which would have made Texas part of the United States. Citizens of the United States had already made several filibustering attempts to wrest Texas from Spain, when James Long in 1819 was named commander of an expedition financed by subscriptions totaling about $500,000. Over 300 young men volunteered, expecting to receive a league of Texas land in exchange for their service.

When James Long left for Texas, Jane was expecting a baby and remained behind with their eighteen-month-old daughter, Ann. The second child, Rebecca, was born on June 16 and twelve days later Jane left hurriedly with both children and Kian, her young slave girl. By the time they reached Alexandria, Louisiana, Jane was sick. She left both children and Kian with friends and plunged on, finally reaching Nacogdoches in August. The citizens of Nacogdoches had declared the independence of Texas, organized a provisional government, and named James Long its chief. Supplies did not arrive as expected from Natchez, and Long made a fruitless attempt to persuade the pirate Jean Lafitte, who occupied Galveston Island, to provide supplies and men for the expedition. Finally in October Spanish authorities sent more than 500 troops to Nacogdoches to drive the Long Expedition out of Texas.

As they fled to Louisiana, the Longs learned their baby, Rebecca, had died. Undeterred by his failure, Long organized a new expedition and by March 1820, he took Jane, their daughter Ann, and the slave girl Kian with him to Bolivar Peninsula, a spit of land extending into Galveston Bay across from the eastern end of Galveston Island. He organized his forces at Fort Las Casas on Point Bolivar and apparently continued to court the elusive Jean Lafitte. In later years, when Jane recounted her experience on Bolivar Peninsula, she claimed that she dined privately with Lafitte in an effort to get his support for her husband's expedition. She also said that she made a flag, which she called "the lone star" for Long's troops to carry with them.

Finally in September 1821, Long and fifty-two men sailed to La Bahía (present Goliad) with plans to capture the presidio. In the meantime, Mexico had won its independence from Spain and had no intention of allowing citizens from the United States to capture Texas. After holding La Bahía for only four days, Mexican forces overpowered Long's troops and they were taken as prisoners to Mexico City where Long was killed about six months later.

Jane, who was expecting another baby, promised James that she would wait for him with several other families at Fort Las Casas on Bolivar Peninsula. After a month, the food supplies began running low, and the Karankawa Indians in the area were becoming increasingly unfriendly. The families began to leave, but Jane insisted on waiting for her husband until she, her daughter Ann, and Kian were all that remained at the fort. With the help of Kian, Jane gave birth to daughter Mary James on December 21, 1821, at a time when it was so cold that Galveston Bay froze. In early 1822, as their food supply dwindled to almost nothing, an immigrant family arrived, and Jane reluctantly moved with them up the San Jacinto River.

When she finally received word that James Long had been killed, she returned to Louisiana. Mary James died in 1824, and Jane Long returned to Texas to claim a league of land in Stephen F. Austin's Colony. Family tradition says that Jane was courted by many of Texas' leaders including Stephen F. Austin, Sam Houston, Ben Milam, and Mirabeau B. Lamar, but she refused all their proposals, apparently remaining loyal to James Long, the love of her life.

After living several years in San Felipe, the headquarters of Stephen F. Austin's colony, she opened a boarding house in Brazoria. The Bolivar Peninsula Cultural Foundation, which maintains Jane Long's memorabilia, states that Jane held a ball at her boarding house in Brazoria when Stephen F. Austin returned in 1835 from prison in Mexico. It was at the ball that Austin made his first speech favoring Texas' independence from Mexico. The foundation claims that during the Texas Revolution in 1836 Jane fled Brazoria ahead of the advancing Mexican Army and that she saved the papers of Mirabeau Lamar, which included his original history of Texas.

In 1837, at the age of thirty-nine, Jane Long moved to her league of land, part of which she sold to developers for the town of Richmond. She opened another boarding house and ran a plantation with the help of twelve slaves. At the beginning of the Civil War, she had nineteen slaves and 2,000 acres valued at $13,300. After the Civil War, she worked her land with tenant farmers. When her daughter Ann died in 1870, the value of Jane's estate had diminished to $2,000. Jane Long died at her grandson's home on December 30, 1880.

Today, the Bolivar Peninsula Cultural Foundation has dedicated a Jane Long Memorial on Bolivar Peninsula, which consists of a monument, Texas historical markers, and three flags—the United States, the Texas, and the Jane Long Flag.

Margaret Hallett Tamed a Town

The story that places Margaret Leatherbury Hallett in early Texas merits being called a "legend" because not every part of her saga meets the truth test. Born on Christmas Day 1787, she was the youngest daughter of a prominent Virginia family and probably the feistiest.

At eighteen she fell in love with John Hallett, a merchant seaman—not exactly the pedigree her parents planned for their daughter. John claimed to be the youngest son of a gentleman from Worcester, England. At an early age, he joined the Royal Navy, but when an officer threatened him, he jumped overboard, and swam to a nearby American ship. Allowed to stay on board, he was brought to the United States and adopted by a merchant seaman. Either Margaret's family did not know his history or they did not care, because it is said that when they insisted that she could do better than a seaman, she said "I would rather marry John Hallett and be the beginning of a new family than remain single and be the tail-end of an old one." Whereupon she left for the Chesapeake Bay area and a chaplain married the couple onboard ship.

Margaret and John lived in Baltimore for several years, and after John fought in the War of 1812 against his former countrymen, one of the accounts says that he and Margaret joined a wagon train of homesteaders heading west. The West to which this story refers was still part of Spain's colonial empire and the Mexicans were involved in a war for independence from Spain (1810 to 1821), and had not at that early date opened their land to homesteaders. It is far more likely that John took his wife aboard a ship that sailed through the Gulf of Mexico to the mouth of the Rio Grande. Again, the legend needs checking because it says the couple settled in Matamoros, a Mexican port across the Rio Grande from present-day Brownsville. The village where they settled was a commercial center used by area cattlemen that did not get named Matamoros for another ten years. It's still an amazing account since they opened a mercantile business in the Spanish Colonial village while Mexicans were fighting for independence from Spain. During that time, their first two sons were born in 1813 and 1815.

The family moved up to the community surrounding the Presidio La Bahía that became known as Goliad and opened a trading post. A third son, Benjamin, and a daughter, Mary Jane, were born at Goliad. Something happened to Benjamin when he was ten; some accounts say Indians carried him off, but no record of the incident survives. In 1833 John acquired a league (4,428 acres) of land from the Stephen F. Austin Colony on the east bank of the Lavaca River in present-day Lavaca County. The family continued operating the trading post at Goliad while John took workers with him to build a log cabin on their new property, dig a well and protect the property with a moat around the cabin that was five feet wide and three feet deep. (The moat is never mentioned again in any of the accounts.) The family remained in Goliad and John continued to travel to their new land until his death, probably in early 1836.

After the fall of the Alamo on March 6, 1836, Margaret and her daughter Mary Jane fled in the Runaway Scrap with all the other families to escape Santa Anna's advancing army. Upon their return, they found their property destroyed and set about rebuilding and replanting. The two oldest sons fought at San Jacinto on April 21 in the battle that won Texas' independence from Mexico. The oldest son, John, Jr., returned home after the war and was killed by Indians. That same year, his brother William went to Matamoros to buy land where he was accused of being a spy, and sent to prison where he died.

Margaret, a forty-nine-year-old widow and her daughter Mary Jane were the only survivors, and when a young man, Colatinus Ballard, rode into Goliad to let Margaret and Mary Jane know that squatters were moving onto the property they owned up on the Lavaca River, the two left immediately for their cabin. Upon arriving they met two friendly Tonkawa Indians and their new neighbors who told stories of constant Comanche attacks. Margaret called a meeting of the settlers and the two Tonkawas who agreed that they must go to San Antonio to seek help from Texas Rangers to rid the land of the raiding Comanches. Margaret prepared food for the trip and issued instructions for the best route. Within two weeks the Rangers had cleared the Comanches from the area.

As more settlers arrived, Margaret stocked her cabin with supplies and began operating a trading post, bartering coffee, sugar, and other merchandise with the Tonkawas and her neighbors in exchange for hides and pelts. She hauled the hides and pelts to nearby Gonzales to trade for corn, which she planted as a crop and began raising cattle and horses that carried her own brand.

As Margaret learned their language, the Tonkawas became good friends, warning her of impending Comanche attacks. One legend says that some Tonkawas came into her trading post asking for free merchandise (same say whiskey). When she refused, one of the Indians began to help himself, and Margaret hit him on the head with a hatchet raising quite a knot. When Chief Lolo came to investigate the incident, he was so impressed with Margaret's independence that he named her "Brave Squaw" and made her an honorary member of the tribe.

Despite being a widow, Margaret never wore black, instead preferring brightly colored clothing. She also wore a chatelaine bag, a purse-like affair that hung by a chain from her waist. Gossips claimed that she carried powder in that bag, and it was not the kind that required a puff. Apparently no one had the nerve to ask what was in the bag.

Margaret donated land in 1838 near her trading post for a town, which was named Hallettsville in her honor. She built a new house in the town and when the legislature of the Republic of Texas authorized a new county named La Baca (it later became Lavaca) Margaret opened her home for county and district court sessions. When time came to select the county seat, the older town of Petersburg claimed the honor. Some stories claim that after two elections failed to secure Hallettsville as the county seat, Margaret Hallett sent an oxcart to Petersburg to retrieve the county records, and that settled the matter.

Although Mary Jane attended a private convent, Margaret gave the land in 1852 to establish the town's first public school and helped organize the Alma Male and Female Institute.

Mary Jane married Colatinus Ballard, the young man who had warned Margaret that settlers were moving onto her land. One of the stories says that Ballard, a native Virginian, was the first cousin of Mary Todd Lincoln.

Margaret Leatherbury Hallett died in 1863 at the age of seventy-six and the Tonkawas took part in her funeral service. She was buried on her league and later her remains were moved to City Memorial Park and a grave marker placed on the site that names her the founder of Hallettsville.

Susanna Dickinson, Alamo Survivor

Nothing tells the Texas story—the struggle for survival, the choices that bring personal tragedy, and the triumph of success—better than the life of Susanna Dickinson. She was only fifteen in 1829 when she eloped in Hardeman County, Tennessee, with the dashing U.S. Army artillerist, Almeron Dickinson, a man almost twice her age. Two years later they joined fifty-four other settlers on a schooner out of New Orleans that was headed for Texas. They received a league of land (4,428 acres) in DeWitt's Colony near present-day Lockhart. In the next three years Almeron acquired ten more lots in and around Gonzales. Life appeared harmonious in those early years: Susanna may have taken in a boarder; Almeron plied his trade as a blacksmith and went into partnership in a hat factory; he joined a band of local settlers in hunting down marauding Indians; and their only child, Angelina Elizabeth, was born in December 1834.

A year later, as turmoil swept across Texas, Gonzales residents in the "Come and Take It" episode, refused the demands of Mexican soldiers to give up their cannon. Within days, Almeron offered his experience with cannons as volunteers marched to capture the Mexican seat of government in San Antonio de Bexar. In early December, Texans drove the Mexican forces from San Antonio, occupied the city, and set up a fortress in the Alamo, a crumbling former mission.

Susanna remained in Gonzales with year-old Angelina until a newly formed troop of Texans looted her house. She fled to San Antonio to join Almeron in late December. When the Mexican Army under General António López de Santa Anna arrived on February 23, 1836, legend says that Almeron swept Susanna and Angelina onto the back of his horse and raced with them to the protection of the Alamo fortress.

In her account of the final battle on March 6, Susanna said that Almeron, who commanded the artillery batteries, hid her and Angelina with the other women and children in the anteroom of the chapel. As resistance failed, Almeron rushed back to his wife saying "Great God, Sue! The Mexicans are inside our walls! All is lost! If they spare you, love our child."

When Mexican soldiers discovered Susanna and the other women and children, Colonel Juan Almonte led them and the slaves to safety at the nearby home of Ramón Músquiz. The following day she and the other women and children were taken before General Santa Anna who gave each of them a blanket and two dollars in silver. He offered to take Angelina to Mexico City to be educated. When she refused to release the child, Santa Anna gave Susanna a letter that she was to deliver to General Sam Houston demanding immediate surrender. To ensure her safe passage, Santa Anna sent a servant of one of his officers to accompany her. Joe, William Travis' slave who had also been released, joined them as they made their way to Gonzales.

Susanna and Joe shared the news of the fall of the Alamo and tried to answer the pleading questions of the families whose men had taken part in the battle. In anticipation of the approaching Mexican Army, General Houston ordered the families to evacuate immediately and head toward safety in Louisiana. Susanna and Angelina joined the long struggle eastward in the rain, mud, and extreme cold in what became known as the "Runaway Scrape."

Susanna was illiterate and did not leave written records, but she continued throughout her life to share her experiences. She claimed to have seen the bodies of Davy Crockett and Jim Bowie. From the house to which she was taken after the fall of the Alamo, she could see the pyres of the dead being burned. For a period after the battle, all she could recall was that she wept for days.

With no means of support and no family, Susanna petitioned the congress of the new republic for financial assistance. Her plea was denied, along with those of the other survivors. Before the end of 1837 she married John Williams. In less than a year his physical abuse prompted her to petition for and receive a divorce—the first granted in what became Harris County. Near the time of her divorce, the Republic of Texas awarded a land bounty of 640 acres to survivors of the battle for Texas Independence, which allowed Susanna to support herself as a laundress and boarding house keeper. In later years she and Angelina were awarded another 1,920 acres as descendants of a member of the Texas Republican Army.

In December 1838, she married Francis P. Herring, whom relatives claim died in 1843 from too much drink. Some accounts claim that Pamela Mann who ran Houston's gaudy Mansion House, which was known as a wild and rowdy place, invited Susanna to live in her hotel, perhaps even working as a prostitute. Others insist that Susanna had proven housekeeping and cooking skills and would not have needed to resort to prostitution for her survival. She may have operated her own boarding house before marrying husband number four, Peter Bellows, in 1847. When Bellows divorced Susanna, he charged her with abandonment and prostitution, apparently referring to her residency in the Mansion House before their marriage. Susanna did not appear in court to challenge the claim because she had already moved to Lockhart where she opened a very successful boarding house.

Before leaving Houston, she had been baptized in Buffalo Bayou by a Baptist minister, Rufus C. Burleson, who praised her for nursing victims of a Houston cholera epidemic. Years later Rev. Burleson wrote in his memoirs, "she was nominally a member of the Episcopal Church...I found her a great bundle of untamed passions, devoted in her love and bitter in her hate...she was joyfully converted. In less than two months her change was so complete as to be observed by all her neighbors...she was a zealous co-laborer of mine in every good work....whenever she did wrong especially in giving way to passion, she would confess and weep over it."

After moving to Lockhart, she met her fifth and final husband, Joseph W. Hannig, a German immigrant, blacksmith, and skilled furniture maker. Susanna sold her land in the old DeWitt Colony and used the proceeds to help Hannig become established in various businesses in Austin. He operated a fine-furniture-making business, an undertaking parlor, and a mill before expanding into a second business in San Antonio.

Hannig built a home in 1869 for Susanna on Pine Street (present-day 5th Street) that is open as a museum today. After several years, Hannig expanded his business interests into real estate and served as city alderman. They moved into a mansion in Hyde Park an area on the outskirts of Austin, and Susanna was able to employ several German servant girls with whom she became friends. Hannig's businesses allowed Susanna to be accepted into the social circles in Austin where she was constantly called on to recount her Alamo experience. Angelina died in 1869, and Susanna raised her four grandchildren, seeing that they were educated in Catholic schools and convents. By the time of her death in 1883, Susanna Dickinson Hannig had become a wealthy and respected member of the Austin community.

Sally Skull, Legend In Her Lifetime

Chroniclers say the tiny, hook-nosed, blue-eyed Sally Skull rode a horse like a man, cursed like a sailor, shot like an Indian, and spoke Spanish like a Mexican. Stories abound of her five husbands—she may have killed one or two, and number five may have killed her.

Sally grew up young, and she grew up tough. Born in 1817 as Sarah Jane Newman, her family moved to Texas in 1821 and settled in the northernmost part of Stephen F. Austin's colony. Besides the constant threat in her childhood of Indians stealing the family's horses and corn, Sally watched as an Indian stuck his foot under the cabin front door to lift it off the hinges and her mother used an ax to chop off his toes. At other times her mother put the children to bed and blew out the candles fearing Indians might shoot them through the cracks between the log walls of the cabin. Finally, the family moved to Egypt, a settlement south of present-day Houston that was less prone to Indian attack.

Like many girls of that time, at age sixteen Sally married. Her husband, Jesse Robinson, a man twice her age, served as a volunteer in the famous Battle of San Jacinto and in several subsequent military campaigns. When they divorced in 1843, he claimed she was a scold and "termagant" and committed adultery with someone she kept in the washhouse. Sally said

Robinson was excessively cruel. They fought for years over custody of their two children.

Sally married again on March 17, 1843, eleven days after the divorce, but not to the accused in the washhouse. Despite three more unions, husband number two, George H. Scull, provided her famous name with a slight variation in the spelling. After the Scull marriage, Sally sold her inherited property around Egypt and disappeared for about ten years. She may have spent that time near her children who attended convents in New Orleans. Those who knew Sally reported that she adored her children and always found other children delightful. However, as her notoriety spread, mothers often chided their children to behave or Sally Skull would get them.

George Scull disappeared from the record by the early 1850s about the time Sally established a horse-trading business twenty miles west of Corpus Christi at the crossing of Banquete Creek and El Camino Real (the old road from Matamoros on the Rio Grande to Goliad and beyond). Several accounts place Sally at the great 1852 fair in Corpus Christi because she is remembered for shooting a man—in self-defense, of course.

Her reputation also spread over her lifestyle choices: she often wore men's pants, she rode her horse astride rather than side-saddle, and she buckled at her waist a wide belt anchoring two cap and ball revolvers. Her only nod to feminine attire consisted of a slatted sunbonnet to protect her once-fair complexion. She hired a few Mexican vaqueros that rode with her on horse-trading trips as far south as Mexico and along the Gulf coast all the way to New Orleans. She purchased up to 150 horses at a time with gold carried in a nosebag around her neck or over her saddle horn.

Sally did not allow anyone to inspect or cut her herds, which may have fueled rumors that after she visited ranches, Indians drove off the best horses that appeared later in Sally's herds. Wives sometimes claimed she made eyes at their husbands while her vaqueros stayed busy running off their horses.

Several tales surround Sally's loss of husband number three, John Doyle, who like George Scull simply disappeared. Some accounts claim Doyle and Sally had a duel and her superior marksmanship won the day. Others said that while in Corpus Christi for a fandango, which she loved attending, she did not wake quickly enough the following morning and Doyle poured a pitcher of water on her head. She leaped from the bed not fully awake, drew her pistol, and became a widow. Another tale tells of her insisting that John Doyle and her vaqueros ride across a swollen river. The rushing current swept away Doyle and his horse. When the Mexicans asked if they should look for his body, she said, "I don't give a damn about the body, but I sure would like the $40 in that money belt around it."

In December 1855, Sally married Isaiah Wadkins and divorced him the following May for beating her, dragging her nearly two hundred yards, and living openly in adultery. After she won the divorce, the Nueces County Grand Jury indicted Wadkins for adultery.

Sally's number five was Christoph Horsdorff or "Horsetrough," a moniker he earned for just sitting around and possibly for being almost twenty years her junior. With the start of the Civil War Sally quit horse trading, fitted out several mule train wagons, converted her Mexican vaqueros into teamsters, and began the highly dangerous and lucrative business of hauling Confederate cotton to Mexico. The Union blockade of all the ports on the Gulf Coast made it necessary for the Confederacy to ship cotton to the mills in England through the neutral Mexican port of Baghdad at the mouth of the Rio Grande. Hundreds of English ships waited for the precious cargo in exchange for Winchester rifles, ammunition, and medical supplies for the Confederate Army. The old route to Matamoros that led through Banquete became known as the Cotton Road as ox-carts and mule-drawn wagon trains lumbered along its sandy route hauling thousands of bales of cotton from all over the South.

Some storytellers believe Horsdorff killed Sally after she was seen riding away from Banquete with him and he returned alone. Later, a man claimed to have noticed a boot sticking out of a shallow grave and discovered her murdered body. No one was ever charged.

J. Frank Dobie, historian and folklorist best described the illusive lady: "Sally Skull belonged to the days of the Texas Republic and afterward. She was notorious for her husbands, her horse trading, freighting, and roughness."

And that's the truth.

Second Woman Hanged in Texas

In 1985 the Texas legislature passed a resolution to absolve Josefa "Chapita" Rodriguez of the murder for which she was hanged on November 13, 1863.

Chapita Rodriguez lived in a lean-to shack where the Cotton Road crossed the Nueces River, north of San Patricio. She offered meals and a cot on her front porch to travelers along the route, which the Confederacy used during the Civil War to ferry cotton to Mexico in exchange for guns, ammunition, and medical supplies. Near the end of August 1863, employees at the nearby Welder Ranch found in the edge of the Nueces River the body of John Savage stuffed in two burlap bags. His head had been split with an ax. A few days before the discovery, Savage arrived late in the evening at Chapita's cabin carrying $600 in gold in payment for the sale of horses to the Confederate Army in San Antonio. A large man who traveled heavily armed with six-shooters strapped to his leg, Savage frequently stayed at Chapita's house.

Most of the records in the case burned in a courthouse fire, allowing rumors and legend to fill in the blanks. Since Chapita was too old (probably in her sixties) and too small to stuff the bulk of Savage into the bags and drag him down river, authorities pointed to Juan Silvera who may have been her illegitimate son.

The sheriff who arrested Chapita and Juan Silvera served as foreman of the grand jury and foreman of the jury that heard the charges at trial. At least three grand jury members also served as trial jurors, and members of both juries had been indicted on felony charges that were later dismissed. Chapita's only defense was her repeating "not guilty." A few days before the trial began, the gold was discovered down river from where the body was found. Despite finding the gold, Chapita was found guilty as charged. The jury recommended mercy because of her age and the circumstantial evidence, but the trial judge Benjamin F. Neal sentenced her to be hanged. Juan Silvera was convicted of second-degree murder and sentenced to five years in prison.

Some accounts claim she was held for a time in the sheriff's home; other stories say she waited in leg irons, chained to the courthouse wall in San Patricio. Children visited the courthouse, supplying Chapita with candy and corn shucks so she could roll her cigarettes.

Many stories suggest Chapita's silence was to protect her son Juan Silvera. Whatever her reason, Chapita rode in a wagon to her fate while sitting atop her coffin and smoking a corn shuck cigarette. She stood to have the noose, dangling from a mesquite tree, placed around her neck. San Patricio residents, many of whom believed her innocent, whispered among themselves that Chapita's execution marked the end of San Patricio. By the mid-1880s life began changing. The introduction of barbed wire closed the open range and the excitement and the business that traveled with the cattle drives came to an end. The railroad by-passed San Patricio, the courthouse burned, and Sinton became the new seat of county government.

Despite Texas' record number of executions, only three women have faced the gallows. Little information exists about the first woman legally executed other than she was a slave named Jane Elkins convicted of murdering a white man in Dallas County and hanged on May 27, 1853. The third execution of a woman occurred in 1998 when Karla Faye Tucker died by lethal injection fourteen years after being convicted in a pickaxe murder.

Saga of Sophia Suttonfield Aughinbaugh Coffee Butts Porter

Two official Texas historical markers sit on the shore of Lake Texoma, the enormous reservoir separating North Texas and Oklahoma. One marker commemorates Holland Coffee's Trading Post, now under the waters of Lake Texoma. The neighboring marker calls Sophia Coffee Porter a Confederate Lady Paul Revere. The colorful lives of Sophia and Holland Coffee came together in 1837 probably while Coffee served in the Congress of the Republic of Texas.

Sophia was born a Suttonfield in 1815 on the remote military post at Fort Wayne (in present-day Indiana). As a beautiful dark-haired girl of seventeen, she ran away with Jesse Aughinbaugh who had been the headmaster at her school. The twosome split up in Texas—Sophia said he deserted her—in 1836 and Sophia, who told many stories about herself, said she was the first woman to reach the battle site at San Jacinto the day after Texas won its independence from Mexico. Although there is no record of their relationship in Sam Houston's published letters or biographies, Sophia claimed she nursed the wounded general back to health, and they remained friends. Some historians believe she was a camp woman who sold her services to the general.

Holland Coffee established his trading post in the early 1830s on the Indian Territory (present-day Oklahoma) side of the Red River and moved across to the Texas side in 1837. The historical marker says Coffee traded with the Indians for many white captives. Some historians think Coffee was out to make money and that, like many of the stories Sophia told of her exploits, not as many rescues took place as later generations believe. Coffee did ransom a Mrs. Crawford and her two children by paying the Indians 400 yards of calico, a large number of blankets, many beads, and other items. In later years, Mrs. John Horn wrote that when Comanches refused to trade for the release of her and her children, Holland wept and then gave her and the children clothing and flour. Although he was accused by settlers of trading whiskey and guns to the Indians for cattle and horses they stole from the whites, his neighbors must have forgiven him because they elected him as their congressman.

Sophia and Holland probably met in Houston, the capital of the new republic. When Sophia failed to get a divorce from Aughinbaugh through the courts, she petitioned the legislature to intervene on her behalf. After several attempts to get a bill through the legislature that was more concerned with passing a Homestead Exemption Law than dealing with a divorce case, Sam Houston finally used his influence and the petition passed both houses with Holland Coffee as a member of the House of Representatives voting aye.

Coffee and Sophia took a 600-mile honeymoon on horseback through Independence in Washington County, to Nacogdoches and along the Red River, stopping at several locales to attend balls in celebration of their marriage. Coffee settled with his bride at his trading post, a popular place for Indians and for drovers heading north with their cattle. Coffee's wedding gift to Sophia was one-third league of land, about 1,476 acres—only the first of her many acquisitions. In her later accounts of life on the Red River, Sophia said her nearest neighbor was twenty-five miles away and that to protect against Indian attack, Texas Rangers guarded their trading post. The horses had to be watched while slaves plowed the fields, and firearms were stacked nearby for easy access during preaching services.

The Republic of Texas built a protective line of forts along the western edge of the frontier and connected them with a Military Road from Austin to Fort Johnson near Coffee's Trading Post. The military base bought supplies, clothing, tobacco, gunpowder, and tools from Coffee, which injected new life into his business. He opened a ferry at a crossing on the Red River and he and Sophia bought land and slaves. New settlers arrived in the area, and in 1845 Holland sold lots on his land for the new town of Preston.

In 1846 Holland Coffee hired Mormons traveling from Illinois to Central Texas to build Glen Eden, a home that expanded over the years into the most impressive house in North Texas where Sophia entertained lavishly. By her own account, she hosted such notables as Robert E. Lee, Ulysses S. Grant (no record exists that either man was there), and Sam Houston. Men from nearby Fort Washita in Indian Territory seemed always to be guests at Glen Eden. Stories vary about how Coffee died in 1846. Some say it began when Sam Houston was scheduled to dedicate the new county courthouse in nearby Sherman and planned to stay with the Coffees at Glen Eden. Coffee's niece had married Charles A. Galloway who offended Sophia by commenting about her former relationship with Sam Houston. She demanded that Coffee horsewhip his new nephew. When Coffee refused to publically air the family problems, Sophia said she had rather be the widow of a brave man than the wife of a coward. Coffee started an "Indian duel," a fight to the death, with Galloway who killed Coffee with a Bowie knife.

At age thirty-one, Sophia, the rich and charming widow of a brave man, managed the 3,000-acre slave plantation, tended her extensive gardens, and continued to host grand parties. On one of her regular visits to New Orleans to sell her cotton crop, she met Major George N. Butts, who returned with her to Glen Eden to manage the plantation. There is no record of a marriage in either Texas or Louisiana, but the relationship was Sophia's happiest—Butts enjoyed the niceties of gracious living—and they paid for their lifestyle with the sale of their cotton and land. They enlarged Glen Eden, filled it with fine furnishings and china from New Orleans. She became known for her rose garden, an orchard of more than a hundred fruit trees, and grape and berry vines for jams and wines. She grew a magnolia tree in the front yard from a seedling given to her by Sam Houston. Albert Sidney Johnston brought catalpa seeds from California, which she planted, in a line down the driveway.

In 1863, William Clark Quantrill with his group of Confederate guerrillas from Kansas and Missouri moved into Sherman and began robbing and killing anyone who did not agree with Quantrill's brand of Confederate support. Although Sophia and Butts were southern sympathizers, Butts got into an argument with one of Quantrill's men and was ambushed one night as he returned from a cotton-selling trip to Sherman. Sophia garnered the sympathy of Sherman residents against Quantrill and got him arrested; he later escaped.

Some historians say the historical marker story calling Sophia Coffee Porter a Confederate Lady Paul Revere may not be altogether accurate. Several tales surround this claim, most of them encouraged by Sophia herself. One says that when James Bourland, commanding a Texas frontier regiment, stopped at Glen Eden on his way back to Fort Washita, he warned her that federal troops were following him. When the Yankees arrived, Sophia fed them dinner and then took them into her wine cellar where they proceeded to get drunk. She locked them in the cellar and then, riding a mule, forded the treacherous Red River to warn Bourland of the Union's plans, thus preventing the invasion of North Texas. Another version of the story says she stripped to her underwear and swam the river and then whistled to get the Confederates' attention.

At age fifty, toward the end of the Civil War, Sophia found the Red River country too dangerous. She packed her gold in tar buckets and took her slaves with her to the safer environment of Waco in Central Texas. There, she met Judge James Porter, a Confederate cavalry officer from Missouri. Rufus Burleson, president of Waco College performed their marriage on August 2, 1865, and the Porters returned to Glen Eden. With her slaves freed, Sophia's net worth dropped, but she and James Porter began buying land at sheriff's auctions and reselling it quickly to increase their holdings.

James Porter apparently influenced Sophia's desire to "get religion." She attended a camp meeting and rushed forward throwing herself at the feet of the preacher. In front of the entire congregation the minister said she must wait for twelve years because "the sun, moon, and stars were against her being a Christian." The Methodist preacher in Sherman, however, welcomed her into the church. She gave a section of land to Southwestern University, a Methodist institution at Georgetown and land for a Methodist Church at Preston Bend. "Aunt Sophia," as she became known in later years, apparently earned the respect of her neighbors. When the Old Settlers Park in Sherman was founded in 1879, one of the speakers at the first meeting was Sophia Porter who entertained the crowd with the stories of her life as a pioneer woman along the Red River.

Glen Eden continued to be a social center, but Sophia no longer allowed dancing. She and James Porter continued giving money or land to churches in the area until his death in 1886. For the next eleven years Sophia and her long-time friend and companion Belle Evans searched the shops in nearby Denison and Sherman and ordered from catalogues new fashions that would restore Sophia's youth. Mrs. Evans also applied Ayer's Hair Dye each week to maintain Sophia's black locks that had attracted so many suitors over the years. On August 27, 1897, when Sophia died quietly at the age of eighty-one in her fine home of fifty-four years, the man at her side was Reverend J. M.

Binkley, the Methodist preacher from Sherman who had accepted her into his congregation.

The Sanctified Sisters

"Charismatic, religious, smart-as-a-whip, trouble-maker"—descriptions given of Martha McWhirter, who moved after the Civil War with her husband George and their twelve children to Belton in Central Texas. George opened a mercantile business, they built a large limestone house, and the couple, active Methodists, founded the nondenominational Union Sunday School.

Martha organized a weekly women's Bible study and prayer group. In August 1866, after two of her children and a brother had died, Martha attended a revival and it failed to offer comfort for her losses. Afterward, she reported that as she walked home, or it might have been the following morning as she was washing dishes, she heard God speak to her and then experienced a "Pentecostal baptism," which may have included speaking in tongues. The events led her to believe she had been sanctified, set apart by God for a special purpose.

With the zeal of the newly converted, she emphasized the importance of dreams and revelations as the source of spiritual guidance rather than the sacraments offered by her church. She encouraged the women in her Bible study to pray for sanctification and to share their dreams and revelations to arrive at a group consensus for their guidance. The new theology led to the removal of five Baptists from their church rolls and several others being elbowed out of their congregations.

The women prayed about trials of everyday life such as authoritarian husbands involved in dishonorable business dealings, drunkenness, and physical abuse. One of their early group decisions—that the sanctified should not have sexual or social contact with the unsanctified—may have resulted from already having more children than they wanted. Whatever led to the decision, it spelled the beginning of some high-profile divorces and angry outbursts from townspeople. In addition to refusing to sleep with their husbands, the women refused monetary support except as payment for work. In the beginning, they sold eggs, butter, and hooked rugs, placing the money into a common pot, enabling them to help a sister whose husband denied her money for necessities and later to hire a lawyer for divorce proceedings.

Distraught women came with their children to Martha's house, escaping angry and often abusive husbands, filling the house beyond capacity. George McWhirter, believing in Martha's sincerity, never understood her behavior, but never publicly criticized her. Eventually he moved into a room above his downtown store. One woman inherited a large house, which they turned into a boarding house for lodging members and the public. Townspeople watched in amazement as wives of prominent men showed determination to make their way financially by taking in laundry, a chore traditionally relegated to black women of the community. Recognizing that they were no longer accepted in polite society, the women took any work offering financial gain. Two women chopped wood and delivered it to homes. Others worked as domestic servants, seamstresses, home nurses, and one became a cobbler. Hard work paid off, and the group prospered, allowing members to rotate working four-hour shifts, and taking turns caring for and teaching their children.

The Sanctificationist code did not exclude men. In later years the women told an interviewer that no man ever stayed with the group longer than nine months because "they want to boss," but "they find they can't." In 1879, two young men from Scotland, who belonged to a similar group at home, came to Belton seeking membership. It was one thing for the men of the town to put up with women being "Sancties," but quite another for males to join. A group of men took the newly arrived gentlemen from their home at midnight and whipped them severely. When they still refused to leave town, they were declared insane in a district court hearing and sent to the asylum in Austin. They were released very quickly, after agreeing never to return to Belton.

A hotel operator in nearby Waco hired some of the women in 1884 for one dollar a day and then asked for more workers. Besides offering a good income, the women learned the hotel business. They built rent houses on the McWhirter property, and opened the Central Hotel across from the railroad depot. At first townspeople boycotted the place, but after George McWhirter died, and it became obvious the hotel was the finest in town and offered the best food of any establishment, it became a popular eating place for locals.

Perhaps being a widow, no longer separated from her husband, or perhaps Martha's donation of $500 to bring in the railroad spur from Temple, or contributing to the fund for building an opera house, caused a change of heart in the community. She won election as the first woman to serve on the Belton Board of Trade—a precursor to the Chamber of Commerce.

Believing the women should see more of the world, led to Martha renting a house in the summer of 1880 near New York's Central Park. She divided the members in three groups, each staying for six weeks. They traveled to the city by rail and returned by ship to Galveston. Martha estimated the total cost at $3,000.

By 1891 when the group incorporated as the Central Hotel Company, they owned several pieces of local real estate, three farms providing food for hotel guests and feed for their livestock. Their net income reached $800 a month.

One of the women became a self-taught dentist charging only the cost of the material because she did not have a license. One member moved to New York, setting up a business selling pianos. By the 1890s, they traveled extensively to New York, San Francisco, and Mexico City, subscribed to many magazines, hired tutors for their children, and no longer held prayer meetings. They continued gathering, discussing dreams, and arriving at group decisions. Although Martha served as the leader, the group operated on feelings and consensus, often sensing when something was wrong, and relying on dreams to tell them what to do. The answer might be selling one of the farms or encouraging a "disloyal" member to get married.

In 1899 the group decided to leave Belton for a locale with a more stimulating environment. Group consensus settled on Washington, D.C. as the best place for pursuing their cultural interests. It's unclear how much the group received from the sale of their Belton property. Some estimates claim $200,000. They paid $23,000 cash for a house at 1437 Kenesaw Avenue, Mount Pleasant, Maryland, and spent another $10,000 renovating the property.

By the time the women settled in the Washington area, newspapers and magazines from around the country had started taking note of the unusual group of religious women who wore no identifying habit, lived a Spartan existence, and made "A Happy Home Without Husbands."

Martha died in 1904 and contrary to predictions, the group of aging women continued living in the house until at least 1918. Another account says a daughter of one of the members lived there until 1983.

A Woman Before Her Time

Jane McManus Storm Cazneau was born in Troy, New York, in 1807, but after a failed marriage and being named in Aaron Burr's divorce, she came to Texas in 1832 with her brother Robert McManus in an attempt to improve the family's shrinking fortune. Although she received a contract from the Mexican government to settle families in Stephen F. Austin's colony, she apparently lacked the funds to get the enterprise off the ground. The German colonists that she landed in Matagorda refused to go farther inland and that seemed to be the end of that adventure. It was not, however, the end of Jane's land speculation and her interest in the future of Texas. She was a prolific writer, and one of the causes she trumpeted in her columns for East Coast publications was Texas independence from Mexico. She also tried to sway U.S. public opinion in favor of annexing the Republic of Texas.

During the Mexican-American War, Jane served as the first female war correspondent and the only journalist to issue reports from behind enemy lines. She was sent to Mexico as an unofficial representative of the *New York Sun* editor Moses Beach's secret peace mission, which was endorsed by President James Polk. Her expansionist interests showed clearly as she began promoting the annexation of Mexico as a way to bring peace.

Jane married William Leslie Cazneau, Texas politician and entrepreneur in 1849, and lived with him for a time in Eagle Pass, a town on the Rio Grande that Cazneau founded in order to open a trade depot and investigate mining potential. She wrote of her experiences in *Eagle Pass, or Life on the Border*, and she continued to write editorials.

William Cazneau was appointed special agent to the Dominican Republic in 1855, and the Cazneaus settled there on their estate, Esmeralda. Jane continued writing her columns and books that advocated her expansionist philosophy, and the couple invested heavily in property all over the Caribbean.

Some writers, including Linda Hudson, author of Jane's biography, *Mistress of Manifest Destiny*, credit Jane with being the first writer to use the term "manifest destiny" in one of her columns. It has been difficult to trace her use of the term since her editorials were handwritten, often unsigned, and she also used the pen names Storm, Cora or Corinne Montgomery. Nevertheless she was such a strong advocate of manifest destiny that she bought into the *New York Morning Star* in order to use the publication to editorialize for the expansion of the south and of slavery into Cuba, the Dominican Republic, and Nicaragua. She was not in favor of the South seceding from the Union because she believed that the division would weaken the United States and slow its expansion. She also stood to lose on her land investments if slavery and its spread to the Caribbean came to an end.

Her influence was widespread; she socialized and corresponded with James Polk, James Buchanan, Jefferson Davis, and Horace Greeley. Former Republic of Texas President Mirabeau B. Lamar dedicated his 1857 book of poems, *Verse Memorials,* to Jane Cazneau.

The Cazneaus fled to another of their properties in Jamaica in 1863 following the destruction of their estate after Spain returned to the Dominican Republic. However, after Spain left the island, the Cazneaus returned and assisted President Andrew Johnson in his efforts to acquire a coaling station at Samaná and in President Grant's effort to annex the Dominican Republic.

William Cazneau died in 1876, and two years later Jane, the woman who often used the pin name Storm, was lost in a storm while sailing from New York to Santo Domingo.

Lady Cannoneer

Texans love stories of pioneer settlers and heroes. Angelina Eberly fits the bill. Born in Tennessee in 1798, Mrs. Eberly married her first cousin, made the journey to Matagorda Bay on the Texas coast in 1822 and finally, with the help of several slaves, opened an inn and tavern in the new village of San Felipe de Austin on the Brazos River.

After her husband died, Mrs. Eberly continued operating the hotel until Texans burned the town in 1836 to prevent it from falling into General Santa Anna's hands during the Texas War for Independence from Mexico. After the war she married again and moved with her new husband in 1839 to the new Texas capital of Austin where they opened the Eberly Boarding House.

History reveals a political atmosphere as contentious during the days of the republic as it is today. The constitution of the new republic allowed the president to serve only one, two-year term, which meant Sam Houston, first president and hero of the war for independence, stepped down to allow the election of his successor and nemesis Mirabeau B. Lamar. Immediately, the new President Lamar inflamed the already inflamed political climate by appointing a site-selection commission that moved the capital of the republic from old Sam's namesake city of Houston to a little village on the Colorado River in the wilderness of Central Texas. The builders had only nine months to erect a city in time to house the next legislative session. The new capital that rose out of the forest was named Austin, in honor of Stephen F. Austin, the father of early Texas settlement.

The temporary capitol, a plank-covered building with a dog run separating the two chambers, faced a wide dirt street named Congress Avenue. The other government agencies were placed in even less pretentious blockhouses made of logs cut from the plentiful cedar trees covering the hillsides. The president's white house was constructed quickly of unseasoned pine from nearby Bastrop and placed on a high hill overlooking the town and the Colorado River coursing below.

One of the early businesses was Mrs. Angelina Eberly's Boarding House where President Lamar and his cabinet often dined. When Sam Houston won reelection in late 1841 for another two-year term, he took one look at the president's crumbling house and refused to occupy the structure. The green timbers had dried and warped, causing cracks in the plastered walls and damage to the roof. Instead, President Houston moved into Mrs. Eberly's Boarding House.

Indians attacked individuals who dared to roam away from the capital. After dark, residents walked at their own risk in the town's streets. Part of the defense plan included a six-pounder cannon, loaded with grapeshot. Sam Houston and his supporters used the Indian threat as one of the arguments for moving the capital away from its location on the western frontier. Finally, when Mexican troops captured San Antonio on March 5, 1842, Houston moved the Congress to Washington, a tiny village on the Brazos River.

Determined to keep the last symbol of the capital in their town, Austin residents demanded the republic's archives, which consisted of diplomatic, financial, land, and military-service records, remain in Austin.

When Mexicans invaded San Antonio again in December 1842, Sam Houston found his excuse for action. He instructed two army officers to take about twenty men and three wagons to Austin in the middle of the night and quietly remove the archives from the General Land Office.

No one ever explained what Angelina Eberly was doing outside in the middle of the night, but when she saw the wagons leaving with the archives, she ran to the loaded cannon and fired it to warn the citizens of the robbery.

The military men traveled about twenty miles that first day up to Kenney's Fort located near present Round Rock. The next morning, when the officers rose to continue their journey, they discovered the citizens of Austin circling the fort with their cannon aimed toward the enclosure. Without further ado, the military men returned the files to the Austin citizens, thus ending what has been dubbed both "The Archives War" and "The Bloodless War."

With most of the republic's business handled in Washington, Austin struggled for several years, the population dropping below 200 and its buildings deteriorating. Finally, in 1845 a constitutional convention approved Texas' annexation to the United States and named Austin as the new state's capital. In 1850 Texas residents finally voted to officially designate Austin as the Texas capital.

Ever eager to find a good business location, Angelina Eberly moved in 1846 to Lavaca (present-day Port Lavaca) on the Central Texas Coast where she leased Edward Clegg's Tavern House while she surveyed the area for the best location for her business. Upon seeing nearby Indianola on Matagorda Bay becoming a thriving seaport, she moved down the coast and opened her American Hotel. At the time of her death in 1860, her estate appraised at $50,000, making Mrs. Angelina Eberly the wealthiest citizen of Calhoun County.

Today, Austin residents honor their cannoneer with a larger-than-life-size bronze sculpture near the corner of Congress Avenue and Seventh Street.

Mary Goodnight, Mother to the Cowhands

Called "Mary" by her husband Charles Goodnight, the best known cattle rancher in Texas, referred to as "Molly" by her distinguished Tennessee family, and known affectionately as "Mother of the Texas Panhandle" by the cowhands she doctored, fed, and counseled, Mary Ann Dyer Goodnight was loved and admired by all.

She was fourteen in 1854 when she moved with her parents to Fort Belknap on the western edge of Texas settlement. Soon, both parents died and Mary began teaching school to support her three younger brothers. She met the young cattleman Charlie Goodnight at Fort Belknap in 1864 and their courtship continued through Goodnight's service in the Civil War. By the time they married in 1870 Goodnight had a well-established reputation for driving cattle along the Goodnight-Loving Trail to New Mexico and eventually to Wyoming before he built a thriving cattle ranch at Pueblo, Colorado.

When Charlie Goodnight and his bride arrived in Pueblo, Mary was shocked to discover two men hanging from a telegraph pole. Goodnight writes in his *Recollections*, "I hardly knew how to reply, but finally stammered out in a very abashed manner: 'Well, I don't think they hurt the telegraph pole.' This seemed to irritate her very much and she said: 'I used to think I knew you in Texas, but you have been out here among the Yankees and ruffians until I don't know whether I know you or not, and I want you to take me back to Texas. I won't live in such a country.' I agreed to this but insisted that she must first have a rest, and during the next few days made it a point to acquaint her with all the good ladies of Pueblo, whom she found quite as human as herself, and the trip back to Texas was soon forgotten."

The Goodnight-Dyer Cattle Company thrived in Pueblo until the financial panic of 1873 and a severe drought led to Goodnight forming a partnership with John George Adair, an Irish financier, to establish the first ranch in the Texas Panhandle in the lush green pastureland of Palo Duro Canyon. Adair, who was interested in investing in the cattle business, put up the financial backing while Goodnight was charged with running the entire operation. Goodnight made the first of many land purchases—12,000 acres for twenty-five cents an acre—and trailed 1,600 head of cattle into the canyon in the spring of 1876. Adair and his wife, Cornelia Wadsworth Ritchie Adair, a highborn lady from New York, had fallen in love with the west on a buffalo hunt and viewed the investment and the trip to see the canyon as a great adventure.

The two couples, one of Mary's brothers, and several cowhands made the 400-mile journey from Colorado to Palo Duro Canyon the following spring. The entourage consisted of 100 head of the finest Durham bulls, four wagons loaded with six months' provisions, equipment, and horses to upgrade Goodnight's Texas herd. Cornelia Adair rode the entire distance on a fine white horse while Mary Goodnight drove the team to one of the wagons.

The Goodnight/Adair outfit reached the rim of Palo Duro Canyon and gazed into the new JA (for John Adair) Ranch—an 800-foot deep gorge, ten miles wide, and almost 100 miles long teaming with 1,000 to 1,500 buffalo—home of Charlie and Mary Goodnight for the next eleven years. It took several days to move all the stock and supplies along the trail that wound for four miles to the Prairie Dog Fork of the Red River at the base of the canyon. After a few days exploring the area, the Adairs left and Mary Goodnight set about adjusting to life in a two-room log cabin at least seventy-five miles from the nearest white neighbor. Goodnight, in his *Recollections* claims that Mary was frightened that first night by the loud noises echoing off the canyon walls made by the buffalo during that spring mating season. Some accounts claim he had to convince her that dried buffalo dung made excellent firewood for her cook stove.

While Charlie Goodnight devoted his boundless energy to enlarging the ranch, improving the stock and blazing the Palo Duro-Dodge City Cattle Trail, Mary acted as surrogate mother for the cowboys—patching their clothes, sewing on buttons, and listening to their troubles. According to Crawford and Ragsdale in *Women in Texas,* Mary's doctoring consisted of "coal-oil for lice, prickly pear for wounds, salt and buffalo tallow for piles, mud for inflammation and fever, and buffalo meat broth for a general tonic."

Despite the constant wind and the loneliness from going six months to a year without seeing another white woman (Comanche squaws came into the canyon with Quanah Parker's band) Mary claimed that was the happiest time of her life. Charlie Goodnight made a peace treaty with the Comanches that both he and Quanah Parker honored: Goodnight would give two beeves every other day to Quanah Parker's band until they could find the buffalo they were hunting as long as the Indians did not take cattle from the JA herd.

Mary Goodnight said in later years that a cowboy brought her three chickens in a sack and they became something she could talk to. They ran to her when she called and tried to talk to her in their language, following her as she went about her chores. She wrote in her diary that during the day she could hear the gunshots of commercial buffalo hunters who swept the plains killing the bison for their hides, even if a calf was standing next to its mother. At night she could hear the orphans bawling, alone and starving among the rotting carcasses that were left behind. She insisted that Charlie bring the orphaned calves home and by nursing them with three gallons of milk a day, she restored them to health and helped establish the Goodnight buffalo herd.

The Goodnights crossbred some of the buffalo with range cattle, calling the new breed "Cattalo." Mary established her own herd and commissioned artist J.C. Cowles to paint scenes of the ranch. In 2011, eighty descendants of the great southern plains bison that Mary Goodnight was instrumental in saving were released to roam on 700 acres of the Caprock Canyon State Park in the Texas Panhandle.

After John Adair died in 1885, Goodnight worked for a couple of years in partnership with Cornelia Adair before he and Mary left the JA Ranch taking as their share a 140,000-acre spread and 20,000 head of cattle near land that became known as Goodnight Station. As railroads, fencing, farmers, and townspeople moved into the Panhandle, Mary helped establish Goodnight College, a post-secondary school, in 1898. As a result of their generosity, churches, schools, and other organizations in the Panhandle were named for the ranching pioneers.

Mary died in 1926 and her headstone reads: "Mary Ann Dyer Goodnight: One who spent her whole life in the service of others."

Harvey Girls Go West

Their uniform consisted of black dresses covered by starched white pinafores, opaque black stockings, black shoes, and hairnets secured with a regulation white ribbon. They were Harvey Girls who could serve a meal in thirty minutes that included fillet of whitefish with Madeira sauce or roast beef au jus and lobster salad. The homemade pie was cut and served in generous quarters unlike the customary one-sixth portions.

As railroads spread across the country, passengers had either carried their own food, endured meals that often included rancid meat and cold beans, or simply did without. Fred Harvey, a dapper British immigrant who worked as a railroad freight agent, observed the terrible conditions on trains and convinced the Atchison, Topeka and Santa Fe Railway in 1876 to let him open a restaurant in Topeka, Kansas. His idea of fine fresh food at a reasonable price proved so popular that his establishments began spreading along the railroad. Harvey Houses reached the isolated cattle towns of West Texas in the 1890s, and crossed the state from El Paso and Amarillo to Dallas and Houston and south to Kingsville. Even in remote towns, up to four passenger trains came through daily carrying from fifty to eighty people who expected to be fed in thirty minutes.

From the beginning, the railroad allowed Harvey to set up his restaurants as he saw fit, which meant fine China and Irish table linens. He demanded civility, cleanliness, and high standards of efficiency. The Harvey girls were not called waitresses; they could not wear makeup or chew gum while on duty. He personally inspected his restaurants and was reported to have sometimes overturned a table that was not set to his standards.

He advertised for "white, young women, eighteen to thirty years of age, of good character, attractive and intelligent." Upon entering their month of training they quickly learned that their work would be demanding—serving meals, polishing silver, brewing fresh coffee every two hours, and following a strict code in dealing with customers. Beginning pay was $17.50 a month, including room, board, and tips. They lived in dormitories with a 10:00 PM curfew, and were supervised by a senior Harvey Girl who served much like a housemother.

Although the environment sounds harsh by today's standards, it allowed young women a rare career opportunity. In later years, married women entered the program and benefited from the chance to add to family income. Some of the women were widows who claimed that they and their children were welcomed like family into the Harvey House environment.

Harvey branched into hotels alongside depots, eventually opening eighty-four facilities. When railroads began offering food service, he reluctantly agreed to staff dining cars with Fred Harvey Company personnel. The Harvey brand began moving in the 1930s into locations away from the Santa Fe Railroad and in 1959 the restaurants started lining the Illinois Tollway. Although the Harvey House era came to an end with the death in 1965 of Fred Harvey's grandson, the company is credited with offering the first "blue plate special"—a good meal at a reasonable price, creating the first restaurant chain in the United States, and opening tourism to the American Southwest by making railroad travel more enjoyable.

Minnie Fisher Cunningham, Paved the Way for Today

After Minnie Fisher graduated at the age of nineteen with a graduate of pharmacy degree from the Galveston School of Pharmacy at the University of Texas Medical Branch in Galveston, she discovered on her first job that she did not earn half the wages of the less-educated male employees. She claimed the memory of that experience in 1901 led to her life's work of championing the status of women.

Minnie Fisher married lawyer and insurance executive Beverly Jean (Bill) Cunningham in 1902, moved to Galveston and began volunteering in local, state, and national women's suffrage organizations. She honed her speaking skills by touring the country urging the passage of equal rights for women and universal suffrage. Cunningham moved to Austin in 1917 and opened the state suffrage headquarters near the capitol. A vote in January 1919 by the Texas state legislature granting full suffrage to women failed when the referendum went before the voters. Then, the United States House of Representatives on May 21, and the United States Senate on June 4, passed a joint resolution on the Nineteenth Amendment. Immediately, Cunningham began campaigning to secure ratification by the Texas state legislature. On June 28, 1919, Texas became the first southern state to ratify the Nineteenth Amendment to the United States Constitution granting women the right to vote.

Cunningham joined a national tour of ratification supporters saying later that she "pursued governors all over the west" urging their states to ratify the amendment. Finally, on August 26, 1920, Tennessee became the thirty-sixth state out of the existing forty-eight to bring the total to the required three-fourths of the states necessary to ratify a constitutional amendment.

Cunningham helped organize the League of Women Voters (LWV) in 1919 and served as its executive secretary. Twenty years later Eleanor Roosevelt recalled that when she heard Minnie Cunningham speak at the LWV's second annual convention, the speech made her feel "that you had no right to be a slacker as a citizen, you had no right not to take an active part in what was happening to your country as a whole."

Cunningham worked for an act in 1921 designed to lower the infant mortality rate and for an act in 1922 that allowed women to have citizenship based solely on their own status and not the status of their husbands. In 1924 she experienced another eye-opener, this time regarding the need for women to get more involved in partisan politics. Eleanor Roosevelt invited Cunningham to join the Democratic Women's Advisory Committee to the Democratic National Committee (DNC) where Cunningham found that despite the DNC authorizing the women's group, it refused to meet with them. Cunningham managed to gain access to the platform committee only because of her membership in the LWV.

In 1928 Minnie Fisher Cunningham became the first woman in Texas to run for the United States Senate. In an effort to raise the status of women among the electorate, she ignored her colleague's advice to assume a combative style that had colored past elections, and ran on a platform advocating prohibition, tax reform, farm relief, cooperation with the League of Nations, and opposition to the Ku Klux Klan. She lost in the state's primary.

Working in College Station as an editor for the Texas A&M Extension Service, Cunningham became interested in the link between poverty and poor nutrition and advocated alongside the Texas Federation of Women's Clubs to enrich flour with basic vitamin and mineral content. In 1938 she organized the Women's Committee for Economic Policy (WCEP), which worked for a fully funded teacher retirement system. While working in Washington for the Agricultural Adjustment Administration, President Roosevelt began calling her "Minnie Fish," a title she carried for the rest of her life.

Returning to Texas in 1944, Cunningham ran for governor in an out-spoken campaign against Coke Stevenson. To raise money for her filing fee, she sold lumber from the trees on her old family farm in New Waverly, and Liz Carpenter served as her press secretary. Cunningham lost the primary, coming in second in a field of nine. When the University of Texas Board of Regents began in the 1940s firing professors as suspected Communists and then dismissed the president for refusing to go along with the charges by claiming he had not disclosed a "nest of homosexuals" among the faculty, Cunningham created the Women's Committee for Education Freedom to stand up to the regents. She helped organize groups to support the New Deal policies and worked tirelessly for Democratic candidates such as Harry Truman, Adlai Stevenson, and Ralph Yarborough.

Cunningham received a guest invitation to the inauguration of President John F. Kennedy in appreciation for her work in helping him carry her predominately Republican Walker County. She financed the campaign in her county through the sale of used clothing.

Despite declining health, Cunningham continued working for policies that benefited women and improved the lives of all the citizens of Texas. She died of congestive heart failure on December 9, 1964.

Lucy Kidd-Key, Tough Victorian Lady

Born into an old southern family in Kentucky in 1839 and given a genteel education in the classics and fine arts, the barely five-foot-tall Lucy Ann Thornton was a bundle of contradictions. A lady ahead of her time who believed women should be educated, she also touted the need for women to hold home and family above all else. After the financial burdens brought by the Civil War and her husband Dr. Henry Byrd Kidd's long illness and death, Lucy was left with three children and mounting debts. She immediately set about recouping the family's financial stability by selling land she inherited from her husband and by bringing suit for $1,500 against a widow with three children who defaulted on a note due for some land. Lucy won the suit. Her husband had held part ownership in a pharmacy and to collect unpaid balances on customer accounts Lucy stationed a Negro servant at the front door of the pharmacy to halt anyone who owed money. In this fashion, Lucy soon shored up the family finances. She then took a job as presiding teacher of Whitworth College in Brookhaven, Mississippi, which with its outstanding music department, grew to be the largest college for women in the south. During her ten years at Whitworth, she developed many principles for educating young women.

Her experience led Methodist Bishop Charles B. Galloway in 1888 to recommend Lucy Kidd to bring life back to the North Texas Female College, which had been closed for a year. Despite her demand that the board of trustees come to her Sherman hotel for the interview, they were quite impressed with the educational credentials and recommendations from Mississippi's governor and lieutenant governor. They probably also thought that Mrs. Lucy Kidd, dressed in black widow's weeds, would bring some of her personal wealth to the college since it was customary at that time for presidents of private schools to invest their personal funds in the institutions and to pay for construction of campus buildings. In fact, Lucy Kidd had less than $10,000 and she carried it sewn into her underwear to keep anyone from knowing her financial status.

She garnered a ten-year contract in April 1888 with the understanding that she would get the buildings back in shape and hire teachers to begin classes the following September. She immediately contacted her old friend Maggie Hill with whom she had taught for years at Whitworth and offered her the position of presiding teacher at a salary of seventy-five dollars a month, payable only when the school started making money. Lucy's eighteen-year-old son Edwin withdrew from the University of Mississippi to become the secretary and financial agent for the college. Her daughter Sarah, who had studied music in New Orleans, New York, and Paris, returned to teach voice at the school. Lucy also convinced four of the best teachers from Whitworth to join her faculty.

She moved her family, servants, and furnishings for the school in July and immediately began traveling to church sessions and camp meeting all over Texas and Indian Territory (present-day Oklahoma) to attract girls and money for the fall semester. In later years Lucy shared stories of the hot, dirty, and exhausting horseback and stagecoach trips she took that summer and of the scary nights sleeping in remote cabins and listening to howling wolves. She also told of one fund-raiser where she was preceded by a preacher who told the congregation that music and musical instruments were tools of the Devil. Then, it was her turn to encourage attendance and financial help for her college that emphasized training in the arts, especially music.

By the time the North Texas Female College opened that September, Lucy Kidd had rounded up 100 students, including the daughter of the governor of Mississippi. More challenges lay ahead. The college consisted of only two buildings and when it rained, a creek running through the middle of the four-acre campus sent mud flowing into the front door of the main building. By the end of the first year she used $850 of her own money to purchase four lots and had a three-story frame dormitory constructed, which was named the Annie Nugent Hall for the daughter of the gentleman who gave the first major gift of $10,000. Over the next three decades the campus grew by another dozen buildings named for generous donors. By 1892 the school boasted telephones, electricity, incandescent lights, zinc bathtubs, running water, and it was the first school in Texas to provide a nurse for its students. The library grew and the school became the only Southern women's college with science laboratories and a $700 refracting telescope.

In 1892 Lucy's marriage to Joseph Staunton Key, a beloved Methodist bishop, posed a name problem for Lucy who enjoyed an amazing career as Lucy Kidd. She solved the dilemma in a daring way for the times: she hyphenated her last name to Kidd-Key. She was also ahead of her time in her educational philosophy. Even as she insisted that "her girls" always be womanly, she believed women had brains and should think for themselves. While she did not oppose women's suffrage, she did not approve of the behavior of some of the women who were organizing for the vote. She wrote that women should be able to take financial care of themselves and their children. Yet, she insisted on surrounding herself with her notion of "womanly" things— flowers and lace in her home and long, flowing dresses that extended into trains.

Townspeople called the students' excursions into the city "the string" because the girls, wearing their navy blue wool uniforms marched two by two with a chaperone at the head and another at the end of the line. Austin College boys gathered at various sites along the route to watch the girls. The students enjoyed tennis and basketball teams and calisthenics. Lucy built a skating rink in the gym and in keeping with her ever-present eye for fund-raising she opened the rink to Sherman residents. When the kitchen staff went on strike in 1908, Lucy hired the older girls to run the kitchen and donated their wages to the new building fund. When the strike ended she treated the girls to an elegant dinner at a downtown hotel.

Lucy's interest in music led to her search for financial backing that enabled her to hire the finest faculty from all over the world. The Conservatory of Music auditorium attracted the top orchestras and singers of the day, including Victor Herbert, Campanini, the United States Marine Band, and the Chicago Symphony Orchestra. She insisted that students have instruments in their rooms, which led by 1910 to 120 pianos on campus.

Enrollment peaked in 1912 with more than 500 students; however, times were changing. There were fewer girls who could afford or wanted to attend what President Roosevelt described as "the only finishing school west of the Mississippi." Less-expensive state supported schools began operating and in 1915 Southern Methodist University in Dallas opened with financial support from the church that had previously gone to North Texas. Lucy's health began declining, and financial shortfalls forced her to pay faculty salaries herself. The class of 1916 was the last to graduate as Lucy made plans for her retirement and to convert North Texas to an accredited two-year junior college. On September 13, 1916, one week after the new school opened, Lucy Kidd-Key died.

Lucy's memory was honored in 1919 when the school was named Kidd-Key College and Conservatory. Her son and daughter ran the school for several years before the Depression brought new financial worries. At the end of the 1934-1935 term, Kidd-Key closed. Today, a Texas Historical marker is all that remains at the old school site but the legacy of Lucy Kidd-Key continued well into the twentieth century as her graduates made names for themselves as educators, writers, musicians, singers, and sculptors.

Ladies Fought Second Battle of the Alamo

The second battle of the Alamo began in the early 20th century as a disagreement between two powerful women over the proper way to preserve the historic structure, which had been allowed after the famous battle in 1836 and the slaughter of the men who fought there to fall into an embarrassing state of neglect and disrepair. Adina Emilia De Zavala, granddaughter of Lorenzo de Zavala, the first Vice President of the Republic of Texas, was a schoolteacher, a prolific writer of Texas history, and an early advocate of restoration of the missions in San Antonio and other historic buildings. About 1889 she organized the "De Zavala Daughters," dedicated to preserving Texas history, which soon became a chapter of the Daughters of the Republic of Texas (DRT).

Although the state of Texas purchased the portion of the site known as the Alamo Chapel from the Catholic Church in 1883, the state did nothing to preserve the structure. The building north of the chapel, which De Zavala and her friends believed had served as the convent when the complex was a Spanish mission and was used for the long barracks where most of the fighting occurred during the battle, had been sold to a wholesale grocer who added a two-story building and altered the façade. Adina De Zavala and her group secured an agreement from the grocer to have first option to purchase the long barracks, which they dreamed of restoring to its former appearance and opening it as a museum.

In 1903, when the group heard that the long barracks might be sold to a hotel syndicate, Adina De Zavala sought the help of Clara Driscoll, a nineteen-year-old heiress who had returned to San Antonio after several years studying in Europe. She was so appalled at the condition of the Alamo that she wrote an article for the *Daily Express* calling the Alamo complex an "old ruin.... hemmed in on one side by a hideous barracks-like looking building, and on the other by two saloons." Clara Driscoll joined the De Zavala chapter of the DRT and went with Adina De Zavala to see the grocer who was asking $75,000 for the structure. Clara Driscoll personally gave the owner $500 for a thirty-day option and the ladies set about raising the purchase price. Despite a nationwide campaign and a legislative appropriation, which was vetoed by Governor S.W.T. Lanham as "not a justifiable expenditure of the taxpayers' money," Clara Driscoll eventually paid $65,000 to complete the purchase. Over the governor's objection, the state reimbursed Clara Driscoll and gave custody of the property to the Daughters of the Republic of Texas.

Cracks began to show in the bulwark of the organization as members divided over what should be done with the grocer's building. Adina De Zavala and her cohorts believed "a large part" of the original convent/long barracks played a significant role in the Battle of the Alamo and remained hidden under the grocer's building. Clara Driscoll and her camp believed the walls of the convent/long barracks overshadowed the Alamo chapel and should be replaced with a dignified park.

Members of the statewide DRT and citizens in San Antonio and Texas divided into De Zavalans and Driscollites, each faction determined to have its way. The two groups within the DRT separated from each other and when Clara Driscoll was given custody of the vacant grocery in 1908, Adina De Zavala locked herself in the building for three days as newspaper reporters from around the country gathered to watch the spectacle. By 1910 the Driscollites seemed to have won the war, but one more battle remained: Governor Oscar Colquitt, deciding that walls under the modern grocery building pre-dated the Battle at the Alamo, ordered restoration of the convent/barracks. In January 1912 as the modern additions were removed, the governor personally watched the process that revealed arches and Spanish stone work, which confirmed the De Zavalans' claim. However, the following year, while the governor was out of state, the lieutenant governor permitted the roof and walls of the upper story to be removed. Fifty-five years later, just in time for the 1968 opening of HemisFair, San Antonio's world's fair, the old building finally received a roof and opened as a museum.

Adina De Zavala continued for the rest of her life organizing groups that restored, marked and preserved historic sites. When she died in 1955 at the age of ninety-three, her casket draped with the Texas flag, was driven past the Alamo one last time. She willed her estate to the Sisters of Charity of the Incarnate Word for a girl's vocational school and a boys' town.

Clara Driscoll spent the remainder of her life devoted to historic preservation, state and national politics, civic and philanthropic endeavors. When she died in 1945 at the age of sixty-four, her body laid in state at the Alamo chapel. She bequeathed the bulk of her estate to the Driscoll Foundation Children's Hospital in Corpus Christi.

Women Pilots Trained in Texas

When the United States entered World War II, the top brass, including General Henry H. "Hap" Arnold, commander of the U.S. Army Air Forces (AAF), had doubts about women's ability to pilot large aircraft. In the summer of 1941, even before the United States entered the war, two famous women aviators Jacqueline "Jackie" Cochran and test-pilot Nancy Harkness Love had presented separate proposals for women pilots to be used in non-combat missions. Meantime, the British government asked Jackie Cochran to recruit American women pilots to ferry aircraft for the British Air Transport Auxiliary, the first organized group of American women pilots to serve in the war.

Finally, after lobbying by Eleanor Roosevelt, the military realized that there were not enough male pilots. In September 1942 Nancy Love gained permission to recruit women for training in the Women's Auxiliary Ferrying Squadron (WAFS) at New Castle Army Air Base in Wilmington, Delaware. Soon thereafter Jackie Cochran returned from Britain to win appointment as director of the Women's Flying Training Detachment (WFTD), headquartered at Houston's Municipal Airport (present-day Hobby Airport). The new recruits were classified as civil service, not military personnel. Calling themselves "guinea pigs," the Houston WFTD were housed in motels and private homes and transported to the airfield each day in trailer trucks. They had no life insurance, there were no crash trucks or fire trucks on the airfield, and they had no uniforms. Since there were no facilities for changing clothes they wore the same gear—GI coveralls in the standard size 52, which they called "zoot suits"—to ground school, to drill, to fly, and to march to and from the mess hall.

When they were moved in early 1943 to better quarters at Avenger Field—the only all-female air base in history—at present-day Sweetwater, they had to pay their own way and pay for their room and board. If they washed out of the program, they had to pay their return fare. After the WFTD and the WAFS merged in August 1943 to form the Women's Airforce Service Pilots (WASP), Jackie Cochran became the director of the program and Nancy Love headed the ferrying division. Cochran recruited women from all over the country but excluded black pilots claiming that since the program was new, innovative, and not very popular, including black pilots might endanger the service's status. More than 25,000 women applied, but fewer than 1,900 were accepted. After seven months of military flight training, 1,074 earned their wings to become the first women to fly American military aircraft—a rate comparable to male cadets in the Central Flying Training Command. The WASPs were all pilots with a minimum of 100 hours when they entered the service, but they were trained to fly "the Army way." Their program followed the same course as male Army Air Corps pilots except for no gunnery training and very little aerobatic and formation flying. The women received 210 hours of flying time divided equally between PT-17s, BT-13s, and AT-6s.

The WASPs flew sixty million miles ferrying 12,650 aircraft from factories to military bases and ports of embarkation. They towed targets for live anti-aircraft artillery practice and flew simulated strafing missions, even dropping tear gas and other chemical agents during the training of ground troops. They accepted the very dangerous task of testing damaged airplanes. As part of bomber crew training, WASPs flew the aircraft while male combat trainees practiced as bombardiers, navigators, and gunners.

When the AAF reached a surplus of male pilots toward the end of 1944, it was determined that the WASP was no longer needed. By the time the WASP was disbanded on December 20, 1944, thirty-eight had been killed in accidents—eleven in training and twenty-seven during active duty. Since they were not considered military, the dead were sent home at family expense and did not receive military honors. Even their coffins could not be draped with the U.S. flag.

In her June 1, 1945 report, Jackie Cochran wrote that WASP safety, accident and fatality rates compared favorably with male pilot records. Despite her report, WASP records were classified secret and sealed, not to be released for thirty-five years. Ironically, Colonel Bruce Arnold, son of General Hap Arnold who had originally been opposed to women pilots, began lobbying in 1975 to have the WASPs recognized as veterans. With the help of Senator Barry Goldwater, who had served as a WWII ferry pilot, Congress passed the G.I. Bill Improvement Act of 1977, granting the WASP corps full military status for their service.

On July 1, 2009, President Barack Obama signed the WASP Congressional Gold Medal into law. On May 10, 2010, three hundred surviving WASPs came to the U.S. Capitol to accept the Congressional Gold Medal from House Speaker Nancy Pelosi and other Congressional leaders.

6

Newcomers Make Their Mark

Friedrich Ernst, Father of German Immigrants

*M*any early Texas settlers escaped a past that they preferred to forget. Johann Friedrich Ernst not only turned his back on his past, he changed his name and became such an outstanding German Texan that he earned the title of "Father of the Immigrants."

Born in 1796 as Christian Friedrich Dirks (or Dierks), the future Texan began service in 1814 in the Duke of Oldenburg's regiment. He rose to the rank of quartermaster sergeant and earned a medallion for participating in the campaign against Napoleon. After five years, the duke made Dirks clerk at the post office. (Some accounts claim he served as head gardener for the Duke of Oldenburg.) In September 1829, apparently aware he was about to be charged by the duke with embezzling a large sum of money from the post office, Dirks took the name Ernst and fled Germany with his wife and five children.

The family settled first in New York where they operated a boarding house and became friends with Charles Fordtran, a tanner from Westphalia, Germany. Fordtran and the Ernst family made plans to settle in Missouri but as they sailed up the Mississippi River they heard of the free land available in Texas and changed their destination. Arriving in Galveston on March 9, 1831, Ernst applied as a family man for a league of land (4,428 acres) from the Mexican government in the fertile rolling hills between present Houston and Austin. Fordtran, a single man, received an adjoining quarter league.

Ernst did not reach Texas prepared for a pioneer life. He did not know how to build a cabin, hated guns, and owned so little farming equipment that he was forced to use a hoe to break the soil for planting. Still, he was so pleased with his new life of political freedom, good climate, and limitless opportunities that he wrote a glowing letter to his friend in Oldenburg describing the wonderful life that Texas offered. The account received wide publicity throughout Germany, prompting many Germans to follow him to the new land. Ernst and his family welcomed the newcomers to their home, even loaning money to help many of the immigrants get started.

Apparently overwhelmed by the size of his land holdings, Ernst traded 1,000 acres for a dozen milk cows. As Germans settled in the area around Ernst, they followed his lead and began growing corn, a crop and diet source totally unfamiliar to the immigrants. Ernst also introduced tobacco growing and made cigars, which he marketed in Houston, Galveston, and nearby San Felipe. He even kept records of the rainfall and temperature at his farm.

He sold pieces of his land as town-size lots to establish in 1838 the community of Industry, the first German town in Texas. The source of the town's name came from either the industriousness of its citizens or Ernst's cigar industry.

Despite efforts of German noblemen in the mid-1840s that brought thousands of German settlers to Texas, Industry still carries the title of "Cradle of German Settlement in Texas." The 2010 census lists a population of 304.

A Steady Onslaught of Immigrants

In 1844, Samuel Addison White saw an opportunity to make some money and develop his barren piece of property that jutted into the waters between Matagorda and Lavaca bays, a protected waterway along the Central Texas coast. Prince Karl of Solms Braunfels, an aristocratic emissary representing a group of German noblemen, had shown up on the shell beach where White had built his small house. Prince Karl was desperate. He had been sent to Texas by noblemen who had created a grand scheme to make a fortune by shipping thousands of farmers, craftsmen, and intellectuals to cheap land in Texas. When Prince Karl reached Galveston in July and discovered that the 9,000 acres his noblemen friends had purchased was unsuitable for settlement, he was overwhelmed by the sudden arrival of a shipload of colonists. He needed a port for disembarkation and a route that offered easy passage into western Texas. White agreed to allow the German immigrants to occupy the beach near his home until the prince could make arrangements for their trek inland.

Prince Karl and White were stunned in late November and December as four brigs carrying 439 immigrants sailed into Matagorda Bay. Each family had paid the Adelsverein (society of nobility) $240 for transportation to Texas, for 120 acres, and for the necessities for survival until they could bring in their first harvest. Instead, they huddled on the wet gravel shore with no trees and no buildings or other protection from the howling winds of a "Texas norther." Prince Karl had secured the services of the Reverend Louis Ervendberg, a German Protestant minister, who conducted Christmas services and offered communion. The group continued their traditional Christmas observances with a small tree—either an oak or a cedar—and the children sang carols. Soon after the New Year, fifteen ox-drawn wagons and fifteen two-wheeled carts were secured and loaded for their journey into Texas as Prince Karl searched for a suitable settlement. He moved ahead of the wagon train and had the good fortune to find a tract where a short, spring-fed river (the Comal) offered excellent waterpower near where it flowed into the Guadalupe River. The weary settlers arrived at their new home on March 21, 1845, one week after the Prince made the purchase. Despite their disappointment with the Adelsverein and the failure to secure their promised acreage, they named the site New Braunfels in honor of Prince Karl's home. In less than a month Prince Karl abandoned the colony even before his replacement had arrived.

Meantime, not all the Germans trusted Prince Karl enough to follow him on the inland search for a new settlement. Johann Schwartz (Swartz) and his family were among those who chose to stay at Indian Point. Schwartz purchased property from Samuel Addison White three miles down the bay and built a home on the site that eventually became the center of the port city of Indianola.

Neither Prince Karl's abandonment, nor the Adelsverein's failure to adequately fund their grand scheme slowed the shipment of more unsuspecting colonists to Texas. Between the fall of 1845 and the following spring, thirty-six ships brought 5,247 men, women, and children to the shore at Indian Point. There were no wagons or carts available to haul their meager supplies to New Braunfels because of Texas and U.S. politics. The impending war with Mexico over Texas' annexation to the U.S. meant that the U.S. military troops had swept through the area confiscating all the means of transportation to haul their supplies to the Rio Grande. Upon hearing from the Adelsverein that more colonists were heading to Texas, Prince Karl's replacement, Baron Johann Ottfried von Meusebach (who had the good sense to change his name to John before he reached Texas) had barracks and tents constructed along the beach for the new arrivals. As the extreme cold of that winter set in, people began dying of respiratory diseases.

The tragedy served as a vehicle to create a community. Dr. Joseph Martin Reuss, who arrived on one of the ships, began his medical practice by caring for the immigrants and opened an apothecary where he prescribed free medicines. When Henry (Heinrich) Huck, a wealthy young German who had settled in New Orleans in 1844, heard about the suffering of those stranded on the Texas coast, he quickly loaded a schooner with lumber and medicine and sailed for Indian Point. Huck opened a lumberyard, helped Dr. Reuss distribute the free medicine, and gave lumber to families for constructing coffins.

Henry Runge had come to the United States through Baltimore, moved to Indian Point in late 1845, and used a tent to open the area's first bank. As the summer heat of 1846 descended on the encampment and a steady flow of new arrivals poured in, the drinking water became polluted, the sanitation facilities proved inadequate, and a plague of mosquitoes, green stinging flies, and house flies descended on the community. Frau Reuss, Frau Huck, Mrs. White, and some of the other women who had become permanent residents prepared broth for the sick and cared for children whose mothers were ill.

The number of dead reached such proportions that they resorted to wrapping victims in blankets and burying them in mass graves. No one knows how many perished; the estimates ranged from 400 to over 1,200. Many people panicked and began walking to the inland colonies, spreading diseases as they moved along the route. Over 200 died along the way.

Samuel Addison White platted a new town on his land in 1846 and began selling lots as many of the German families decided to remain on the coast and begin their new life at Indian Point—a choice that would give them the prosperity and freedom they had imagined when they listened to the false promises of the Adelsverein.

Ferdinand Lindheimer, Father of Texas Botany

If you have heard of the Texas prickly pear cactus, the Texas yellow star daisy, milkweed and loco weed, or the Texas rat snake, you may be surprised to know all five derive their scientific name from Ferdinand Jacob Lindheimer—a botanist who scoured the wilds of Texas in the 1830s and 40s to discover several hundred new plant species.

Raised in a wealthy German family and university educated, Lindheimer taught at Frankfurt's Bunsen Institute where he became affiliated with a group seeking government reforms. Finding himself at risk for his political associations, which alienated him from his family, he fled to the United States. Lindheimer settled first in Illinois, near some of his former German colleagues. From there he traveled with another German group to a plantation near Vera Cruz, Mexico, where he began his lifelong fascination with collecting plants and insects.

Excited by reports of the Texas Revolution in 1836, Lindheimer joined a company of volunteers heading to Texas. They missed the action, however, arriving the day after the final battle at San Jacinto. For the next year Lindheimer served in the Texas army.

At the invitation of George Engelmann, a botanist and friend from Frankfurt, Lindheimer traveled to St. Louis where he agreed to collect plant specimens in Texas for Engelmann and Asa Gray, a Harvard botanist. Lindheimer roamed the Texas coast and Hill Country for nine years with his botanical cart and his dogs, collecting plants, which he identified, dried, and shipped to Engelmann at the Missouri Botanic Gardens and Asa Gray at Harvard.

When a group of German noblemen organized the Adelsverein in 1844 to settle immigrants in Texas, Lindheimer helped their leader Prince Carl of Solms-Braunfels find the settlement site, which became New Braunfels, at the confluence of the Comal and Guadalupe rivers. Prince Carl awarded Lindheimer a piece of property on the Comal River where Lindheimer built his home.

Lindheimer collected his first specimen of the nonvenomous Texas rat snake (Elaphe obsoleta lindheimeri) in New Braunfels. Reaching lengths of more than six feet, the Texas rat snake consumes large quantities of rodents, birds, frogs and lizards. Because of his years roaming through Texas, Lindheimer held the respect of area Indians and occasionally hosted Santana, war chief of the Comanche, in his home.

Married and raising a family of four children, Lindheimer gave up his travels in 1852 and for the next twenty years served as editor and then publisher of the *New Braunfels Herald-Zeitung*. He also ran a private school for gifted children and served as the first justice of the peace for Comal County.

Believing a lack of bees needed to pollinate the fruit in the area accounted for the low fruit production, Lindheimer convinced Wilhelm Brückisch, a scientific beekeeper from Silesia (Prussia) to come to Texas. Brückisch arrived with his wife, three sons, two daughters, and several hives of Italian black bees and settled across the Guadalupe River from New Braunfels. Credited as the first person in Texas to begin the commercialization of bees, Brückisch established an apiary on the river and published numerous books and articles on beekeeping.

As rumblings of secession from the United States grew in intensity, Lindheimer is credited with keeping down much of the discontent felt in other German communities with his editorials admonishing his German readers opposing the Civil War to support the Confederacy as a means of maintaining regional stability. Historians say his postwar writings indicate his true loyalty lay with the Union.

At least twenty institutions hold Lindheimer's plant collections, including the Missouri Botanical Gardens, the British Museum, the Durand Herbarium and Museum of Natural History in Paris, and the Komarov Botanic Institute in St. Petersburg.

Lindheimer died in 1879 and is buried in New Braunfels. Today, the Lindheimer home on the banks of the Comal River serves as a museum and is listed on the National Register of Historic Places. Visitors see framed botanical specimens, the sword given to Lindheimer by Prince Carl, the family Bible published in 1701, Lindheimer's desk and several pieces of furniture made by some of the New Braunfels German cabinet makers.

Indianola, Gateway to the West

Waves lap the sunbaked shell beach of a ghost town that never should have been. Despite its locale at near sea level, the thriving port of Indianola rivaled Galveston in the mid-19th century as a major shipping point on the Texas coast.

Disillusionment with the Adelsverein, a group of German noblemen that organized a large wave of immigration to Texas, led many of the new arrivals to decide not to continue inland to German settlements, but to remain on the coast. They began a community at the landing site, and built docks into the shallow bay to receive the steady stream of new immigrants.

By 1849 a village had developed at Indian Point, and the residents changed its name to the more melodious "Indianola."

During the Mexican-American war the United States War Department built a wharf and opened an Army Supply Depot to serve as the disembarkation point for personnel destined for posts as far away as El Paso del Norte (future Fort Bliss) and along the western edge of Texas settlement. Hundreds of freight wagons and Mexican carts loaded with silver from the mines of Chihuahua, Mexico, rolled into Indianola to meet ships that transported the silver to the mint in New Orleans.

If anything proved to the citizens of Indianola that their seaport was making a name for itself in Washington, D.C., it was the arrival of thirty-three camels in May 1856, followed by a second shipment of forty-one camels the next February. The entire affair was an experiment initiated by the Secretary of War, Jefferson Davis, to test the viability of camels as beasts of burden in the Southwest.

Indianola was a southern town, but it boasted a seaport's connection to the more cosmopolitan world of commerce, business cooperation, and a diverse blend of residents newly arrived from all over Europe. The soil—gritty shell beaches cut by a crisscross of shallow bayous and lakes—did not lend itself to cotton growing. The vast slave plantations thrived much farther east and north along the rivers and in the rich bottomlands. Planters who came to Indianola to purchase supplies could also buy slaves at auction on the front porch of Indianola's Casimir House, an elegant hotel and social center that used slaves to serve its guests. Most of the blacks in Indianola were free, having bought their freedom or been freed by previous owners. Despite Texas laws that forbid free blacks from remaining in the state, Indianola residents paid little attention to the ex-slaves who were needed to work on the docks and operate pig farms on the huge Powderhorn Lake that sprawled behind the low-lying port city.

During the fall of 1860, talk of Lincoln's possible election caused little concern and no apparent disruption in the cooperation between northern business people pouring into the port and local shipbuilders producing steamers at a brisk pace. The newspaper editor touted the rosy financial picture, expecting it to continue indefinitely.

Before the first war shots were fired, the United States military personnel that had manned the posts along the western edge of Texas settlement to protect colonists from Indian attack began marching through the streets of Indianola to the docks where federal ships waited to carry them away. The federal blockade of the Gulf of Mexico soon forced the Indianola merchants to close and many residents to flee the city. Despite bombardment by federal troops in October 1862 and a three-month occupation of Indianola in early 1864, residents quickly returned after the war, and began rebuilding the destroyed docks and their homes and businesses. The eagerness to return their port to a thriving commercial center and to assist families that had been impoverished by the war played well for an economy that thrived on its maritime commerce.

The problem of high tide washing into the downtown streets was virtually ignored as profits soared, freight wagons by the hundreds clogged the thoroughfares leading to the docks, and ships sat patiently at anchor waiting for access to the busy port. In September 1875, Indianola overflowed with visitors from all over the region who had come to witness the murder trial of participants in the infamous Sutton-Taylor Feud. Few people noticed the increasingly bad weather until the road out of town became impassable and the railroad tracks washed away. By the time the storm ended, several hundred had died and most of the business houses were destroyed having been washed into the huge Powderhorn Lake. Many residents moved inland, but those who remained were determined to rebuild their city.

As railroads were built from rival ports undermining Indianola's shipping enterprise, businessmen began to look at developing the town as a resort to take advantage of its clear water, excellent fishing, and fine restaurants.

In August 1886, a fierce hurricane moved into the Gulf of Mexico. By the time it reached Indianola it was one of the most powerful storms in recorded history. Structures that had survived the 1875 storm soon gave way to the force of wind and flood. A lamp exploded in a disintegrating building and the wind fanned flames across the entire downtown. At dawn the port city of Indianola was gone, and the survivors moved, many without ever looking back at the ghost town they left behind.

Log Church Cathedral

A one-room church, built originally of hand-hewn logs in 1866, sits on a lane leading off a country road in Wesley, a farming community between Houston and Austin. Wesley boasts the first Czech school in Texas that started here in 1859 when the town was called Veseli meaning "joyous." The church building housed the community school and the place of worship for the first Czech-Moravian congregation in Texas.

Reverend Bohuslav Emil Lacjak, serving as teacher and pastor in 1888, began painting the interior of the wood building using an art technique called trompe l'oeil, a method of creating realistic imagery in three dimensions to give the impression of a basilica-style cathedral, which resulted in rustic-appearing brick walls, columns, and geometric decorative patterns.

Unfortunately, Reverend Lacjak was killed in an 1891 hunting accident before he could explain the meaning of his work. He clearly had not completed his creation because the outlines of more designs are still visible. The congregation believes the gray bricks, highlighted in black that stretch to the top of the windows, depict the strength of the walls of Jerusalem. The Star of David atop white pillars casting dark shadows reminds congregants of the pillars of Solomon's Temple. The continuous chain design around the edge of the ceiling represents the unbroken link of brotherhood and the word "Busnami" above the pulpit area translates as "God with us."

Czech immigrants, searching for cheap land, began arriving in Texas in the 1850s. Although most of them were Roman Catholics, ten to fifteen percent were Protestant and most of those were United Brethren. They came to Texas after generations of persecution by the Catholic Church in their homeland. They held worship services in homes until they built this little one-room chapel. The building was enlarged and the steeple added in 1883. One hundred years later, the congregation built a new church next door, which serves a community of about sixty. The "log church cathedral," listed on the National Register of Historic Places, is open as a museum reminding all Czech-Moravians of their rich heritage.

7

When Texas Left the Union

Texas Unionists

*W*ith the election of Abraham Lincoln in November 1860, the United States headed relentlessly toward civil war. Not all southerners supported secession. Almost 2,000 Texans were sufficiently opposed to separating from the Union that they joined the Federal Army. Other Unionists, those who did not want to break up the United States, handled their positions in different ways. For instance, Sam Houston was adamantly opposed to destroying the Union. He had been elected governor of Texas in 1859 despite campaigning vigorously against secession. He had worked for years after Texas won its independence from Mexico to secure statehood for Texas. After the Secession Convention voted to secede on February 2, 1861, he refused to sign the loyalty oath to the Confederacy. He was removed from office on March 6, and returned to his home in Huntsville where he died in July 1863.

Robert E. Lee was a Unionist who was heartsick over secession. But, when he was offered a generalship in the U.S. Army, he turned it down because he could not bring himself to fight against his beloved state of Virginia. General Robert E. Lee, like so many others, remained in the Confederacy.

Edmund J. Davis, a judge in the Brownsville district, opposed secession, and his views probably caused him to lose his bid to represent his district at the Secession Convention. After Texas seceded, Davis refused to take the oath of loyalty to the Confederacy, and like Sam Houston, the state vacated Davis' judgeship. He fled to Louisiana and then with John L. Haynes and Andrew Jackson Hamilton, Texans who also opposed secession, he went to Washington to meet with President Abraham Lincoln. With Lincoln's support for providing arms, the first and largest unit—the First Texas

Cavalry Regiment—was organized on November 6, 1862, in New Orleans under the command of Edmund J. Davis (who later served as Texas governor during the period of reconstruction). The regiment remained in Louisiana, except for brief forays into Texas, until November 2, 1863, when it landed on the south Texas coast as part of the 6,000-man Rio Grande Campaign. The invasion force was tasked with stopping the Confederate wagons loaded with cotton that came down through Texas to reach the old port at Bagdad on the Mexican side of the Rio Grande. Waiting offshore were hundreds of European (mostly British) ships eager to receive the cotton in exchange for Winchester rifles, ammunition, medical supplies, and other essentials for the Confederate Army.

After only a month on the Rio Grande, the regiment's ranks grew by more than 50 percent as refugees, Unionists, and Confederate deserters fled south. Texas was the only southern state that bordered a neutral country, and the Rio Grande served as the dividing line that offered an escape route. Although the officers of the First Texas Cavalry were primarily men from mainstream southern backgrounds, the rank and file consisted in large part of Spanish-speaking Texans and first-generation immigrants, including German Unionists from settlements in the Hill Country. Most of the troops did not own slaves and saw no reason to fight for those that did.

With the occupation of Brownsville and the increase in the number of volunteers, the Second Cavalry Regiment was formed and then both regiments merged into the First Texas Volunteer Cavalry. In preparation for a federal invasion of Texas from Louisiana, most of the Union troops were pulled out of the Rio Grande Campaign and only a few hundred were left in the area between Brownsville and Brazos Santiago, a port across from the southern tip of Padre Island on the Gulf coast.

Seizing the opportunity, Confederate troops retook Brownsville on June 29, 1864, and chased the remaining Federal troops, including the remaining Texas Volunteer Cavalry, to Brazos Santiago. One month after Robert E. Lee surrendered at Appomattox, the federal infantry on Brazos Santiago made an ill-advised decision to advance toward Brownsville. The Confederates who had been keeping a watchful eye on the Union troops met them at Palmito Ranch on May 12, 1865, killing, wounding and capturing more than two-thirds of the Yankee force to win what has been called the last battle of the Civil War.

True to the Union

One of the few Union monuments south of the Mason-Dixon Line stands in Comfort, Texas, honoring a group of Union sympathizers killed by Confederate troops. Most of the Unionists, young German immigrants recently arrived in the United States to escape oppression in their native country, saw themselves as freethinkers, intellectuals who did not believe in slavery. They did not own land of sufficient size to need slave labor, and they did not want to separate from the country that recently welcomed them to its shores.

The young freethinkers established Comfort and several communities on the western edge of the Texas frontier. Their mercantile businesses supplied the United States army outposts, and they opposed secession because of the disruption to their lucrative trade.

After Texas seceded from the Union, all the federal troops manning the posts along the western frontier were called back to the United States, leaving the western communities exposed to Indian and outlaw attack. A group of young men formed a militia to protect the western counties.

The Confederates, suspecting the group posed a serious threat to the government, declared martial law. When Confederates demanded that all men sixteen years and above join the army, about sixty-eight young intellectuals under Major Fritz Tegener headed to Mexico, which remained neutral throughout the Civil War.

Failing to select a defensive position or even post a guard, the young Germans camped along the west bank of the Nueces River about fifty miles from the Mexican border. Lieutenant C.D. McRae and his Confederate force of ninety-four followed the retreating Unionists and attacked before dawn on August 10, 1862. After holding off three charges, the Unionists realized the impossibility of their position. The survivors crawled through the Confederate line, leaving behind nineteen dead and nine wounded. Lieutenant McRae's men executed the wounded a few hours after the battle.

Two Confederates were killed and eighteen wounded, including McRae. Of the Unionists who escaped, Confederates later killed seven, and six more drowned as they tried swimming the Rio Grande into Mexico. Eleven returned home, and most of the others made it to Mexico and California.

In 1865 a group of German Texans traveled to the battle site, gathered the scattered bones of the dead in tow sacks, and carried them back to

Comfort for burial in a common grave. The following year the community erected a monument at the gravesite titled "Treue der Union" (Loyalty to the Union).

Houston's Civil War Hero

A handsome, redheaded Irish saloonkeeper led a group of forty-six Irish dockworkers in a Civil War battle that Jefferson Davis called the most amazing feat in military history. At the outbreak of the war, Richard "Dick" Dowling joined the Davis Guards, and soon became the company's first lieutenant. After gaining a reputation for its artillery skills in the January 1, 1863, Battle of Galveston in which the Confederates regained control of the island, Dowling's company was assigned to Fort Griffin, a nondescript post at the mouth of Sabine Pass on the Texas/Louisiana border.

The twenty-five-year-old Dowling showed leadership beyond his years by keeping his rowdy men occupied with artillery practice—firing the fort's six cannons at colored stakes placed on both sides of a shell reef that ran down the middle of the pass dividing it into two channels. The east side of the passage led along the Louisiana border and the west paralleled the earthen embankment of Fort Griffin.

On September 8, 1863, Dowling's Company F watched a Union navy flotilla of four gunboats and 5,000 men approach the pass. Waiting until the first two gunboats entered the parallel channels, the little band of forty-six Irishmen opened fire with all six cannons, striking the boiler and exploding the *Sanchem* on the Louisiana side of the reef and then striking the steering cables of the *Clifton* on the Texas side of the pass. With both channels blocked by disabled ships, the Union force sailed away. In less than one hour Dowling's men captured both Union vessels, killed nineteen, wounded nine, and took 350 prisoners without suffering a single casualty.

Dick Dowling rose to the rank of major before the end of the war and he returned to Houston as its hero, hailed as the man who stopped federal forces from coming ashore and marching westward to capture Houston and Galveston. Jefferson Davis presented a personal commendation, calling the Sabine Pass Battle the "Thermopylae of the Confederacy." The ladies of Houston presented Dowling's unit with medals made from Mexican coins smoothed down and inscribed on one side with "Sabine Pass, 1863."

Dowling claimed genuine Irish roots. Born in County Galway, Ireland in 1838, he moved with his parents and six siblings to New Orleans to escape the Great Irish Potato Famine of 1845. Orphaned by the 1853 Yellow Fever epidemic that took the lives of his parents and four siblings, Dowling finally made his way to Houston and within four years opened his first saloon.

By 1860, the mustached Irishman with a good sense of humor owned three saloons; the most popular, called "The Bank," sat on the square with the Harris County Courthouse and became Houston's social gathering place. Dowling also immersed himself in Houston's business community—investing in local property, helping set up Houston's first gaslight company, and installing gaslights in his home and in "The Bank." He helped found Houston's Hook and Ladder Company fire department and the city's first streetcar company.

After the war, Dowling returned to his earlier business interests and expanded into real estate, oil and gas leases, and ownership of a steamboat. Unfortunately the 1867 Yellow Fever epidemic, which swept across Texas from the Gulf coast, ended Dowling's life on September 23, 1867.

Survived by his wife Elizabeth Ann Odlum and two children Mary Ann and Felize "Richard" Sabine, Dowling was honored by the city of Houston's first public monument, which stands today in Hermann Park.

Palmito Ranch, Last Battle of the Civil War

Official Civil War records claim the battle at Columbus, Georgia, on April 16, 1865, was the last fight of the war and that the Battle of Palmito Ranch along the lower Rio Grande was a "post-Civil War encounter" because it occurred more than a month after General Robert E. Lee's surrender on April 9th. The reasons for the Texas battle are also open to argument although it is clear that some of the officers and enlisted men on both sides were not yet ready to quit the fight. In March 1865, believing the Union had won the war, Lieutenant General Ulysses S. Grant gave permission for Major General Lewis Wallace to meet the Confederate commanders of the Brownsville area in hopes of securing a separate peace agreement. The Union terms offered at the meeting on March 11th required Confederates to take an oath of allegiance to the United States to state that there would be no retaliation against the troops, and it also said those who wished to leave the country would be allowed to do so. When the Union's proposal went up the Confederate chain of command, not only did Major General John G. Walker denounce the terms, he wrote an angry letter to his subordinates for agreeing to meet with the Union in the first place. Even on May 9th the commander of the Confederate Trans-Mississippi Department, Lieutenant General Edmund Kirby Smith told a gathering of governors of the Confederate states west of the Mississippi that despite Lee's surrender he proposed continuing the fight.

After receiving a false report that the Confederates were abandoning Brownsville, the Union commander on Brazos Island at the mouth of the Rio Grande sent 300 men to the mainland with instructions to occupy Brownsville. Confederates got word of the advance on May 12 and met the Federals for a brief skirmish at Palmito Ranch twelve miles down the river from Brownsville. Both sides sent for reinforcements, but the Confederates were supplied the following day with mounted cavalry and a six-gun battery of field artillery that offered far more firepower than the Federals that had an increase in infantry to only 500. At 4:00 P.M. on May 13, the battle began and immediately the federal line started falling apart. Within four hours the Union troops retreated seven miles back to Brazos Island. At that point Confederate Colonel John Salmon "Rip" Ford, commander of the southern division is quoted as saying, "Boys, we have done finely. We will let well enough alone, and retire." Ford wrote in his report of the battle that it had been "a run" and the clash showed "how fast demoralized men could get over ground." The accounts also differ on the number of losses: from a handful to a few dozen Confederates wounded, while the Union had from sixteen to thirty killed and wounded.

At the same time the Battle of Palmito Ranch raged, governors of the Confederate states of Arkansas, Louisiana, Missouri, and Texas were instructing Lieutenant General Edmund Kirby Smith to dismiss his armies and end the war. A few days later, Federal officers from Brazos Island arrived in Brownsville to arrange a truce with the Confederate Commander of the Brownsville area.

8

Cattle and the Men and Women Who Drove Them

Shanghai Pierce, Cattleman Extraordinaire

*I*t was unusual for a cattleman to come to Texas as a stowaway on a ship. But that is exactly how nineteen-year-old Abel Head Pierce made his way to Port Lavaca in 1854. Discovered when the ship reached the high seas, he earned his passage by mopping the deck and hauling cargo at ports-of-call along the six-month journey.

Soon after landing with only the clothes on his back and seventy-five cents in the pocket of his too-short britches, Pierce met William Bradford Grimes, "the most important cattleman in the region." Grimes hired the greenhorn to split rails, apparently thinking the six foot-four giant with the booming Yankee accent needed to learn some lessons about the cattle business. Immediately Pierce informed his new employer that he wanted to be paid at the end of the year in cows and calves because he planned to go into the cattle business.

Pierce set about his work on the ranch with industry, rising early, and quickly taking on other responsibilities. In his eagerness to prepare for his future as a cattleman, Pierce hired a blacksmith to forge his own brand and then proudly showed the "AP" to Grimes. Chris Emmett in his delightful book, *Shanghai Pierce: A Fair Likeness,* says at the end of the year, when time came for payment, Grimes "cut four old cows and three scrawny calves from the run of range cattle...." As winter set it, the cows died, leaving Pierce with only the calves to show for a year of work. Grimes bragged that he gave Pierce his "first degree in the cattle business."

The origin of the moniker "Shanghai" claims an unclear pedigree.

Glorying in his self-appointed image as a storyteller and entertainer, Pierce relished an audience whether gathered around a campfire among cowboys or in later years among dignitaries. At times he alluded to school days in Rhode Island when "Shanghai" was a fighting word. Then, he claimed it became a "brand of distinction." He said, "I do not have time to fight everybody who wants to fight me. If I take that much time off I will not have time to take their money away from them." His nephew said in later years that he "looked so much like the long-necked, long-legged rooster from Shanghai that they named him after his counterpart." Chris Emmett tells of another version, usually whispered, "Because he 'shanghaied' so many people out of their property." He often made fun of his size by claiming he was born in Rhode Island, but the state got too small for him. When he lay down, his head landed in the lap of somebody in Massachusetts and his feet bothered someone in Connecticut.

Shanghai did not leave Grimes' employ when Grimes cheated him out of his first year's pay. Instead, he stayed on to work for the richest cattlemen in South Texas. Shanghai rounded up mavericks and branded them for Grimes at $1 a head. He told a fellow cowboy at the end of the year, "I'm damn glad he [Grimes] didn't ask me whose branding iron I used this year." This spelled the beginning of Shanghai Pierce's cattle acquisitions.

At the end of the Civil War, when some of the men bragged about their accomplishments and tried to tease Shanghai about being the regimental butcher, he boasted: "By God, Sir, I was all the same as a major general: always in the rear on advance, always in the lead on retreat."

After the war, when the only profit from beef lay in hides and tallow (the carcasses were fed to the hogs or thrown away), he went into the slaughter business. Finally, Shanghai Pierce became one of the first to drive a herd along the Chisholm Trail to market in Abilene, Kansas. He quickly proved to be a cunning and able businessman, eventually acquiring up to 35,000 head of cattle and 250,000 south Texas acres.

In 1881, when the railroad came through his land, Shanghai dreamed of Pierce's Station becoming the county seat. He did not get his wish, but he found another interest. He wrote the railroad asking that two cars of lumber be deadheaded at Pierce because: "I am pioneering in another matter. I am trying to introduce religion in the community." He ordered pews and a pulpit. Shanghai proudly showed the new facility to all visitors. One gentleman asked, "Colonel Pierce, do you belong to that church?"

"Hell, no!" Pierce shouted. "The church belongs to me."

Shanghai believed ticks caused fever in cattle and, after touring Europe, he decided Brahman cattle were immune to ticks because "'Bremmers' sweated and the ticks fell off, and the cattle got fat thereafter." After his death in 1900, his estate and another rancher, Thomas O'Connor, undertook the importation of Brahmans, the beginning of a new cattle industry for Texas.

During Shanghai's European tour, the fine statues all over Europe caught his attention, and upon his return he commissioned a marble statue of himself created by sculptor Frank Teich. They agreed on payment of the $2,250 only if he felt satisfied that the statue represented a fair likeness of him. As workmen placed the life-size marble statue atop a ten-foot granite pilaster, mounted on another ten-foot piece of gray granite, Pierce sat with a friend watching the finishing touches. A small black boy approached the statue and after walking round and round the figure and looking again and again at Shanghai, the boy said, "Mr. Shanghai, that sure does look like you up there."

"Ugh, by God." Shanghai snorted. "I'll take it."

Shanghai Pierce died on December 26, 1900, from a cerebral hemorrhage and was buried beneath his massive likeness.

Margaret Borland, Trail Driver

She buried three husbands and then hit the cattle trail in 1873 with her children and a grandchild in tow. Margaret Heffernan was born in Ireland, and when she was five years old, her family was among the early Irish immigrants that settled on a land grant in South Texas. In 1829 her father, a candle maker in Ireland, became a rancher in the McMullen and McGloin Colony on the prairie outside San Patricio. Stories vary about how Margaret's father died—either by an Indian attack or by Mexican soldiers in the lead up to the Texas Revolution. Another story claims that with the outbreak of the war for independence, Margaret's mother fled with her four children to the presidio at Goliad, and they were spared the massacre because they were so fluent in Spanish that they were thought to be Mexicans. (I know of no record of women and children being massacred at Goliad.)

Margaret married at nineteen, gave birth to a baby girl and was widowed at twenty when her husband lost a gunfight on the streets of Victoria. A few years later Margaret married again, had two more children, and lost that husband to yellow fever in 1855. Finally, about three years later Margaret married Alexander Borland, who was said to be the richest rancher in the county. Margaret bore four more children. One of her sons-in-law, the *Victoria Advocate* newspaper editor and historian, Victor Rose, wrote of Margaret Borland: "a woman of resolute will, and self-reliance, yet was she not one of the kindest mothers. She had, unaided, acquired a good education, her manners were lady-like, and when fortune smiled upon her at last in a pecuniary sense, she was as perfectly at home in the drawing room of the cultured as if refinement had engulfed its polishing touches upon her mind in maiden-hood."

Margaret partnered with her husband in the ranching business; however 1867 proved to be another year of tragedy. Alexander Borland died in the spring while on a trip to New Orleans. Later that year a dreadful yellow fever epidemic that swept inland from the Texas coast killed thousands, including four of Margaret's children and one infant grandson.

As the owner of the ranch, Margaret managed its operations and enlarged her holdings to more than 10,000 cattle. The Chisholm Trail had proved so profitable that in the spring of 1873 Margaret led a cattle drive of about 2,500 head from Victoria to Wichita, Kansas. She took a group of trail hands, two sons who were both under fifteen, a seven-year-old daughter, and an even younger granddaughter. After reaching Wichita, Margaret became ill with what has been called both "trail fever" and "congestion of the brain." She died on July 5, 1873, before she had time to sell her cattle.

Although at least four women are known as "Cattle Queens" for having taken the cattle trail, it is thought that Margaret Heffernan Borland was the only woman to ride the trail without being accompanied by her husband.

English Nobleman in Big Spring

Texas claims its share of frontier characters—buffalo hunters, Indian fighters, gunslingers, and cowboys—who roamed and sometimes helped settle the vast western regions. The remittance man, although a less well-known frontier character, represents a few hundred wealthy Europeans, mostly Englishmen, who found themselves exiled to the wilds of West Texas. Although these nobles lost their positions at home, their families continued financial maintenance (remittance) in an effort to keep them out of sight.

Joseph Heneage Finch, Seventh Earl of Aylesford, fits the bill as a remittance man. He held claim to one of the finest estates in England until his life blew up in a scandal that shook British nobility, including such personages as the Prince of Wales (future King Edward VII), and Lord Blandford Churchill, uncle of the future Sir Winston Churchill. It seems Finch accompanied the Prince of Wales on a goodwill trip to India in 1875–1876 only to abruptly leave his sponsor and return home to confront his unfaithful wife and her lover. After a divorce that shook the highest levels of English society, Finch lost his estate, and left for adventure in America.

Upon arriving in New York, Finch met Jay Gould, president of the Texas & Pacific Railroad, who described the cheap land and good turkey and antelope hunting in West Texas. With former buffalo hunter John Birdwell serving as his guide, the earl bought a 37,000-acre ranch northeast of the new railroad town of Big Spring in 1883 and stocked it with $40,000 worth of cattle. Birdwell warned Finch that cowboys "don't cater to big names and such, so we'll just call you 'Judge.'" From then on, the "Judge" became popular with the local cowhands for his tales of hunting in India with the Prince of Wales and for footing the bill for their drinking parties.

Storytellers say Finch bought a saloon, tended bar himself, and at the end of the party gave the establishment back to its former owner. We know he satisfied his yen for mutton, which did not sit well with local cowboys and cattlemen, by building his own meat market, the first permanent building in Big Spring. He lined the walls of his lodge with an amazing collection of hunting gear and after the structure burned, he bought the Cosmopolitan Hotel. Some folks say he bought the hotel because he and his friends needed a place to party for one night. He gave the hotel back the next day with the understanding that there would always be a room for him and his buddies. On January 13, 1885, after throwing a lavish Christmas dinner and drinking party that lasted two weeks, the Seventh Earl of Aylesford died in his hotel room at the age of thirty-six. A Texas Historical Marker in Big Spring tells the English nobleman's story.

Panhandle Nobility

In the late 1870s, word spread across England of the fabulous money—returns of thirty-three to fifty percent on investments—in American cattle ranching. Two British aristocrats, Sir Edward Marjoribanks, the Baron of Tweedmouth and his brother-in-law the Earl of Aberdeen, established the

"Rocking Chair Ranche" in 1883. Courting dreams of a vast English-style estate, the "cattlemen" bought 235 sections (one section equals one square mile or 640 acres) in Collingsworth and Wheeler counties of the Texas Panhandle and stocked it with 14,745 head of cattle and 359 ponies. They built a ranch house, corrals, and a store as the nucleus of their envisioned cattle empire and named the site Aberdeen.

The inhabitants of the Texas Panhandle in the 1880s, in true frontier spirit, did not take to the high-minded notions of the English. West Texans considered themselves equals whether they owned extensive cattle ranches or only a few steers and a dugout. The English ranchers, unfortunately, held to their Old World attitudes regarding master and servants. In response to their references to cowboys as "cow servants" their establishment became known as *Nobility Ranche*.

J. John Drew, an Englishman who partnered in the original scheme to sell ranch land to British investors became general manager of the Rocking Chair. He got along well with the "cow servants" and knew cattle, but he wasn't scrupulously honest.

Baron Tweedmouth's younger brother, Archibald John Marjoribanks became assistant manager and bookkeeper at the ranch. Uninterested in the life of a rancher, and known among the cowboys as "Archie" or "Old Marshie," Archibald never associated with or rode with the cowboys. He spent his days drinking and gambling in Mobeetie saloons and hunting with his purebred hounds while drawing an annual salary of $1,500. Soon, even men who prided themselves on always being fair in their cattle dealings began openly rustling cattle from *Nobility Ranche*, apparently with Drew's knowledge.

Everyone in the Eastern Panhandle, except Archibald, knew that rustlers and disgruntled cowboys were openly stealing from the ranch. Drew, who maintained the loyalty of the ranch employees, kept for himself 100 cows for every one stolen and reportedly shipped more cattle for himself than he recorded for the ranch. For a time the ranch prospered, but the thievery began to show in the financial reports. Without prior notice Lord Aberdeen, Baron Tweedmouth, and other investors showed up at ranch headquarters demanding an inventory. Drew directed the cowboys to drive the cattle around a nearby hill and back several times to make the count increase by several hundred and satisfy the "Lords of the Prairie" that the ranch operated an increasingly large herd.

Additionally, a feud developed in 1890 between settlers and squatters of Southern Collingsworth County, who wanted Pearl City to be the county seat, and the Rocking Chair faction that had laid out Wellington to be the seat of government.

The Rocking Chair cowboys also caused the Great Panhandle Indian Scare in January 1891 when they killed a steer for supper, accidentally incinerated the carcass of the animal and in the process let out some loud whoops and celebratory gunfire. Although Indians had been run out of the Panhandle for at least ten years, settlers living in the remote region continued to be nervous. A woman living near the commotion rushed with her two children to report the blood-curdling war whoops. The news of an impending slaughter went out over the telegraph at the train station. Citizens barricaded themselves, waiting in terror for the attack. A hardware store in Clarendon sold out of guns and ammunition. Finally, the Texas Rangers mustered to defend the terrified citizenry discovered that the noise came from Rocking Chair Ranche cowboys having a good time. It took three days to calm the frightened community, and the episode became known as The Great Panhandle Indian Scare.

By 1891 the Rocking Chair herd was so reduced that the entire range had to be searched to produce two carloads of calves for market. The owners tried bringing charges against Drew, but community feelings against the Englishmen made it impossible to impanel a jury. The ranch was sold in 1895, and all that remains is the town named Wellington and Rocking Chair Hills in the northern part of Collingsworth County.

Niles City, "Richest Little Town in Texas"

Three miles north of Fort Worth's business center, Niles City, a tiny strip of land spreading over a little more than one-half square mile and boasting a population of 508, incorporated in 1911. Within its bounds sat the Fort Worth Stock Yards, Swift & Company, Armour & Company, two grain elevators, and a cotton-oil company, which placed the city's property value at $12 million. Six railroads came through the town with the Belt Railway owning and operating a roundhouse. Niles City had a town council and enjoyed complete utility service, good roads, and fine schools.

The town was named for Louville Veranus Niles, a successful Boston businessman who reorganized the Fort Worth Packing Company in 1899 and was instrumental in convincing Armour and Swift to locate in Niles City in 1902. There were no fine homes in the town, just the houses belonging to the plant workers and about seventy rental houses erected by the Fort Worth Stock Yards for its employees. Niles City claimed other important venues including the Live Stock Exchange Building, the horse and mule barns, and the Cowtown Coliseum, where the Fat Stock Show offered the first indoor rodeo in the United States. Many big name entertainers performed at the Coliseum including Enrico Caruso who drew a crowd of about 8,000 in 1920. The Swift and Armour packing plants added significantly to the economy, employing about 4,000 workers from Fort Worth and the surrounding area.

All of the wealth packed into such a small piece of real estate proved too tempting for Niles City's neighbors. In 1921 the Texas legislature passed a bill allowing a city of more than 50,000 to incorporate adjacent territory that did not have a population greater than 2,000. To protect itself from annexation, Niles City quickly took in another square mile of extraterritorial industries including the Gulf Oil Company refinery and its pipeline plant, and two school districts attended by the children of Niles City. The move increased the town's population to about 2,500 and its taxable property to $30 million. The legislature passed a second bill raising the population needed to halt annexation to 5,000. In July 1922 Fort Worth held a special election in which voters passed amendments to the city charter allowing Fort Worth to incorporate Niles City, which occurred on August 1, 1923.

Today the Stockyards, the Cowtown Coliseum, and Billy Bob's, the world famous honky tonk, are located on the grounds of the town once known as "the richest little town in Texas."

9

Rails, Roads, and Bridges

Los Ebanos Ferry

*N*amed for the ebony trees in the area and for the tiny town hugging Texas' southern border, this ancient crossing on the Rio Grande serves as the only government-licensed, hand-operated ferry between the U.S. and either its Mexican or its Canadian border.

For years before Spain began issuing land grants on the Texas side of the Rio Grande, colonists in Northern Mexico crossed this old river ford on their way to La Sal del Rey, a massive salt lake where they loaded the precious mineral in wooden carts for the trip back to Mexico.

In the 1740s José de Escandón, an appointee of the Viceroy of New Spain, led his men across this old ford on an expedition to locate the most favorable sites for Spanish colonization and Christianization of the Indians.

In 1875 an incident at this crossing resulted in the naming of a Mexican national hero. Despite Texas Ranger Captain L.H. McNelly's efforts to drive Juan Cortina and his bandits across the border and out of Texas, cattle thefts increased. A rancher reported Cortina's men driving seventy-five head of stolen cattle toward this crossing known then as Las Cuevas, named for the Mexican ranch on the opposite bank. Word spread claiming Las Cuevas Ranch headquartered the great bandit operation, and 18,000 cattle waited there to be delivered to Monterrey.

Captain McNelly's men pursued the Mexicans across the river after dark, attacked a ranch, and killed all the men only to discover that they had stopped at the wrong ranch. They returned to the river and posted guards in the brush waiting for a counterattack.

152

When General Juan Flores Salinas, who owned Las Cuevas Ranch, learned of the earlier attack, he led twenty-five mounted Mexicans to the river only to die along with some of his men in the surprise ambush. The following day the Mexicans agreed to turn over the thieves and return the stolen cattle. Incensed over the indiscriminate killing, Mexicans across the region proclaimed General Salinas a national hero. His statue dominates the plaza across the river in the little village of Ciudad Díaz Ordaz.

Over the years, bandits and illegals used the ford, and during Prohibition as many as six boatloads of liquor crossed here every night. In 1950 the U.S. Border Patrol opened an entry station here. It remains the smallest of eight official ports of entry into Texas from Mexico and it offers a glimpse of an earlier time when residents on both sides of the border enjoyed casual visits between neighbors sharing a common river.

Depending on the swiftness of the river, it takes from two to five men pulling hand over hand on heavy ropes to propel the wooden ferry loaded with three cars and a maximum of a dozen foot passengers across the 70-yard expanse. The anchor cable that keeps the vessel from drifting off down river has been tied, since 1950, to the massive Ebony tree on the Texas side of the river. The giant tree, thought to be 275 years old, is listed in *Famous Trees in Texas*.

Most travelers choose to park their cars and join walking passengers who board the barge-like vessel on its round trip. Fence building under Homeland Security may close the old waterway. The time may be short for travelers to experience the last hand-drawn ferry on a U.S. international border.

Butterfield Stage Across Texas

The famous Southern Overland Mail Route, better known as the Butterfield Stage in romantic Wild West movies, actually operated its twice-weekly mail and passenger service for less than three years from September 15, 1858 until March 1, 1861. Two trails from the east started from St. Louis and from Memphis, Tennessee. When the trails met at Fort Smith, Arkansas, they joined and continued west. The line swooped south through Texas in what was called the "Ox Bow" to avoid the snows and mountain passes of the central regions of the country. The stages crossed the Red River into Texas on Colbert's Ferry near present Denison and then headed west for the 740-mile, eight-day trip to Franklin (present-day El Paso). The stages ran night and day averaging speeds of five to twelve miles per hour. Primitive stations offering water and a change of horses lay about every twenty miles along the flat, desert-like trail and were spaced between stops at Fort Belknap, Fort Phantom Hill, and Fort Chadbourne. The route crossed the Pecos River, skirted the base of the Guadalupe Mountains, and reached the dividing point between the route's east and west divisions at present-day El Paso.

Passengers who did not want to make the grueling trip straight through could stay over, get some rest, and take a later stage. However, if the next few stages were full, a traveler might be marooned for up to a month. Almost everyone agreed the food was awful. Waterman Ormsby, a reporter for the *New York Herald,* was the only passenger that made the entire distance on that first trip from St. Louis. He sent dispatches along the way to his paper describing the journey. He wrote, "...the fare, though rough, is better than could be expected so far from civilized districts. It consists of bread, tea, and fried steaks of bacon, venison, antelope, or mule flesh—the latter tough enough. Milk, butter, vegetables were only met with towards the two ends of the trip." He described another meal of shortcake, coffee, dried beef and raw onions. He said that often there were not enough plates or tin cups to serve the passengers. Mail delivery took top priority, which often resulted in mailbags being crammed into the coach with the passengers. On the stretch from Fort Belknap in Texas to Tucson, Arizona, the handsome Concord-made coaches weighing more than two tons were replaced by lighter-weight "celerity" or mud wagons and the team of four to six horses stepped aside for mule power that proved to be a lot less attractive to Indians. The mud wagons had light frames that made it easier to maneuver the deep sands and mud. The roofs were made of thick duck or canvas and the open sides allowed the free flow of air as well as dust and rain.

Until Congress authorized the U.S. postmaster general to offer a contract to deliver mail from St. Louis to San Francisco, all mail bound for the West Coast had to be shipped through the Gulf of Mexico, freighted across the Isthmus of Panama to the Pacific and shipped up the coast to California. John W. Butterfield and his associates won the U.S. government contract in September 1857 to haul mail and passengers across the southern part of the country to California. It took a year to assemble the necessary equipment—a huge investment in 250 Concord Stagecoaches, 1,200 horses, and 600 mules. They dug cisterns or water wells and built corrals at 139 relay stations and hired 800 employees, including drivers, conductors, station keepers, black-smiths, and wranglers. The government contract called for the Butterfield Overland Stage Company to receive $600,000 a year, plus the money it earned on passenger fares and the receipts for mail. Postage cost ten cents per half-ounce and passengers paid $200 for the one-way 2,795-mile trip. The coaches departed each Monday and Thursday morning in the east from near St. Louis and in the west from San Francisco for the 25-day journey.

At the conclusion of that first trip west, Waterman Ormsby, the *New York Herald* correspondent wrote: "Had I not just come out over the route, I would be perfectly willing to go back, but I now know what Hell is like, I've just had 24 days of it."

Despite passengers' complaints of discomfort, the Concord coaches, unlike other conveyances that rode on steel springs, were suspended on "thoroughbraces," leather straps fashioned for each coach from over a dozen oxen hides that were cured to be as tough as steel. In 1861, when Mark Twain's brother Orion Clemens was appointed Secretary of the Nevada Territory, Twain accompanied him on the trip west and wrote of the journey in *Roughing It*. Twain describes their stagecoach as "a swinging and swaying cage of the most sumptuous description—an imposing cradle on wheels."

Continued debt and competition from the Pony Express that proved mail could be delivered cross-country in ten days forced Butterfield out of the Overland Stage Company. Wells Fargo took over the operation and in antic-ipation of the Civil War, the southern Ox Bow route through Texas made its last run on March 21, 1861. With the start of the Civil War on April 12, Wells Fargo moved all the equipment north and continued the operation as the Central Overland Trail from St. Joseph, Missouri to Placerville, California.

On March 30, 2009, President Barack Obama signed Congressional leg-islation authorizing the study of the designation of the Butterfield Overland Trail National Historic Trail.

Millions in Silver Hauled Across Texas

Hundreds of freight wagons, each drawn by six to eight mules, and brightly colored Mexican carretas, each pulled by four to six oxen, formed dusty weaving trains on the Chihuahua Road from the silver mines of northern Mexico to the port town of Indianola on the Central Texas Coast. The trail across Texas opened in 1848 at the end of the Mexican-American

War when the U.S. laid claim to Texas and the entire southwest all the way to the Pacific Ocean. The following year, the California Gold Rush set the get-rich-quickers into a frenzy looking for a shorter route across the country than the old Santa Fe Trail that ran from Missouri to Santa Fe, New Mexico.

The new port of Indianola on Matagorda Bay offered dockage for U.S. military personnel and equipment bound for the western settlements of Texas as far as El Paso (future Fort Bliss), and it provided the perfect jumping-off place for settlers and gold-hungry Americans heading west. The ships, anchored at piers stretching out into the shallow bay, took on the Mexican silver and transported it to the mint in New Orleans. The vessels returned with trade goods destined for the interior of Texas and the towns developing in the west and the villages of Mexico.

The Chihuahuan Road headed northwest from Indianola, made quick stops in San Antonio and Del Rio, twisted north along the Devils River, forded the steep ledges along the Pecos River, and then plunged southwest through the Chihuahuan Desert to cross the Rio Grande at Presidio, entering the mineral-rich state of Chihuahua, Mexico.

The Spanish, as early as 1567, had discovered northern Mexico's mineral wealth—gold, copper, zinc and lead—but silver was overwhelmingly the richest lode. By the time Mexico opened its commerce with the U.S. after the Mexican-American War, there were six mines in the area near Ciudad Chihuahua, capital of the Mexican state of Chihuahua.

The raw outcroppings of the richest mine, Santa Eulalia, had been discovered in 1652, but persistent Indian troubles chased away the Spanish explorer who had found the site. Fifty years later, three men who were fugitives from the law hid in a deep ravine tucked into Santa Eulalia's steep hills. They stacked some boulders to create a fireplace, and as the flames grew hotter, the boulders began leaking a shiny white metal, which they recognized as silver. Knowing their fortune awaited, they sent word via a friendly Indian to the padre in the nearby mission community of Chihuahua They offered to build the grandest cathedral in New Spain if the padre would absolve their sins and pardon them of their crimes. It worked. The fugitives received absolution and pardon, they became fabulously wealthy, and they built the Church of the Holy Cross, Our Lady of Regla, the finest example of colonial architecture in northern Mexico. Miners flocked to the Santa Eulalia mine and Ciudad Chihuahua grew into a large and wealthy city.

Millions of dollars in silver and trade goods were hauled over the road between Indianola and Chihuahua, except for the years of the Civil War. The road served as the corridor for western settlement until 1883 when the Texas and Pacific Railroad from the east met the Southern Pacific from California. The new Southern Transcontinental Railroad opened a direct route between New Orleans and California. The final blow to the Chihuahua Road arrived with the devastating hurricane of 1886 that turned the thriving seaport of Indianola into a ghost town.

Sam Robertson, Visionary

The railroad and visionaries like Sam Robertson deserve much of the credit for development of the Rio Grande Valley of Texas. Before arrival of the railroad, the Valley was a no man's land. Towns such as Brownsville and Matamoros, Mexico, relied on the Rio Grande and the Gulf of Mexico for access to the outside world. Travel from Brownsville to Corpus Christi took days of slogging through the vast jungle of mesquite, cactus, chaparral and brush-covered country known as the Wild Horse Desert.

In 1903, as Robertson fulfilled a contract to lay the first rails from Corpus Christi to Brownsville, he noticed the peculiar topography of the area along the Rio Grande looked much like that of the Nile River—higher by several feet than the surrounding landscape. Unlike other river valleys that drain into nearby streams, years of flooding left behind silt, resulting in the Rio Grande flowing at a higher level than the surrounding terrain—an ideal situation for harnessing the water for gravity irrigation into the fertile land along its banks. Robertson also observed dry riverbeds left behind after the Rio Grande flooded and then changed course, cutting new channels. Locally known as resacas, the 400-foot wide dry canals or oxbows twisted through the area north of Brownsville offering readymade irrigation potential.

Robertson convinced local investors to join him in purchasing 10,000 acres to begin land development, and laying out of the town of San Benito along one of the curving resacas. They cut a canal from the Rio Grande to introduce irrigation water into the dry resacas and began selling land to northern farmers looking for new opportunities in the Rio Grande Valley. The farmers, forced to rely on horses, mules, and dirt roads to get their produce to market, preferred land next to the railroad.

In 1912 Robertson decided to take the railroad to the farmers and began constructing the San Benito and Rio Grande Valley Railroad. Soon, all the spurs and intricate network of lines snaking across the valley became known as the Spiderweb Railroad, and the train that traveled the route became known as the "Galloping Goose" for the frequency with which it jumped the track, forcing passengers to help lift it back on the rails.

Making two round trips daily at a grand speed of fifteen miles per hour, the train picked up both passengers and freight. Some farmers built tiny loading platforms beside the track, while others merely flagged the engineer to take on travelers or a few bushels of produce.

By 1924 the Missouri Pacific took over the line, but the little railroad, whose track never extended beyond 128 miles, had served an important role in opening the rich Rio Grande Valley to worldwide markets.

Robertson's visions extended to establishing ice plants for refrigerated railcars carrying vegetables to city markets. He served as San Benito's first postmaster and two terms as sheriff before joining General John J. Pershing's army chasing the Mexican bandit Pancho Villa into Mexico. During World War I Robertson proved his competence building light rail lines to the front trenches and remained in Europe after the war to help rebuild Germany's rail system.

Upon Robertson's return to San Benito, he embarked on his final grand scheme—developing Padre, the barrier island paralleling Texas' southern shore, as a resort community. He built a "trough" causeway from the northern end of Padre to the mainland near Corpus Christi. A trestle supported four parallel troughs, wooden slots constructed wide enough to accommodate a standard car tire within its walls. With automobile wheels set firmly in each trough, traffic flowed both directions across the causeway.

In his zeal to attract tourists, Robertson opened ferries at Port Aransas and at the south end of Padre Island. Then, he built a hotel and constructed a toll road along the island.

Although the unusual trough causeway boasted 1,800 cars the first month and 2,500 cars the second, interest began waning after the 1929 Stock Market Crash. By the next year, Robertson's dream appeared doomed; he could not pay his debts. He sold his interest in the development and must have watched in horror as the 1933 hurricane destroyed all the structures on and leading to Padre Island.

Sam Robertson died in 1938, twenty-four years before his dream came true. Congress established Padre Island National Seashore and President John F. Kennedy signed the bill into law on September 28, 1962.

Southern Transcontinental Railroad

The outbreak of the Civil War forced the U.S. Congress to change its plans for the first Transcontinental Railroad to be built along the 32nd parallel, which extends across Texas roughly from Shreveport, Louisiana, to El Paso. Instead, Congress selected a northern route along the 42nd parallel. In 1869 the Central Pacific Railroad from Sacramento, California met the Union Pacific from Council Bluffs, Iowa, and drove the "Last Spike" at Promontory Summit, Utah, just north of the Great Salt Lake. In a never-to-be-forgotten ceremony, a transportation network of railroads linked for the first time both coasts of the United States.

The northern route created a major improvement in east-west transportation but the need remained for a southern route. The U.S. Congress chartered the Texas & Pacific Railroad in 1871 to build a line westward from Marshall, Texas, to meet the Southern Pacific coming from San Diego. The Texas Legislature, eager to have the rail line stretch across the state, accepted the only federally chartered railroad in Texas and paid Texas & Pacific twenty sections (a section is one square mile or 640 acres) of land for every one mile of track that it laid—a total of fourteen million acres.

The construction progressed piecemeal due to contract disputes until Jay Gould and his syndicate bought an interest in the project and with solid financial backing reached an agreement with the Southern Pacific to meet at Sierra Blanca, ninety-two miles east of El Paso. Construction pitched forward at a furious rate as each line worked to be first to complete the designated mileage. The Southern Pacific used Chinese workers for most of its labor force as it crossed rugged terrain that required water to be hauled in to its crews. The grueling work halted for the Southern Pacific on November 25, 1881, when the railroad reached Sierra Blanca. With the arrival of the Texas & Pacific on December 15, the second Transcontinental Railroad spanned the nation.

Waco's Suspension Bridge

After the Civil War, Waco was a struggling little town of 1,500 nestled on the west bank of the Brazos River. No bridges crossed the Brazos, the longest body of water in Texas. During floods, days and even weeks passed before travelers as well as cattle on the Shawnee and Chisholm trails could safely cross the river. Although money was scarce and times were hard during recovery from the war, a group of businessmen formed Waco Bridge Company and secured a twenty-five-year contract to construct and operate the only toll bridge for five miles up and down the river.

John A. Roebling and Son of New York designed the 475-foot structure, one of the longest suspension bridges in the world at that time. Waco's bridge served as the prototype for Roebling's much-longer Brooklyn Bridge completed in 1883.

The fledgling Waco company ran into problems from the beginning. Work started in the fall of 1868 with costs, originally estimated at $40,000, growing to $140,000 forcing the investors to continue issuing new stock offerings. The nearest railroad stopped at Millican, over 100 miles away, which meant that coils of wire and cable, steel trusses, and custom-made bolts and nuts had to be hauled to Waco by ox wagon over rutted, sandy roads. The contractor floated cedar trees down the Brazos for shoring up the foundation in the unstable riverbed. Local businesses made the woodwork and the bricks.

The bridge opened to traffic in January 1870 with tolls of ten cents for each animal and rider; loose animals and foot passengers crossed for five cents each, and sheep, hogs, or goats crossed for three cents each. It was not long until residents on the far side of the river began complaining about the tolls. Businessmen who used the facility joined them in their protests.

Landowners along the river began allowing cattlemen, travelers, and local citizens to cut across their property to reach other fords on the river. The uproar increased for the next nineteen years, until September 1889, when the Waco Bridge Company sold the structure to McLennan County for $75,000 and the county gave the bridge to the city.

Vehicles continued using the bridge without paying a toll until 1971 when it was converted to a pedestrian crossing. Today lovely, shaded parkland edges both sides of the river and the bridge enjoys a listing on the National Register of Historic Places and designation by a Texas Historical marker.

The Crash at Crush

William George Crush, general passenger agent for the Missouri, Kansas & Texas Railroad, conjured up a rip-roaring publicity stunt to generate revenue. Katy RR officials agreed that promoting a train wreck between two old locomotives would stir a lot of interest and bring in revenue by selling $2 round-trip tickets to transport spectators to the event.

Crush sent out circulars and bulletins throughout the summer of 1896 advertising the "Monster Crash." Newspapers all over Texas and the surrounding states ran daily crash progress reports. Katy workers laid four miles of track about fifteen miles north of Waco, built a grandstand for "honored guests," set up a restaurant in a borrowed Ringling Brothers circus tent, and laid out a huge carnival midway with medicine shows, refreshment stands, and game booths. They even built a depot with a 2,100-foot-long platform and a sign modestly announcing to visitors that they had arrived at Crush, Texas.

At daybreak on September 6, 1896, the first of 33 fully loaded excursions trains arrived, some so crowded that passengers rode on the roofs of the cars. Many others came by wagon and on horseback. They picnicked, listened to political speeches at the three speakers' platforms, and surged around the bandstand and special facilities for reporters.

By 5:00 P.M. with an estimated crowd of more than 40,000, old engine No. 999, painted bright green, and No. 1001, painted a brilliant red, faced each other and then backed for 3.5 miles in opposite directions. William George Crush mounted upon a handsome white horse and wearing a white suit, removed his white hat, held it high above his head, and then whipped it down as the signal to start engines. The crowd screamed as trains, whistles blaring, began barreling down steep inclines toward the valley below, picking up speed as they churned forward. Both engineers tied the throttles wide open and jumped to safety. The cars trailing each engine bore brilliantly colored streamers and advertisements.

When the locomotives met in a shuddering, grinding clash both boilers exploded sending pieces of metal and wood flying like lethal missiles in all directions. Two men and a woman were killed, at least six received injuries including Waco's most prominent photographer who was blinded.

William George Crush lost his job that day. And Katy rehired him the following day. The railroad paid damage claims with cash and lifetime rail passes. Souvenir hunters helped clean the site by carrying off pieces of the tragedy.

In the early 20th century, Scott Joplin memorialized the event with his march "Great Crush Collision."

The Four Gospels Railroad

The twenty-two-mile rail line did not begin in 1909 as anything other than a central Texas business scheme to move Williamson County's huge cotton crops, cattle, wheat, and passengers to the "Katy" Railroad at Bartlett. Farmers and residents along the line were so happy to have a railroad that when the last of the track was laid into Florence on December 27, 1911, an excursion train arrived loaded with 250 to 300 people who paid $1 for the round trip. They dressed in their Sunday best and enjoyed the daylong celebration.

It was after The Bartlett Western Railroad changed owners a couple of times and was sold in 1916 to Thomas Cronin that the route took on a new flair. Cronin had retired from a highly successful career with the International and Great Northern Railroad and was looking for a new challenge. He found it in the BW. Cronin began by turning the operation into a family affair, naming his daughter Marie the vice-president, his daughter Ida treasurer, and Ida's husband William Branagan general manager; nephew Thomas Wolfe, who had been injured in his former railroad position, came along in a wheelchair and may have simply supervised. The entire clan moved into an apartment in downtown Bartlett on the second floor of a brick commercial building next to the Katy Railroad and a few blocks from the Bartlett Western depot.

Marie and Ida Cronin grew up in the East Texas railroad town of Palestine, but both girls studied in Paris. Marie had remained in Paris until the beginning of World War I and earned an international reputation as a fine portraitist. Upon her return, she won commissions for several of the portraits that hang in the Texas State Capitol. Ida, a gifted singer-organist, studied music in Paris, retuned to Palestine, married William Branagan and became very active in Catholic women's work. This rather unusual family set about developing a relationship with the 2,200 townspeople of Bartlett and soon found the community welcoming, if not a little surprised by their new neighbors.

Marie Cronin, called "Mamie" by her family, took the town by surprise with her flamboyant European-style clothing, wide-brimmed Parisians hats, and way more makeup than women of Bartlett found acceptable. She moved her art studio to the second floor of the BW depot where she could perform her duties as vice-president for the railroad and continue with her painting. Ida Cronin Branagan, as BW treasurer, set about renaming four of the small flag stations, locales where farmers waited to load their cotton or other produce for market or to catch the train for a trip to Florence or Bartlett. The stops consisted of a roof with benches on each side. Ida had the gospel names framed along with appropriate verses for each stop to offer passengers an opportunity to read while waiting for the train. For instance, the first stop after Bartlett was Caffrey and it had text from St. Matthew. The John Camp station heralded verses from St. Mark. The railroad siding at Atkinson noted St. Luke scripture, and St. John marked the stop at Armstrong. Passengers began calling the line the "Four Gospels Railroad," but it also became known as the "Bullfrog Line" because it jumped the track so often. The folks in Florence called it the "dinky" and others said the initials BW stood for "Better Walk."

Despite derisive remarks, the BW in 1916 earned $3,817 in passenger revenue and $30,327 from freight. Cronin set about improving the BW service and maintenance of its equipment, bridges, and roadbed. At some point a tractor was fitted with flanged wheels, allowing it to pull flat cars loaded with up to 130 bales of cotton. Crews carried sand to sprinkle on the tracks when the train, carrying a heavy load, had difficulty gaining traction on the up or down grade. When the BW secured the mail contract, it used Ford trucks equipped with railroad wheels. Although cotton was the largest commodity transported over the BW, it also carried the needs of the communities along its route including lignite, livestock, forest products, fruits, vegetables, drugs and, furniture. Cronin overhauled the trolley-style passenger car and tried, unsuccessfully, to get financing to extend the line to connect with the Santa Fe in Lampasas.

Ida Cronin Branagan fell in 1926 while getting off the BW and died from her injuries. That same year Thomas Cronin died, leaving Marie to serve as president of the BW while William Branagan continued as general manager. Marie, William, and cousin Thomas remained as a family living in the old commercial building.

Marie Cronin relished her role as president of a railroad, even riding the BW to give attention to every detail. She appeared perfectly confident in herself and her abilities and showed more self-assurance than the people of Bartlett expected from a woman. One person said she "always dressed like she was going to meet the Queen." Others said her strong voice dominated the room and she showed other eccentricities such as her long-time desire to be a lawyer. Despite never having studied the law, she took the bar exam many times without success. Many others found Marie friendly and generous to everyone without regard to race. One account claims she gave her Willys-Graham to her chauffeur because he needed a car for his family.

In the 1920s and '30s the BW struggled with damage from frequent flooding that tore out the tracks and continually drained the family's savings. The boll weevil spread across Texas by 1926 causing cotton prices to drop from $1.59 to $0.45 a bale, starting the downward spiral of revenue for the BW. Some family members have said Marie enjoyed being president of a railroad so much that she waited longer than reasonable to admit that the BW needed to be shut down. One nephew says Marie was what would be described today as a Type-A personality. The Texas Railroad Commission finally granted Marie Cronin's request to close the BW on October 11, 1935. No one denies, however, that Marie Cronin and her family added color, charm, and a sense of excitement to life along the Bartlett Western Railroad.

Texas Interurban Railways

In 1901 the first electric interurban, or trolley, began operating on a 10.5-mile track between Denison and Sherman in North Texas. The thirty-minute trip on the seventy-pound steel rails cost twenty-five cents. The line proved so popular that a second route between Dallas and Fort Worth opened the next year. A fourteen-mile track began operating between Belton and Temple and by 1909 the original line extended all the way south from Denison to Dallas. In five years the line moved further south to Waco and other lines began between Beaumont and Port Arthur, El Paso and Ysleta, and Houston, Baytown, and Goose Creek.

The Interurban between Houston and Galveston started carrying passengers in 1911 after Galveston completed its amazing rebuilding following the devastating 1900 storm. The city constructed a seventeen-foot seawall, raised the entire level of the island, and opened a new $2 million causeway to the mainland with tracks to accommodate the electric interurban line, railroad tracks, and a highway. The Houston-Galveston Interurban boasted an observation car on the rear and the fastest schedule of any steam or electric railroad. It made the fifty-mile downtown-to-downtown trek in seventy-five minutes with the help of a thirty-four-mile "tangent," one of the longest sections of straight track that allowed the carriage to travel at fifty-five miles per hour. Passengers rode to Galveston for an evening on the beach or in the gambling houses and then took the late interurban back to Houston.

Other areas offered special excursions between cities. Baseball teams grew up along the interurban lines, and passengers flocked to see games of the Class C and D "Trolley League."

The frequent service, convenient stops within cities, and lower fares of the interurbans overcame all competition with steam railroads. At the peak of the service in 1920, nearly four million passengers enjoyed the trolleys— the carpeted cars with lounge chairs, spittoons, and rest rooms. By 1931, ten systems across the state covered over five hundred miles.

The advent of the automobile and the convenient travel it offered spelled doom for the interurbans. The lines began closing, their tracks being paved over to make way for their competition, the automobile. On December 31, 1948, the old Denison to Dallas line made its last run.

10

Big Dreams

Houston Rises From the Mud

*H*ouston reigns as the largest city in Texas and the fourth largest in the United States, but it hasn't always enjoyed top billing. In 1832 brothers Augustus C. and John K. Allen came to Texas from New York and joined a group of land speculators. During the 1836 Texas War for Independence from Mexico, the Allen brothers outfitted, at their own expense, a ship to guard the Texas coast and to deliver troops and supplies for the Texas army. Their operation along the coast offered an opportunity to look for a good site for a protected deep-water port.

Some stories claim that after Texas won independence from Mexico in April 1836, the brothers tried to buy land at Texana, a thriving inland port at the headwaters of the Navidad River located between present Houston and Corpus Christi. Despite a generous offer, the landowner countered with a demand for double the price. One of the brothers reportedly became so angry that he climbed on a nearby stump and declared, "Never will this town amount to anything. I curse it. You people within the sound of my voice will live to see rabbits and other animals inhabiting its streets." (Today, Texana rests under an 11,000-acre lake, a recreational reservoir on the Navidad River that is part of Lake Texana State Park.)

Soon, the Allen brothers moved to their second choice, a site on the west bank of Buffalo Bayou, a muddy stream that wound its way for fifty miles to Galveston Bay and the Gulf of Mexico. They purchased about 6,500 acres for $9,500 and wisely named the new town for Sam Houston, the hero of the Texas War for Independence and the future president of the republic. By August 1836 the brothers placed newspaper ads claiming the new town was destined to be the "great interior commercial emporium of Texas." The ads also said that ships from New York and New Orleans could sail to the door of Houston and that the site on the Buffalo Bayou offered a healthy, cool sea breeze. They did not mention the heat, humidity, and mosquitos and that Buffalo Bayou was choked with tree branches and logs.

The Allen brothers had the town laid out with wide streets on a grid pattern parallel to the bayou to accommodate their future port. They sold town lots at a brisk rate, and donated property for churches and other public institutions. The first small steamship arrived in January 1837 after a fifteen-mile journey that took three days during which passengers helped clear logs and snags from the channel. The travelers found a "port city" of twelve inhabitants and one log cabin.

The Allen's slickest advertising ploy turned out to be their bid to get the government of the new Republic of Texas to relocate in Houston by offering to construct, at their own expense, a capitol and to provide buildings for public officials at a modest rental of $75 a month. It worked. By the time the government moved to Houston in May 1837, the town boasted a whopping population of 1,500 and 100 houses.

Arriving shortly after the opening of the government, the famous naturalist John James Audubon reported wading through ankle-deep water to get to President Sam Houston's "mansion." He found the two-room log dog run filthy, with papers cluttering a desk and camp beds crowded into one room. President Houston's chambers were just as dirty and he observed the furniture in the capitol was drenched with water since the building had no roof.

When travelers arriving in Houston found food and accommodations in short supply, the Allen brothers opened their large home, free of charge. Their accountant estimated the hospitality cost the Allen brothers about $3,000 a year, but the expense brought rich returns.

The brother's deal to provide the capitol and all the official office space carried the stipulation that if the government moved from Houston, the property reverted to the Allens. In 1839, after the election of President Mirabeau B. Lamar, the Texas government moved from the bogs along the coastal prairie to an Indian-infested wilderness on the banks of the Colorado River and named the place Austin.

With the loss of the capital, Houston plunged into financial turmoil that threatened to bankrupt the city. Multiple yellow fever epidemics hurt the town's image along with a growing reputation for drunkenness, dueling, brawling, and prostitution. In the midst of it all, Houston welcomed the Masons, the Presbyterians and the Episcopalians, and the town became the seat of county government. Businessmen invested in the cotton trade, small steamboats ferried supplies to and from the thriving seaport at Galveston and enterprising merchants used ox wagons to haul goods to settlers in the interior and to return with cotton and other farm commodities.

Following years of regular dredging and widening of Buffalo Bayou to accommodate larger ships, the Houston Ship Channel finally opened in 1914, creating a world class waterway that helped Houston become the "great interior commercial emporium of Texas" just as the Allen brothers advertised in 1836.

The Menger Hotel, San Antonio Landmark

In 1855, German immigrants William and Mary Menger built a one-story boarding house and brewery on the dusty plaza next to the Alamo. A sheep pen (where Rivercenter Mall now stands) served as the Mengers' other neighbor. Mary's cooking and William's beer proved so popular that local hacks picked up guests at Main and Military plazas and brought them to dinner. Travelers arrived by stagecoach from New Orleans and California.

Within four years, the Mengers erected a two-story stone hotel on the site, and other additions followed. Prominent military personnel stationed at or visiting nearby Fort Sam Houston—such as generals Ulysses S. Grant, Robert E. Lee, and John Pershing—frequented the Menger. Poet Sidney Lanier praised the atmosphere and many of O. Henry's characters in his short stories had dealings at the Menger.

In 1876, before John "Bet-A-Million" Gates made his first million, he set up a barbed wire fence in Alamo Plaza in front of the Menger and filled it with Longhorn cattle to demonstrate to the skeptical, big time ranchers who stayed at the Menger that barbed wire would hold the restless cattle. The performance proved so successful that orders for barbed wire poured in with such fury that the company Gates represented had trouble meeting the demand.

Theodore Roosevelt stayed at the Menger first in 1892 while on a javelina hunting trip. The hotel's famous solid cherry bar with its French mirrors and gold plated spittoons is a replica of the taproom in the House of Lords Club in London. Roosevelt put the bar on the map in 1898 when he gathered men there to recruit the First United States Volunteer Cavalry, the regiment known as the "Rough Riders" of the Spanish-American War.

The Menger's Colonial Dining Room grew famous throughout the southwest for its wild game, mango ice cream, and snapper soup made from the turtles caught in the San Antonio River.

The hotel grew until it eventually encompassed the entire block, changing to Kampmann family ownership and then to the Moody family interests. Through the years, each owner added to the charm of the prestigious structure. The Menger remains part of San Antonio's heritage from the days the city was known as the "Paris of the Wilderness."

Camels In Texas

Texans make a lot of extravagant claims. Sometimes they are true, like the story about having camels in Texas. Jefferson Davis, Secretary of War (1853–1857) under President Franklin Pierce, convinced Congress to appropriate $30,000 to buy and import camels for military use as beasts of burden. Davis claimed that because camels carried tremendous loads, traveled long distances without water and could survive on whatever plants grew along their route, they were well suited to the desert-like conditions of the West.

On May 13, 1856, citizens of the Indianola seaport on the Texas Gulf Coast rushed in droves to the dock to watch the unloading of thirty-two adult camels and one calf wildly rearing, breaking halters, kicking, and crying as three Arab and two Turk handlers made a valiant effort to control the beasts. Before the day ended the camels regained their land legs and amid the tingling of bells hanging from their saddles, they plodded docilely toward the corral constructed by the War Department.

A horseback rider rode ahead of the camels shouting to get horses and mules out of the way since the sight and smell of the strange beasts sent both horses and mules into frightened frenzies causing runaway wagons and tossed riders. The townspeople followed the parade thoroughly enjoying the commotion. Some accounts claim that the War Department ran out of lumber for the corral and resorted to stacking up the plentiful prickly pear cactus for fencing. The camels ate the prickly pear.

Major H.C. Wayne, who purchased the camels and accompanied them to Texas, reported to Secretary Davis that Indianolans voiced skepticism about camels being stronger than their mules and oxen. In a PR stunt, Major Wayne directed one of the handlers to take a camel to the Quartermaster's forage house for four bales of hay. Major Wayne mingled among the crowd listening to the derisive comments of those absolutely certain the kneeling camel could not rise under the burden of two bales weighing 613 pounds. Then, two more bales were added for an incredible 1,256 pounds. To the astonishment of the onlookers, the camel rose on command and walked away.

After three weeks of exercising to prepare the camels for the 200-mile trek to Camp Verde on the western frontier of Texas, the procession moved majestically across the prairie. A Victoria woman along the route gathered some of the camel hair and knitted socks for President Franklin Pierce. He sent a thank you letter, but did not mention wearing the things.

The experiment proved so successful that another forty-one camels arrived in 1857. They carried supplies for a team surveying a wagon road from New Mexico to the Colorado River and on to California. They hauled supplies in the first expedition to explore and map the Big Bend on the Texas/Mexican border.

A Methodist circuit rider, John Wesley DeVilbiss wrote that he was conducting a brush arbor camp meeting south of Camp Verde when six camels walked into the meeting carrying wives and children of Camp Verde military officers. At the end of the day, the visitors climbed aboard the docile beasts and plodded away.

When Texas seceded from the Union, Federal troops abandoned the western frontier and the camels were left to roam. The Confederates used some camels to pack cotton bales to Mexico where international ships waited to barter for guns and medical supplies. One camel carried all the baggage for an entire infantry company.

Although the camels fulfilled all expectations as beasts of burden, they were eventually sold and allowed to die out. They never gained acceptance because they smelled terrible, they frightened horses and mules, and their American handlers, who preferred the more docile mules, hated them.

A Century of Chautauqua

A Methodist preacher and a businessman started a training program for Sunday school teachers in 1874 at an outdoor summer camp on Chautauqua Lake in western New York State. It grew in popularity and soon "daughter"

Chautauquas began springing up all over the United States. In the early days, the most popular lectures were inspirational and reform speeches. Over the years, the fare lightened with the addition of current events, story-telling, and travelogues—often in a humorous vein.

A few Waxahachie residents traveled to the summer adult education center that had become famous for its great speakers, musicians, preachers, and scientists. Their enthusiasm led to Waxahachie erecting a pavilion in 1900 for its first Chautauqua Summer Assembly. Two years later Waxahachie built an octagonal-shaped Chautauqua auditorium that seated 2,500. The all-wood building, constructed at a cost of $2,750, was circled by large windows that slid upward into the wall to create an open-air facility, and boasted electric lights. Hundreds and then thousands of enthusiastic farm families and small-town residents from all over North Texas came in wagons and on horseback to camp for a week to ten days; they slept in tents and under their wagons, and for the first time in their lives they enjoyed a chance to hear humorists, watch jugglers, listen to statesmen talk of patriotism, and hear actors read from Shakespeare.

The list of programs and the response of the audiences paints a clear picture of how eagerly rural and small-town residents grasped for an opportunity to know about the world and to be challenged with new information in the days before widespread communication. A professor from San Antonio's Trinity University captivated the audience with experiments showing the many uses of liquid air. In 1906 a standing-room-only crowd arrived for a demonstration of wireless telegraphy. A packed house paid fifty cents a ticket to hear William Jennings Bryant, the famous populist orate on "The Price of a Soul."

The attendees enjoyed plenty of social life. A Chautauqua Parlor offered popular piano and vocal solos and tables set up for games of Forty-Two. The local Young Men's Chautauqua erected a social tent complete with electric fans and ice water. Later, they added sofas and rugs. The group became known as the "matrimonial agency" because of the number of couples who met there and later married.

Music brought in crowds especially when the U.S. Marine Band performed in 1914. Scottish music and the Highland Fling became a 1922 hit. The next year an electrical storm interrupted for twenty-five minutes a lecture and demonstration of electricity and the radio.

World War I themes turned to patriotism and the war effort. A war tax boosted the new ticket price of $2.50. A 1918 program highlighted war inventions—two-wheeled automobiles or gyrocars, airplanes with gyroscopes, ultra-violet rays, and hearing torpedoes—for a spellbound audience.

By the 1920s at the height of its popularity, twenty-one companies operated ninety-three Chautauqua circuits in the United States and Canada. Often, one performer finished his presentation and left for the train as another arrived. New York City actors brought plays such as "The Melting Pot," "Little Women," and Gilbert and Sullivan's "H.M.S. Pinafore."

Will Rogers, on his third U.S. tour, made a stop in Waxahachie in 1927. As the audience waited for his show, they listened in delight to a radio program amplified with music. Although he spoke for 101 minutes, some in attendance left disappointed because he did not do his famous trick roping, for which he named himself the "poet lariat."

The advent of the automobile, the popularity of the radio, and the Great Depression began to slowly erode the attendance at Chautauqua. Ticket sales declined, forcing local supporters to underwrite more and more of the Chautauqua expenses. By 1930 the Chautauqua Assembly in Waxahachie came to an end.

The old building slowly declined until members of the community formed the Chautauqua Preservation Society and began restoration. Today, Waxahachie, like so many communities all over the United States continue to offer Chautauqua entertainment and educational events. The original institution continues to thrive each summer on the shores of Chautauqua Lake, New York.

Rosenwald Schools

Black children in the South attended segregated schools that were dilapidated. They used castoff books from white schools. At times they attended classes in churches and lodge halls because the local school board did not provide buildings for black students. Two men worked to change all that. Booker T. Washington, founder of Tuskegee Institute and Julius Rosenwald, a Chicago philanthropist, instituted a program that eventually built 464 schools in Texas and almost 5,000 across the South.

Julius Rosenwald, son of German-Jewish immigrants, became part owner in Sears, Roebuck & Company in 1895, and from 1908 until 1925 he served as president. As his wealth grew he increased his gifts, especially to educational and religious institutions. His friendship and work with other philanthropists such as Paul J. Sachs of Goldman Sachs, led to Rosenwald meeting Booker T. Washington.

In 1911, Rosenwald wrote, "The horrors that are due to race prejudice come home to the Jew more forcefully than to others of the white race, on account of the centuries of persecution which we have suffered and still suffer." After Rosenwald gave Tuskegee Institute $25,000 for a black teacher-training program in 1912, Booker T. Washington convinced Rosenwald to allow part of the money to be used for a pilot program to build six schools in rural Alabama. Impressed with the results, Rosenwald donated $30,000 for construction of 100 rural schools and then he gave additional money for building another 200 schools. By 1920 the Julius Rosenwald Fund began a rural school building program for black children that continued for the next twelve years in fifteen states, including Texas.

To qualify for the grants, which ranged from $500 for a one-teacher facility to $2,100 for a school large enough for ten teachers, the local black community had to raise matching money in the form of cash, in-kind donations of materials, and labor. Many of the schools were in freedmen communities where the residents were eager to offer education for their children. Black men often cut the lumber, hauled the material, and served as carpenters. The land and building had to be deeded to local authorities, and the property had to be maintained as part of the school district. The district was required to furnish new desks and blackboards for all classrooms as well as two hygienic privies for each building. Classes had to be held for more than five months of the year.

Floor plans were specific as well. The design included large windows on the east side of the building to allow for maximum natural lighting and small high windows on the west side to insure cross ventilation while keeping out the hot afternoon sun. Many white schools adopted the Rosenwald designs because they were found to be so efficient.

During the twelve-year program in Texas over 57,000 black students were served by almost 1,300 teachers. Black citizens contributed $392,000, white citizens gave $60,000, tax funds totaled $1.6 million, and the Rosenwald Fund contributed $420,000.

Julius Rosenwald, who died in 1932, said it was easier to make a million dollars honestly than to give it away wisely. With that in mind and in light of changing social and economic conditions, he directed that all the Rosenwald

Fund be spent within twenty-five years of his death. By 1948 when the fund ended Rosenwald and his fund had given over $70 million to schools, colleges, museums, Jewish charities, and black institutions.

Ten to fifteen Rosenwald schools survive in Texas, and some are being restored as museums and community centers. In keeping with the original fundraising efforts, citizens are raising the money to bring back these historic buildings. Women in the Pleasant Hill area are selling quilts to restore the Rosenwald School, a Baptist Church near Seguin is using the Sweet Home Vocational and Agricultural High School as their fellowship hall and nutritional center, and a YouTube video tells the story of the West Columbia Rosenwald School. The Texas Historical Commission began in the mid-1990s to inventory the history of the Rosenwald School building project and to apply for listing on the National Register of Historic Places.

Post, Founded by a Cereal Magnate

C. W. Post was an inventor. His imagination ran the gamut—designing better farm implements, improving digestion with breakfast foods, creating a model town, and making rain by detonating dynamite—a genius that lived before folks talked about bipolar; they called him peculiar.

Born in 1854, Post grew up in Illinois, attended two years of college at the future University of Illinois, and at seventeen dropped out of school to work as a salesman and manufacturer of agricultural machines. He married at twenty, had a daughter, Marjorie Merriweather Post, and during the next fifteen years he secured patents on farm equipment such as cultivators, a sulky plow, a harrow, and a haystacker. The periods of intense work, followed with bouts of depression, led in 1885 to Post suffering his first nervous breakdown.

Leaving his stressful manufacturing occupation, Post moved his family to Fort Worth in 1886 where he bought a 200-acre ranch, began a real estate development company that laid out streets, built homes, and constructed a woolen mill and a paper mill. A second breakdown came in 1891, followed by extensive travel in search of a cure. Post entered a sanitarium in Battle Creek, Michigan, run by John Harvey Kellogg, a medical doctor who used holistic treatments that focused on nutrition, enemas, and exercise. Dr. Kellogg, along with his brother, invented corn flakes as a breakfast cereal. Following Dr. Kellogg's regime, Post soon recuperated, and because he decided that coffee was poison, he devised a breakfast cereal drink called Postum. In 1897 he created Grape Nuts cereal and in 1904 he called his new corn flakes Elijah's Manna until the religious community complained. The name soon became Post Toasties.

Post and his wife, after living apart for several years, divorced the same year that Post Toasties hit the market, and Post remarried before the year was out. His breakfast foods business was raking in millions. Advised by his doctor to move to a drier climate, Post bought 225,000 acres of ranchland and platted his vision of a model town in the Texas Panhandle at the foot of the Llano Estacado, or Caprock, one of the largest mesas or tablelands on the North American continent.

Calling his new town Post City, he threw himself into his new business, the Double U Company (meaning double utopia), which was charged with fulfilling his grand plan—a place where ordinary families could find a home or a farm site at a reasonable price and borrow with little money down at low monthly rates. Although Post hired a manager for the enterprise, he directed every minute detail of the new town from his homes in Michigan and later in California, racing madly back to Post to solve each problem. Until 1910 when the Santa Fe Railroad arrived, the nearest railhead lay eighty miles away, which meant bouncing over unpaved ruts in mule-drawn hacks to reach his flourishing village. Since the new town had to be built from scratch on the semi-arid plains, Post purchased two-dozen freight wagons and mules to haul the supplies for building the infrastructure and constructing every home and business. Post sent plans for the houses, mostly bungalows, which he favored, and for the aesthetics, including shade trees planted thirty feet apart on each side of the highway for two miles leading in and out of town. He built a school, churches, and a department store. He took great pride in the hotel, insisting that Postum and Grape Nuts be served at every breakfast. He tried, unsuccessfully, to force the workmen whom he hired from the surrounding ranches to eat his special breakfast diet. He paid excellent wages, but he was demanding, expecting the same perfection from those who worked for him as he demanded of himself.

Parks sprouted over town, Bermuda grass covered the lawns, and orchards began producing fruit. Determined to keep out the bad element, Post hired someone to see that his model community did not serve alcohol in any establishment, and if a business did not follow the guidelines, it was shut down immediately. Brothels, of course, were not permitted.

Two big problems plagued the place—water and weather. Post had wells and reservoirs dug and hauled and piped water from the top of the Caprock, all without sufficient success to meet the needs of the growing community. Stories he had read of the rainstorms that occurred after major battles in the Napoleonic Wars and the tales that Civil War veterans told of rain following heavy cannon fire, led to his rainmaking experiments. In 1910 he tried attaching two pounds of dynamite to a kite and igniting it, but then decided that was too dangerous. He placed four-pound dynamite charges along the rim of the Caprock and detonated one every four minutes for several hours. In 1912, Post exploded 24,000 pounds of dynamite and a little rain fell after that battle, as Post called each effort to force rain from the clouds. Success was intermittent—sometimes light rain fell, other times it did not. He had almost instant rain after he placed 3,000 pounds of dynamite in 1,500 sticks; however, critics said Post held his experiments during the time of the year when rain usually fell.

By 1914 Post was again suffering from overwork, exhaustion, and abdominal pains. He remained at his California home, claiming to wean his town from his constant attention. The public realized for the first time that Post was not well when he cancelled a speech in New York that he was scheduled to deliver denouncing President Woodrow Wilson's income tax law. In March, a private railroad car raced from California to Mayo Clinic in Rochester, Minnesota, where Post had surgery for acute appendicitis. The surgery was called successful, but after Post returned to his California home, his health did not improve. Believing he had stomach cancer, Post committed suicide on May 9, 1914, some accounts say from a gunshot wound.

Marjorie Merriweather Post, his twenty-seven-year-old daughter, inherited his businesses and his vast fortune—one of the largest of the early twentieth century. She used her business acumen, which she had learned at the side of her father, to expand his enterprises into the General Foods Corporation, becoming the wealthiest woman in America. She lived the lavish life of a socialite, an art collector, and an internationally recognized philanthropist.

Lance Rosier, Mr. Big Thicket

A Texas historical marker on FM 770, a few miles east of Saratoga in deep East Texas credits Lancelot "Lance" Rosier as being one of the individuals responsible for the creation of the Big Thicket National Preserve, a sprawling wonderland of biodiversity so unique that UNESCO designated the region as a Biosphere Reserve in 1981. A self-taught naturalist, Lance Rosier was born and grew up in the heart of the Big Thicket, roaming the forest, growing familiar with every trail, every baygall (shallow, stagnant water), and the name of every plant. An avid reader of botanical publications, he became the foremost authority on the flora of the Big Thicket. Rosier served as a guide for Hal B. Parks and Victor L. Cory, botanists in the 1930s who authored the *Biological Survey of the East Texas Big Thicket,* the "Bible" of those wishing to preserve the area.

The Big Thicket has always presented a challenge to those who wanted to exploit its riches and to men like Rosier who worked to preserve its unique character. As early as the 17th Century, when Texas was part of the Spanish Colonial Empire, the forest of ninety-eight-foot Longleaf pine trees measuring five and six feet in diameter towered over dense growths of six-foot palmetto trees, beech trees, fern, cacti, orchids, and carnivorous plants. The padres who established Spanish missions in East Texas traveled a route that circled north of the 3.5 million-acre swatch of Southeast Texas from near Nacogdoches to near present Beaumont. Long before the Spanish arrived, mound-building Caddo Indians and other tribes from along the Gulf coast used the thicket for hunting deer, bear, panthers, and wolves. At the end of the 18th Century Alabama and Coushatta Indians migrated into the region and settled in the thicket in the 1830s.

Called "the thicket" because of the dense plant growth and cypress swamps, the region offered ideal hiding places for emigrants coming to Texas to escape legal problems such as bankruptcy and criminal charges in the United States. During the Civil War, when the Confederate government began conscription in 1862, men who did not want to get in the war, men who did not own slaves and saw no reason to fight for big plantation owners, hid out in the thicket. They survived on the abundance of fish, small game, and wild berries. They set up secret locales where their families brought them coffee and tobacco in exchange for honey, wild game, and fish the families sold in nearby Beaumont.

Lance Rosier grew up listening to the stories about the thicket and the timber barons who began clear-cutting the forests in the mid-1800s turning the region into a lumber bonanza after the railroad arrived in the 1880s. By the time Spindletop blew in south of Beaumont in 1901, the lumbering had reduced the thicket to about 300,000 acres and the oil industry brought more frantic development into the area.

After serving in the army in World War I, Rosier returned to his homeland and worked as a timber cruiser (someone who measures a plot of forest to estimate the quality and quantity of timber in that stand) and he led Big Thicket tours for anyone seeking his expertise including scientists, photographers, students, scholars, and conservationists. Rosier also led politicians such as Texas Governor Price Daniel and Speaker of the U.S. House Sam Rayburn as they explored possibilities of making the Big Thicket a Texas state park.

A shy and retiring little man, Rosier is said to have lent a sense of spiritual zeal to his quest to save the thicket. He catalogued hundreds of species of new plants and discovered plants that had been considered extinct. Rosier worked with the original East Texas Big Thicket Association that began in 1927 hoping to save the land and waterways. When that project met political headwinds, he led a new movement that became the Big Thicket Association in the early 1960s. Lance Rosier died in 1970, four years before his dream was fulfilled—the United States Congress passed a bill in 1974 establishing an 84,550-acre Big Thicket National Preserve—a string of pearls consisting of nine land units and several creek corridors. Today, the preserve manages twelve land units covering over 105,000 acres. The Lance Rosier Unit at 25,024 acres is the largest and most diversified preserve in the thicket. It encompasses the land where Rosier was born and roamed as a child.

Gainesville Community Circus

In 1930, when the Gainesville Little Theatre discovered a $300 deficit, the theatre board decided to solve the financial problem by organizing a burlesque circus using local residents as performers. The editor of the *Gainesville Register* was an authority on circuses, townspeople visited professional shows for inspiration and ideas, and every member of the show spent their after-work-hours practicing. The show proved so popular that it ran for three performances and the theatre ended up with $420. From the beginning, the entire operation was a volunteer effort—no one got paid—and they purchased their own costumes and made most of their equipment.

No one was turned down. If a volunteer could not master the high wire or perform acrobatic tricks or swing from a trapeze, he could be a clown. The tax collector and the postmaster created the clown gags. A local car dealer donated a stock car that an auto mechanic converted into a funny Ford, a trick machine that appeared to be driverless, squirted a stream of water from the radiator, blew horns, and rang bells. A junior college student went through four grueling months of exercises required to hang by her knees from a trapeze while holding in her "iron jaw" a girl spinning below. A housewife and young mother learned to climb hand over hand up a rope and whirl high above the ring in a Spanish web. An eleven-year-old girl wowed the crowds on the loop-the-loop trapeze and a gasoline station operator served as the principal bareback rider who stood on a galloping horse while balancing two girls on his shoulders.

When visitors from nearby Denton saw the show, they invited the circus to perform for their 1932 County Fair, which launched The Gainesville Community Circus road shows. After completing their regular day job, the circus performers drove to surrounding towns to present their three-ring circus under a big top. Profits went back into improving trapeze rigging, expanding to seven tents, and adding a 22,000 square foot big top that seated 2,500. The troupe purchased six ornamental tableau wagons, a calliope, and hundreds of costumes.

From 1930 to 1952 the circus offered 359 shows in fifty-seven different cities, cancelling only one in Ardmore, Oklahoma, in 1939 when a tornado destroyed the big top. In 1937 over 51,000 spectators crowded Fort Worth's Will Rogers Coliseum to see the traveling show. By 1941 it was touted as the third largest circus in the country. During its twenty-five year history about 1,500 Gainesville residents performed in the circus. A fire in 1954 destroyed the tents and equipment, but the performers struggled to rebuild the circus. After a few small shows, the troupe tried in 1958 to make a formal comeback but as the former circus president and chief clown said, "Television and air conditioning killed" the circus.

The memories are kept alive at the restored Santa Fe Depot Museum where photographs and costumes are displayed and a 1937 Paramount Pictures newsreel shows a behind-the-scenes look at the famous Gainesville Community Circus.

11

Oil Patch

Tol Barret Drills Texas' First Oil Well

*I*n Texas, known for its strutting, lavish-living oilmen, Tol Barret, the pioneer who in 1866 drilled Texas' first producing oil well, doesn't fit that moniker. His home, which is located five miles south of Nacogdoches in deep East Texas, sits in the middle of a pine tree plantation.

Everyone knows about Spindletop, the 1901 oil discovery that thrust Texas and the world into the big-time petroleum business. A few people know that in 1895 the city fathers of Corsicana hired an experienced Kansas outfit to increase the town's water supply. To the embarrassment of the politicians, the drillers accidently discovered oil, which they quickly abandoned. Tol Barret, who brought in Texas' first oil well in 1866, slipped under the radar.

Barret arrived as a child in deep East Texas and grew up aware that oil seeped into water wells, that hogs wallowing in creek beds got slimy with oil, and he probably knew that a water well in a nearby county caught fire in 1848 and burned for a year—all signs to the self-educated young man that contrary to the view of "experts" there was oil in those pine tree covered hills.

Confirmation that the experts were correct came in 1859 when the first well in the US was drilled in Northwest Pennsylvania. Undeterred, Barret had leased a tract of land that same year with plans to drill for oil, but lack of equipment and the Civil War interrupted.

After serving in the Confederate Army, Barret came home, formed the Melrose Petroleum Oil Company with four other men, and renewed his lease. Mounting an auger eight feet long and eight inches in diameter on a tripod, he used a steam engine for drilling and a mule to pull the auger out of the hole. In that fashion, he bored to 106 feet, where, in early fall of

1866 he struck oil. This first Texas oil well produced 10 barrels a day. Barret secured financing through a Pennsylvania firm and brought a Pennsylvania operator to begin a second well. When oil prices plummeted from $6.59 to $1.35 a barrel, and the well didn't come in at 80 feet, the driller shut down and headed home. Broke, and unable to convince Pennsylvania oil operators of the merits of Texas petroleum, Barret gave up. He spent the remainder of his life managing his wife's farms and a mercantile store in Melrose.

He lived until 1913, long enough to see that he had been correct. An oil boom hit in 1887 in the field where Barret had drilled, and the granddaddy of them all––Spindletop––gushed in 1901. Texas, indeed, became the oil capital of the world.

Patilla Higgins Believed in Big Hill

Patilla Higgins is one of those people that put Texas on the world oil map, and he rarely gets a mention. He came on the scene in the mid-1880s in a brawl with a local deputy marshal that cost Higgins his arm and the marshal his life. Since the scrape occurred after dark, a plea of self-defense got Higgins off the hook.

Two years later, Higgins got born again at a Baptist revival and gave up forever associating with his wild crowd, swearing, drinking, gambling, and even smoking. Thanks to his new lifestyle, a fellow Baptist and wealthy lumberman, George Carroll, hired Higgins as a buyer of east Texas timberland.

Meanwhile, Higgins began teaching Sunday school and taking his class on picnics to "Big Hill," a salt dome rising from the flat prairie land south of Beaumont in southeast Texas. For entertainment, he showed the kids how to punch cane poles into the hillside and light the gas that escaped.

Higgins only attended three or four years of school, but he read extensively and became convinced that despite the so-called experts' claims to the contrary, oil lay in abundance under Big Hill. Eventually Higgins convinced Carroll and two others to form the Gladys City Oil, Gas and Manufacturing Company and hire Higgins as manager. Higgins selected the name "Gladys" in honor of a seven-year-old girl in his Sunday school class. He held such a firm belief that oil waited to be discovered that he drew plans for a model industrial complex named Gladys City adjacent to the future oil field.

The drillers ignored Higgins' insistence that oil lay at 1,000 to 1,100 feet, which was deep for those days, and were ready to quit after four dry wells in a row. One man, Anthony Lucas, a mining engineer, continued to believe in Higgins' theory. Lucas convinced Carroll and his partners to get financial backing from Dick and Andrew Mellon, sons of T. Mellon, the Pittsburg banking giant. The $300,000 deal cut Higgins out of the business.

On January 10, 1901, what Anthony Lucas described as a "geyser of oil" blew in on Big Hill. Oil spewed 800,000 barrels over one hundred feet above the well for nine days before it could be capped. Spindletop ushered in the petroleum age, and Patilla Higgins finally gained respect from the community. Anthony Lucas, however, became the hero.

Patilla Higgins did not suffer in the deal. Six more gushers blew in before Higgins' own well came in on April 18. The derrick floors, which measured seventeen feet across, were so close together that a person could walk a mile without stepping on solid ground.

It is said that Higgins sued Carroll and his partners for $4 million, and settled out of court "satisfied." He continued as a wildcatter, making and losing fortunes until his death at 92. Some say he ended up one of the wealthiest men in Texas.

As for Gladys City, it developed as a boomtown of frame shanties, not the model city of Higgins' dreams. Today, Spindletop Gladys City Boomtown, operated by Lamar University, offers a self-guided tour of the grounds and fifteen re-constructed buildings filled with objects from the oil boom era.

Edgar B. Davis Gave Away Millions

Travelers driving south from Austin on US 183 know when they reach Luling––it's the smell of oil. Pumping stations (pump jacks) operate all over town—even in the downtown. Nobody in Luling minds the smell. In fact the residents appreciate the oil so much that all nine of the pumping stations are decorated. You'll see Uncle Sam, a girl eating a watermelon slice (it's also watermelon country), a grasshopper, and Tony the Tiger.

The story of Luling's oil business dates back to 1919 when the little town of 1,500, a railroad running parallel to its dusty main street and wooden sidewalks, was struggling to recover from the effects of WWI. That's when Edgar B. Davis, a loud-talking, over-sized bachelor from Massachusetts with a strong Yankee accent, showed up. The residents welcomed the jovial fellow who had already made a million in the shoe business and over $3 million in the rubber business. He had come to Luling because his brother Oscar asked him to look into a $75,000 investment he had made in oil leases that weren't producing.

His brother died and against the advice of everyone, including geologists, Davis bought his brother's interest, ordered the drilling to go from 1,700 to 3,000 feet, and promptly drilled six dry wells in a row. Almost broke and deeply in debt, Davis drove out to the seventh well site on August 9, 1922. Suddenly, black gold shot straight up in the air, announcing the arrival of Rafael Rios No. 1. Within two years the field produced 43,000 barrels of oil a day. In 1926 Davis sold his leases to Magnolia Petroleum Company for $12 million (half in cash), an oil deal considered the largest in Texas up to that time.

If that were the end of the story, it would just be another ho-hum tale of a rich man almost going broke and rebounding into even more wealth. This is no ordinary story. Although Edgar B. Davis did not belong to a church, he held a strong belief that Providence guided his life. He planned a "thank offering" for his friends, associates, and employees. He bought 40 wooded acres on the north side of town and built an athletic clubhouse for blacks. South of town, on the banks of the San Marcos River, he bought 100 acres and laid out a golf course and clubhouse facilities for whites. He fully endowed both sites. Then, he hosted a barbecue, strung Japanese lanterns, built polished, outdoor dance floors, imported bands, and brought in singers from the New York Metropolitan Opera. Estimates of attendance ranged up to 35,000. The food reportedly cost $10,000 and included all the accoutrements, even Havana cigars.

Next, the man who believed that he was an instrument of God gave bonuses to his employees of 25 to 100 percent of their total salary—an estimated $5 million. But, he wasn't done. With the firm belief that he had been "directed" to deliver Luling and the surrounding counties from the oppressive one-crop cotton economy, Davis purchased 1,200 acres west of town and established the Luling Foundation. This experimental farm continues to conduct research in all facets of farming including experimental and management programs in cooperation with Texas A&M University.

Several strange tales circulate about Edgar B. Davis. Perhaps the strangest is that Davis continued to wildcat and during the Depression, he found himself in such financial straits that the bank was about to foreclose on his home. In a series of mysterious late-night raids, his house was burned to the ground. The explanation for why a community would burn the home of a man held in such high regard stems from the belief that if Edgar B. Davis couldn't keep his home, nobody else was going to get it.

Before Davis died in 1951 at age 78, he rebuilt his fortune. He was buried on the grounds of his destroyed home. Today, the Seton Edgar B. Davis Hospital, an acute care facility that opened in 1966, operates on the home site of the man who believed that the more one gives, the more one has.

12

Legends in Their Day

A Love Story

Jim Shankle was born in 1811 on a Mississippi plantation. When he married Winnie, she already had three children. Soon after the marriage, their master sold Winnie and her children. Jim heard enough of the business deal to know that they were taken to a plantation in East Texas. He grieved for several days. Then, determined to find his family, he ran away. With a price on his head as a runaway slave, he headed west, always moving at night, foraging in fields for his food, and hiding in the fields when he heard others on the road. Not daring to use a ferry, he swam both the Mississippi and the Sabine rivers.

After a 400-mile journey, he reached East Texas and moved at night from plantation to plantation asking about Winnie. Finally, Jim found her as she collected water at a spring. For several days, Winnie hid Jim and brought food to him at night. Some accounts say Winnie's master found Jim, other stories say she told her master about her husband. Whatever the truth, the plantation owner agreed to buy Jim.

In addition to Winnie's three children, they raised six of their own. When emancipation came following the Civil War, they became farmers and began buying land with their partner Steve McBride. Eventually, they owned 4,000 acres where the black community of Shankleville developed with schools, churches, a cotton gin, sawmills, and gristmills.

Steve McBride married one of the Shankle daughters and though he could not read, he established McBride College (1883-1909), fulfilling his dream of helping others receive the education he had been denied.

Winnie Shankle died in 1883 and Jim died five years later, ending a love story that has become a legend.

Bigfoot Wallace, Came to Texas for Revenge

It's hard to know what's truth and what's myth regarding the adventures of William Alexander Anderson Wallace. He was a nineteen-year-old working in his father's Virginia fruit orchard in 1836 when he heard that his brother and a cousin had been killed in the Goliad Massacre during the Texas War for Independence from Mexico. That was all the six-foot-two-inch, 240-pound fellow needed to send him to Texas to "take pay out of the Mexicans." He arrived after Texas had won independence and become a republic, but he wasn't ready to stop fighting. He tried settling on a farm near La Grange, but the life didn't suit him. According to his own account, which he embroidered to suit his audience, it was while living on the edge of the frontier that he woke to discover that Comanches had raided in the night, taking all his horses except for one old gray mare that had been staked away from the other animals. Wallace jumped on the old horse in pursuit of the Indians. He dismounted in a hickory grove and crawled near their camp where the band of forty-two Indians had started eating his horses. Tying off his pant legs and his shirtsleeves, he filled his clothing with the hickory nuts until his body bulged into a new grotesque size. He claimed to have crawled (how did he manage that?) near the camp, shot one of the Indians, and then stood to his bulging height. The startled Indians quickly regained their composure and began firing arrow after arrow into his hickory nut armor. When Wallace continued standing the Comanches ran for the hills. Wallace untied his clothing and the hickory nuts tumbled out three inches deep on the ground. He brought his wagon, gathered the nuts, which the arrows had already cracked, and took them home to feed his pigs.

He soon ventured west to the new Texas capital of Austin, which was being carved out of the hills and cedar trees in hostile Indian country. In fact, it was Wallace's encounter with an Indian who was a lot bigger than Wallace that earned him the life-long nickname of "Bigfoot." He claimed to have earned two hundred dollars a month hewing logs for the new buildings being quickly constructed for the capital. He and a partner went out into Comanche Territory, cut cedar and other logs and floated them down the Colorado River to the new town. During one of his absences, a neighbor discovered that his house had been ransacked and huge moccasin tracks led from his house to Wallace's home. Since Wallace wore moccasins, the neighbor stormed over accusing Wallace of the robbery. It seems there was a Waco Indian, much taller and much heavier than Wallace who also wore moccasins. Everyone called him Chief Bigfoot because his foot measured over fourteen inches and his big toe protruded even further. To calm the neighbor, Wallace took him home and placed his own foot in the giant prints to prove that Wallace was not the guilty party. Wallace's roommate, William Fox, thought the encounter so funny that he began calling Wallace "Bigfoot," a moniker that lasted the rest of his life. Ironically, the next year Chief Bigfoot killed and scalped William Fox. Wallace tried to take revenge, but the giant Indian survived Wallace's attack.

After Bigfoot Wallace saw the last buffalo run down Austin's Congress Avenue, he decided the capital was getting too crowded and moved on to San Antonio, which lay on the extreme edge of civilization. He joined local residents in their fight against encroaching Indians and Mexicans who, having not accepted Texas independence, made forays into the new country as far north as San Antonio. In 1842, after another Mexican raid of San Antonio, Bigfoot Wallace joined the Somervell and Mier expeditions, which were intended to put a stop to the Mexican incursions. Some of the volunteers turned back, deciding their Texas force was not large enough to counter the power of the Mexican Army. Bigfoot Wallace was among the 300 determined to continue into Mexico. A strong Mexican force at Mier promptly defeated them and began marching them to Perote Prison in Vera Cruz. The prisoners tried escaping into the Mexican desert, but were quickly found and under orders from Santa Anna were sentenced to a firing squad. Army officials convinced Santa Anna to execute only every tenth man, and to accomplish that plan, seventeen black beans were placed in a jar of white beans. The unlucky seventeen who drew a black bean were quickly shot. Bigfoot Wallace drew a gray bean, and the Mexican officer decided to classify Wallace as one of the lucky white bean drawers. Instead of a quick death, he and the other fortunate men were marched to Perote Prison where they remained in dungeons for two years before being released.

Bigfoot Wallace had not gotten the urge to fight out of his system. Upon returning to San Antonio he joined Jack Hayes' Texas Rangers in the

Mexican-American War and when it ended in 1848, he served as a captain of his own ranger company, fighting border bandits and Indians. They were known for forcing confessions, hanging those they believed were guilty, and leaving the dangling bodies as a warning to other outlaws. One of his ranger buddies, Creed Taylor, complained of constantly losing his stock to bandits and Indian raids. When a Mexican raider known as Vidal and his gang stole a bunch of Taylor's horses, Bigfoot and his rangers went after the Vidal gang. They found them asleep and by the time the fracas ended, all the bandits were dead. That's when Bigfoot and his rangers decided to make an example of Vidal. They beheaded him, stuffed his head in his sombrero and secured it to his saddle pummel. They tied Vidal's body in his saddle, mounted it on one of the stolen horses, and sent the horse off in a run. The vision on a dark night of a body swaying wildly on the back of the galloping black stallion with the gruesome head hanging in plain sight may not have stopped horse thieves, but it scared so many people that as late as 1900, people from Mexico to New Mexico to Texas were claiming to have seen El Muerto, The Texas Headless Horseman.

Bigfoot began freighting mail over the 600-mile route from San Antonio to El Paso. A month of hard riding was required to get through the Texas desert and cross the old Comanche Trail leading into Mexico. Although killing or wounding the fearless fighter would have been a feather for any warrior, Bigfoot managed to make the trips, suffering only one badly shot up mail coach. He claimed that on one occasion he lost his mules to Indians and had to walk all the way to El Paso. Just before reaching town, he stopped at a Mexican house, where he ate twenty-seven eggs, then went on into town and had a "full meal."

The Civil War brought new challenges for Bigfoot Wallace. He did not agree with secession, but refused to abandon his own people. Instead, he spent the war guarding the frontier settlements against Comanche raids.

Bigfoot Wallace never married, and he spent his later years in Frio County in a village he founded named Bigfoot. He welcomed visitors and delighted in regaling them with his stories of life on the Texas frontier. He told his friend and novelist John C. Duval in *The Adventures of Bigfoot Wallace, the Texas Ranger and Hunter* that he believed his account (with the Mexicans) had been settled. Soon after his death on January 7, 1899, the Texas legislature appropriated money to move his body to the State Cemetery in Austin.

Gail Borden, Pioneer Inventor

A brilliant eccentric, Gail Borden reportedly rode about Galveston on a pet bull. He invented a "locomotive bath house," a portable affair that allowed women to bathe privately in the waters of the Gulf of Mexico before he was "discouraged" by the city authorities. And he worked for the Galveston City Company laying out the streets while designing a self-propelled terraqueous machine that was supposed to move on land and on water. During its maiden voyage, it reportedly dumped its occupants into the Gulf.

Born in Norwich, New York, Gail Borden, Jr. (1801–1874) moved with his family to Indiana where he received about a year and a half of formal education. Before coming to Texas in 1829, he began to show his lifelong concern for others by helping rescue a freedman from rustlers.

After settling in Texas, he farmed, raised stock, and began serving as a surveyor for Stephen F. Austin's colony. He prepared the first topographical map of Texas, and as the war for Texas independence from Mexico became a certainty, Borden and some partners started the *Telegraph and Texas Register* newspaper to keep the citizenry informed of the pending conflict. Throughout the war, the *Telegraph* was moved across Texas just ahead of General Santa Anna's advancing army. Ten days before the Texas victory at the Battle of San Jacinto, the Mexican army captured the *Telegraph* printers and threw the press into Buffalo Bayou. As soon as Texas won its independence, Borden traveled to Cincinnati and bought a new press, which he continued to move across Texas following the new republic's congress as it began to meet in Columbia and then on to the new capital of Houston.

Borden drew the map laying out the new capital on the muddy banks of Buffalo Bayou. In 1837, the year after Texas became a republic, Borden moved to Galveston to serve as the first collector of customs at the port. Active in the Baptist church, he worked in the temperance movement, served as a local missionary to the poor and to travelers visiting Galveston. He and his first wife, Penelope, reportedly were the first Americans to be baptized in the Gulf of Mexico west of the Mississippi River. He served as a trustee of the Texas Baptist Education Society, which founded Baylor University, and as an alderman he helped temporarily rid Galveston of gamblers.

He apparently began inventing around 1840 with a scheme to market jelly made from the horns and hooves of oxen. He tried preserving a peach mixture using hydraulic pressure. Penelope's death in the yellow fever epidemic of 1844 prompted Borden to abandon his other projects and search for the cause of the disease. Recognizing that yellow fever struck during the summer heat and disappeared with the first cold front, he built a large-scale icebox, using ether to cool its interior. He imagined a refrigerator large enough to cool the entire population of Galveston during the summer months. When his giant refrigerator for people did not materialize, Borden devoted himself to creating a meat biscuit that he believed would provide nutrition for the U.S. Army and for travelers. He boiled eleven pounds of meat to get one pound of extract, which he combined with flour and baked into a biscuit. It was recognized for its nutritional value and earned a gold medal in London at the 1851 International Exposition. Borden built a factory in Galveston, introduced the meat biscuit at Texas' first state fair in Corpus Christi, and moved to New York to be closer to distribution centers. Sales fell flat because it tasted terrible, which ended his expensive investment.

Still convinced that he could improve the food supply by developing concentrated food products, Borden condensed milk by using a vacuum pan with a heating coil to remove the water without burning or souring the milk. In this fashion he produced the first condensed milk in 1853 that could be stored and shipped long distances. He started a dairy company in Connecticut, and for the first time in his life, he was in a perfect position to capitalize on his invention. During the Civil War he provided condensed milk for the Union Army. Still the experimenter, Borden created processes for condensing fruit juices, extract of beef, and coffee.

After the war, he returned to Texas, founded the town of Borden west of Houston, and established a meatpacking plant, a sawmill and a copperware factory. His Borden Milk Company with Elsie the Cow as its logo became known throughout the world.

John Twohig, Breadline Banker

A story published by the University of Incarnate Word in 1913 in the *Invincible, A Magazine of History* tells the tale of John Twohig who ran away at fifteen from his Cork County Ireland home and apprenticed on a British merchant ship sailing between New Orleans and Boston. Lured by the financial prospects of Texas, Twohig carried a stock of goods to San Antonio in 1830 and opened a mercantile business. He took part in the Siege of Bexar, the two-month-long fight in the fall of 1835 that resulted in Texans driving the Mexican army out of San Antonio. There is no record of him joining the forces in the Alamo before it fell in March 1836. However, in September 1842 when Twohig heard that the Mexican army was on its way to occupy the city for a second time that year, he invited the poor to take what they wanted from his store. Then he blew up the building to keep the Mexicans from getting the gunpowder and other supplies. In retaliation for the act, Twohig was captured with about fifty other San Antonians and marched to Perote Castle, the dreaded prison near Vera Cruz. In July 1843, Twohig and about a dozen prisoners dug a tunnel and escaped. One account says he walked through Vera Cruz to the docks disguised as a peddler and boarded a ship for New Orleans.

When Twohig returned to San Antonio in 1844, he reopened his mercantile business and began operating an extensive trade with Mexico. He purchased land on a crossing of the Rio Grande, which lay only 142 miles from San Antonio. In 1850 he surveyed the land, laid out a new town, and named it Eagle Pass. Twohig was forty-seven in 1853 when he married Bettie Calvert of Seguin and began enlarging his home on the San Antonio River. The couple built several guesthouses along the river and held lavish dinners for such notables as Sam Houston, Ulysses S. Grant, and their good friend Robert E. Lee. On February 18, 1861, as Texas prepared to secede from the Union, Lee had dinner with the Twohigs and wrote the following day thanking them for their hospitality and expressing regret that he had to leave under such sad circumstances.

A devout Catholic, Twohig was known for giving money to anyone in need, especially the Brothers of the Society of Mary who came from France to start a school. In addition to financial help, Twohig advised the Brothers to build their St. Mary's Institute on the San Antonio River. The school developed into St. Mary's University. He served as godfather for two or three generations of children, several of whom recalled receiving a gold piece every time they saw him. Pensioners knew that they could go to his bank at closing time every Saturday afternoon, and Twohig would always draw from his own pocket a gift of money.

The Sisters of Charity built an orphanage in San Antonio and relied on Twohig for support. An eccentric jokester, he often "fined" his wealthy friends who would later receive a note from the orphanage thanking them for their gift. He became known as the "Breadline Banker" because on Saturdays, the poor women of San Antonio gathered at his house to receive loaves of bread, which arrived by the barrel. Twohig's sister Miss Kate had moved from a convent in New York to live with the couple. Bettie Twohig and Miss Kate passed out the loaves of bread, keeping track of how much bread they distributed by dropping beans or matches into a tumbler. After Bettie Twohig died, Miss Kate stayed with her brother, maintained his house, and continued distributing the bread.

By 1870 when Twohig had moved exclusively into banking, with connections all over the United States and London, he was ranked as one of the 100 wealthiest men in Texas. His real property was estimated at $90,000 and personal property estimated at an additional $50,000. At the time of his death in 1891, his estate was valued at half a million. He left his house to his sister Kate until her death and the remainder to the Catholic Church. Miss Kate continued after her brother's death to give away the bread.

The Twohig house, which sat across the San Antonio River from his bank, deteriorated over the years. In 1941, the Witte Museum moved each stone of the Twohig house to its campus and carefully reconstructed it for use as staff offices and for special events.

Buffalo Soldiers in Texas

During the Civil War more than 180,000 black soldiers served in segregated Union Army regiments. Realizing that many of the black units had achieved outstanding combat records, the U.S. Congress reorganized the peacetime army to include black enlisted men in the Ninth and the Tenth United States Cavalry. By 1869, black units manned the Twenty-fourth and Twenty-fifth United States Infantry—all under the leadership of white officers. As these soldiers moved to posts in Texas and across the Southwest and the Great Plains, the Indians began calling them "Buffalo Soldiers." Most accounts claim they earned Indian respect for their fierce fighting ability. Others say the title came from a combination of the Indians' regard for the buffalo and the black soldiers' tightly curled hair that resembled the hair on the bison's face. Accepting the respect of their adversaries, the Buffalo Soldiers adopted the image of the bison on their regiment crest.

The army paid the black recruits $13 a month plus food, clothing, and shelter—more than most black men could earn after the Civil War. Their enlistment was for five years and when they reached Texas they took part in most of the major Indian campaigns. They were stationed at almost every fort on the frontier from the Rio Grande to the Panhandle, helping to build and repair the outposts. They escorted mail teams, stagecoaches, cattle herds, and survey crews. They built roads, strung miles of telegraph lines, and performed ordinary garrison duties in the isolated western outposts. They recovered thousands of head of stolen livestock and spent months on the trail of horse thieves and Indian raiders.

Thirteen enlisted men and four regiments earned the Medal of Honor by the end of the Indian wars in the 1890s. Many went on to serve in the Spanish-American War, the Philippine Insurrection, and Pershing's punitive expedition into Mexico against Pancho Villa. However, by the turn of the last century the Buffalo Soldiers faced increasing racial prejudice. Resentment and anger that developed during Reconstruction in the South drove a wedge between citizens and anyone in a Federal uniform, especially a black man transformed from slave to person of authority. Buffalo Soldiers were stationed outside segregated communities and were subjected to increasing harassment by local police, beatings, and occasional sniper attacks. One example of the increasing tensions between white citizens occurred in Brownsville in 1906 when the newly arrived Twenty-fifth regiment was falsely accused of a murder. When members of the unit could not name the culprits, President Theodore Roosevelt followed recommendations to dishonorably discharge 167 men because of their "conspiracy of silence." It was 1972 before an inquiry found them innocent, and President Nixon granted the two surviving soldiers honorable discharges, without back pay. When Congress finally passed a tax-free pension the following year, only one Buffalo Soldier survived, and he received $25,000 and was honored in ceremonies in Washington, DC and Los Angeles.

Buffalo Soldier regiments were not called to duty during World War I, however many of the experienced personnel served in other black units. After the Ninth and Tenth cavalries were disbanded, their men served in other units during World War II. The Twenty-fifth saw combat in the Pacific before being deactivated in 1949. The Twenty-fourth, the last Buffalo Soldier regiment to see combat, served in the Pacific during World War II and in the opening days of the Korean War, before being deactivated in 1951.

In 1948 President Truman issued an executive order abolishing racial discrimination in the United States Armed Forces, but it was fifteen years later before Secretary of Defense Robert McNamara issued a directive obligating military commanders to stop discrimination based on sex or race in facilities used by soldiers or their family.

Scott Joplin, King of Ragtime

By the time he was seven Scott Joplin was proficient on the banjo and had started experimenting with the piano at the house where his mother worked as a cleaner. Born about 1867 into a musical family—Joplin's father, a former slave, played the violin for plantation parties and his mother, a freeborn African-American, sang and played the banjo—Joplin grew up amidst music making. The family moved into Texarkana around 1875 where Joplin's father worked as a laborer on the railroad and his mother cleaned houses.

Although several local teachers helped Joplin with piano lessons, young Joplin's world changed when Julius Weiss, a well-educated German who had immigrated to the United States to teach music, heard the eleven-year-old Joplin play the piano. Weiss had moved to Texarkana as the private tutor for children of a wealthy lumberman. Weiss offered Joplin free lessons in piano, sight-reading, and skills to enhance his natural instinct for harmony. Soon, Joplin's father left his mother and six children over what some claim was his father's belief that all the piano playing kept Joplin from working to help with the family income. Whatever the cause, Weiss helped Joplin's mother purchase a used piano and Joplin continued seriously studying music and practicing after school. Weiss introduced him to folk and classical music, including opera, and instilled in him a desire for education. Weiss left Texarkana in 1884 after the death of his employer, but Joplin apparently stayed in touch with his mentor and in later years, when Weiss was old and broke, Joplin sent regular gifts of money to Weiss until his death.

For a time Joplin played piano for a vocal quartet and taught guitar and mandolin. Some accounts claim he taught at the local Negro school. In the late 1880s Joplin became a traveling musician, playing piano where black piano players were accepted—churches, brothels, and saloons. He returned to Texarkana in July 1891 to perform with the "Texarkana Minstrels" to raise money for a monument for none other than Jefferson Davis, President of the Southern Confederacy. By this time Joplin's music was called "jig-piano," a pre-ragtime rhythm popular throughout the mid-South.

The 1893 Chicago World's Fair did not welcome black performers, but the twenty-seven million visitors attending the fair also visited local saloons, cafés, and brothels where they heard ragtime for the first time. Many accounts credit the fair with introducing ragtime and by 1897 the *St. Louis Dispatch* described ragtime as "a veritable call of the wild, which mightily stirred the pulses of city bred people."

Joplin played in black clubs, formed his own six-piece dance orchestra, and published his own compositions *Please Say You Will* and *A Picture of Her Face* in 1895. He may have been in Texas that September for the train crash that was promoted as a public relations stunt by the Katy Railroad, because the following year the *Great Crush Collision March*, which has been called "a special...early essay in ragtime," was published in Texas.

Joplin taught piano to future ragtime notables Arthur Marshall, Brun Campbell, and Scott Hayden. Accounts of Joplin's financial success vary widely. The contract for *Maple Leaf Rag* called for Joplin to receive one percent royalty on all sales with a minimum sale of twenty-five cents. Some versions of the story claim Joplin was the first musician to sell one million copies of a piece of instrumental music; however, later research indicates that the first print run sold 400 copies over a year and garnered four dollars for Joplin. Later sales earned him a steady income of about $600 a year.

In the early 1900s, while living in St. Louis, Joplin produced some of his best-known pieces, including *The Entertainer, March Majestic,* and *The Ragtime Dance*. After the death of Joplin's second wife, for whom he had written *The Chrysanthemum*, he wrote *Bethena*, called by some admirers "among the greatest of ragtime waltzes."

Convinced that education held the key to success for African-Americans, the theme of education ran through much of his work. By 1907 Joplin made New York his base for touring along the East Coast and settled there permanently as he worked on *Treemonisha,* a black opera that appeared to parallel Joplin's early life. Although it is now considered one of the most important of his compositions, it failed to be recognized for its worth until after his death.

Joplin contracted syphilis that by 1916 caused his health to deteriorate and his playing to become inconsistent. He died at the age of forty-nine in a Manhattan mental hospital on April 1, 1917.

He was inducted into the Songwriters Hall of Fame in 1970. The following year the New York Public Library published his collected works, and his music was featured in *The Sting,* the 1973 Academy Award-winning movie. In 1976 he was posthumously awarded the Pulitzer Prize for *Treemonisha,* the first grand opera written by an African American. His works included a ballet, two operas, a manual for aspiring ragtime musicians, and many works for piano including rags, marches, and waltzes. The biographical film *Scott Joplin* was released in 1977; the United States Postal Service issued a Joplin commemorative stamp for its Black Heritage series in 1983; Joplin was inducted into the Big Band and Jazz Hall of Fame in 1987 and the list goes on—quite a record for the "King of Ragtime," son of a former slave.

13
Grand Treasures

Elissa, Texas' Tall Ship

She is a pricey lady, but Galvestonians claim her as their own and money seems not to be a concern when it comes to preserving this beauty. She only visited the island twice but she is a prize the city is proud to sail and show. Built in 1877 in Aberdeen, Scotland, at the beginning of the age of steam, she is one of the last of her kind—a three-masted, iron-hulled sailing ship—measuring 205 feet from her stern to the tip of her jib boom.

After years of traveling the world, by 1961 she had been reduced to smuggling cigarettes between Italy and Yugoslavia. Aware the Galveston Historical Foundation wanted a sailing vessel to display as a visual link between the city's thriving 19th century port and its major businesses lining The Strand, Peter Throckmorton, a marine archeologist, spotted the much-altered old square-rigger in a Piraeus, Greece, scrapyard. Once aboard, Throckmorton discovered a plaque identifying the *Elissa*. More investigation revealed the dilapidated hulk as the oldest ship registered with Lloyds of London and its log showed two visits to Galveston.

When she first arrived in Galveston on December 26, 1883, she carried one passenger and a cargo of bananas. The following January 25 she left port loaded with cotton, bound for Liverpool, England. Her next visit occurred on September 8, 1886, when she arrived from Paysandú, Uruguay, probably carrying a cargo of hardwood or sugar. She sailed for Pensacola, Florida, on September 26 carrying only her ballast.

Over the years, the *Elissa* knew at least seven owners and carried names such as *Fjeld*, while berthed in Norway; *Gustaf*, while sailing out of Norway; and even *Christophoros* when purchased by Greeks. Each new name reflected the identity of her owners and brought physical changes such as

197

losing her grand sails and acquiring her first engine in 1918 and having her bow snubbed in 1936.

Even after Throckmorton discovered *Elissa*, the Galveston Historical Foundation did not purchase her until 1975 for $40,000. Despite the GHF sending a restoration team to Greece to make her seaworthy, replacing twenty-five percent of the hull, and removing tons of rust and rotten wood, *Elissa* could not sail and had to be towed across the Atlantic and the Gulf of Mexico to Galveston. As she made the journey across the Atlantic, the *Elissa* became the first object to be granted placement on the National Register of Historic Places while still outside the bounds of the United States.

No blueprints existed to guide the restoration, but the new owners realized she must be made seaworthy to attract the support needed to complete the enormous task. Experts arrived from Europe, Africa, and all over the United States to direct a corps of volunteers who descended on the fine old ship, varnishing the woodwork and going aloft to "tar" the rigging to keep it from rotting.

On July 4, 1982, with the restoration completed at a cost of $3.6 million, Texas had its "Tall Ship." The *Elissa* sailed the Gulf of Mexico and began receiving a long list of awards for its restoration, for its volunteer program, and for the most prestigious accolade from the National Trust for Historic Preservation in 1984—the Preservation Honor Award.

In 1985 *Elissa* made her first voyage as a restored sailing ship to Corpus Christi, Texas. The following year she sailed to New York harbor for the Statue of Liberty celebration and tall ship parade where she held the honor of being the oldest of the event's Class A vessels.

Over the years the *Elissa* represented Texas from Brownsville to Pensacola and received designation as a National Historic Landmark. Anchored at Galveston's Pier 21 next to the Texas Seaport Museum, *Elissa* reigns as one of Galveston's prime tourist attractions and meets the challenge to retain her place in Texas history.

The Grandest House on the Texas Coast

Today, Fulton Mansion would be called the empty-nest home of George W. Fulton and Harriet Gillette Smith since at the time of its construction in 1877 the Fulton's six children were already grown. When the three-and-a-half-story, nineteen-room Second Empire style mansion rose along the shore of Aransas Bay, it was the grandest house on the Texas coast. The Fultons, with the help of seven servants, entertained lavishly in their elegant new home.

Fulton, like his cousin Robert Fulton of steamboat fame, was a brilliant engineer and used his skills to design a house with features that were rare for that time—hot and cold running water, gas lights, a refrigeration system, central heat, and flush toilets. Despite sitting only yards from Aransas Bay, the Fulton Mansion withstood massive storms, including the 1919 hurricane that produced a ten-foot tidal wave that destroyed most structures in the area. Fulton designed a shellcrete (a form of concrete made from the plentiful local shell) foundation. Walls, both inside and out, were made of one-by-ten-inch pine boards stacked side-by-side to form a solid ten-inch-thick frame. Shellcrete filled in between every fourth or fifth board in the floors creating a structure as stable as a grain elevator.

Fulton could afford to construct the massive house because of his wife's inherited land and his own entrepreneurial spirit. Fulton, born in 1810, had worked in Indiana as a schoolteacher, watchmaker, and creator of mathematical instruments until he organized a company to fight in the Texas Revolution. They arrived too late for the action, but Fulton joined the Army of the Republic of Texas in 1837 and for his service received 1,280 acres. Fulton worked for the General Land Office, which introduced him to the legal maneuvering necessary to acquire land. In 1840 he married Harriet who was the daughter of Henry Smith, governor of Texas for a short time in 1835 before the war for independence from Mexico. After Smith failed to win the presidency of the new Republic of Texas, he continued to serve in several government positions, to purchase land along the coast, and to promote the development of his property.

Meantime, George Fulton and Harriet left Texas and spent the next twenty years in Ohio and in Baltimore where they raised and educated their children. After Harriet's father died and the Fultons cleared the titles on Smith's coastal land, they returned to Texas. Using his knowledge of land titles, Fulton purchased acreage, and combined with the land Harriet inherited from her father, Fulton acquired 25,000 acres. After joining with partners in the Coleman-Fulton Pasture Company, the holdings peaked at 265,000 acres, creating one of the largest cattle companies in Texas. The lavish lifestyle that ensued from the business allowed the partners to live like cattle barons and the Fultons to build their grand mansion.

Much of the partners' wealth came from the hide and tallow factories lining the shore of Aransas Bay near the Fulton's home. Hundreds of thousands of cattle and mustangs were slaughtered and their carcasses reduced to tallow in great boilers. The hides were cured and shipped along with the tallow, bones, and horns on waiting steamers headed for the East Coast.

Ever the inventor, Fulton received a U.S. patent for shipping beef using artificial cooling and for a steam engine modification. He introduced new livestock breeds that are still prevalent in Texas. Before barbed wire became available, the company used smooth wire to fence some of the ranges. A wooden plank fence enclosed one 2,000-acre pasture near present Rockport. Fulton gave land for the railroad, and towns—Sinton, Gregory, Portland, and Taft—developed on the company's vast holdings.

The most elegant of Fulton's achievements, which survives today, is the Fulton Mansion, listed on the National Register of Historic Places. In October 2015, the Texas Historical Commission completed a $3.1 million restoration and reopened the home to the public.

Texas Capitol Paid for in Land

The first big land giveaway in Texas started in 1749 when the Spanish Colonial government began establishing villas along the Rio Grande. Mexico continued the practice of granting empresarial contracts to men eager to establish colonies in Texas. The Republic of Texas issued land grants to pay its debts, including payment to the army and volunteers for their service in the war for independence from Mexico. After Texas joined the Union and negotiated to keep its public land, the state offered land to encourage development of farms and ranches, to attract new industry, to fund its public schools, and to entice railroad construction. Finally, the state Constitution of 1876 set aside land to fund construction of the state's fourth capitol.

The third capitol burned on November 9, 1881, increasing the urgency to name a contractor for construction of the new building. By 1882 the State of Texas initiated one of the largest barter transactions in history to pay wealthy Chicago brothers, John V. and Senator C. B. Farwell, three million acres of Panhandle land in exchange for building the $3 million State Capitol at Austin.

When the builders discovered that the limestone planned for the structure discolored when it was exposed to the elements, owners of Granite Mountain, a solid rock dome about fifty miles northwest of Austin, donated enough "sunset red" granite to construct a Renaissance Revival design modeled after the national capitol in Washington. Convict labor hauled the huge blocks of granite to a newly built narrow-gauge railroad that carried 15,700 carloads of granite from the quarry to the building site in Austin. Upon completion of the 360,000 square foot capitol in 1888 and placing of the statue of the Goddess of Liberty atop its dome, the building reached a height of 311 feet—almost fifteen feet taller that the National Capitol.

Since the land used to pay for the capitol stretched across the unsettled Texas Panhandle from present Lubbock to forty miles north of Dalhart, the capitol syndicate decided to establish a ranch until the land could be sold. Representatives went to England in 1884 to secure $5 million from British investors to finance the purchase of cattle, fencing, and the entire infrastructure for the huge enterprise.

Trail boss Abner Blocker drove the first herd to the ranch in 1885 only to discover that a brand had not been selected. Trying to create a design that could not be easily changed, Blocker drew "XIT" in the corral dust with the heel of his boot, and it stuck as the brand and ranch name. In later years the story spread that the brand stood for "ten (counties) in Texas" because the ranch spread into ten counties. Other folks speculated that it meant "biggest in Texas."

The vastness of the operation required dividing the ranch into eight divisions with a manager over each. A 6,000-mile single-strand wire fence eventually enclosed the ranch, the largest in the world at that time. By 1890 the XIT herd averaged 150,000 head, and the cowboys branded 35,000 calves a year. Fences divided the ranch into ninety-four pastures; 325 windmills and 100 dams dotted the landscape. Cowhands received pay of twenty-five to thirty dollars a month. XIT men and their "hired guns" sometimes formed vigilante groups to combat problems of fence cutting and cattle rustling. Wolves and other wild animals took a heavy toll, especially during calving season. Lack of ample water, droughts, blizzards, prairie fires, and a declining market resulted in the XIT operating without a profit for most of its years.

The schoolteacher wife of one of the managers, Cordelia Sloan Duke, kept a diary, writing notes on a pad she carried in her apron pocket while she "looked after" her own family and the 150 cowboys who worked the ranch.

She successfully encouraged eighty-one cowboys and their families to keep diaries. Eventually, she and Dr. Joe B. Frantz published a book, *6,000 Miles of Fence: Life on the XIT Ranch of Texas*. Through Mrs. Duke's efforts, an authentic account of the work and lifestyle of that early phase of American life has been preserved in the cowboys' own language.

With British creditors demanding a positive return, the syndicate began selling the land for small farms and ranches. Although the cattle had been sold by 1912, the last parcel of land was not sold until 1963. One hundred years after the land exchange, the tax value on the property reached almost $7 billion.

The XIT Ranch, built on land that served as payment for building the largest state capitol in North America, is remembered at the annual Dalhart XIT Reunion Parade where a horse with an empty saddle honors the range riders of the past.

14
Power of Design

Treasures of the Lower Pecos

*T*ravelers heading northwest on US 90 out of Del Rio parallel the Rio Grande through arid canyon lands carved by the intersecting Pecos and Devils rivers, one of the most significant archeological regions in North America. Tucked into overhanging limestone ledges and deeply recessed caves are rock shelters where evidence of human habitation dates back about 10,000 years. Over 300 paintings, sprawled across the limestone walls of these hidden rock shelters, created between 3,000 and 4,000 years ago, are among the world's finest pictographs (drawn or painted images) and the largest collection in North America. Some of the multi-colored scenes, painted and drawn by hunter-gatherers who called the canyons home, spread more than 100 feet and depict characters twenty feet tall. The oldest images, known as Pecos River style, are the most common and often feature shaman rituals representing journeys to the spirit world. Some of the shamans are painted to look like they are ascending; others appear to be hovering with protective out-stretched arms. Panthers with great long tails leap across the limestone canvass and splay fierce claws among rabbit, snake, and crab-like shamans. In later work beginning about 500 B.C., fertility rituals, copulation, and birthing scenes are depicted.

The only large array of petroglyphs (images carved, pecked, or cut into stone)--hundreds of geometric and abstract designs created about the year 1000--has been discovered on gently sloping bedrock on private property. Work continues to remove sediment revealing older, more graceful techniques, including motifs of atlatls (spears that pre-date the bow and arrow) as well as animal tracks and human footprints.

The artistic styles evolved slowly over time among these isolated people living in a small region with no influence from outside forces until about 1600 to 1800 when Spanish explorers and Plains Indians began to make forays into the region, bringing disease and warfare. Depicting the changes brought by the intrusion, the art first shows the novelty of domestic livestock and the curiosity of a people who wore little clothing upon seeing hats, boots, weapons, and the armored horse. Although no missions were established in the Lower Pecos, structures appear similar to missions topped with a Christian cross. Then the destructive consequences of diseases, warfare, and starvation created by the outside invasion appear in scenes of soldiers, horsemen, and destroyed churches.

The introduction of the horse culture among these indigenous people seems to explain the appearance of the more recent art in canyons near water supplies and access to grazing areas away from the steep cliff sides of earlier pictographs. The scenes depict hand-to-hand combat, horse theft, thunderbirds, and sun symbols.

Since the 1920s researchers ranging across all the disciplines have been studying the art and the lifestyle of the ancient canyon-dwellers who for thousands of years did not cultivate crops, but sustained their livelihood by hunting and gathering. Although more than 250 sites in Texas are known for prehistoric pictographs, only the Lower Pecos Canyonlands exhibit a rock-art tradition of a single group of people over an extended period of time.

For centuries, the arid environment preserved the wall art as well as the grass beds, baskets, mats, string bags, and sandals made from fibers of native plants such as lechuguilla, sotol, and agave—priceless evidence of the culture of the prehistoric era. However, modern treasure hunters began destroying and defacing the art, and it was not until the 1930s that archeological expeditions began collecting the materials primarily for display in museums. Serious archeological research and efforts to protect the site began in the late 1950s when Mexico and the United States made plans to construct the huge Amistad Dam at the confluence of the Devils River and the Rio Grande in the core of the Lower Pecos Canyonlands. When the dam was completed in 1969, its reservoir spread over 89,000 acres, covering much of the prehistoric treasures.

Study and preservation have continued, and today visitors enjoy guided tours to the Fate Bell Shelter conducted by the Seminole Canyon State Park & Historic Site and White Shaman Tours led by the Rock Art Foundation.

Nicholas Clayton, Texas' First Architect

In the last half of the nineteenth century, the most powerful men in Texas called Galveston home. The Strand, a street stretching five blocks along the docks, wore the moniker of Wall Street of the Southwest. Two dozen millionaires officed along the route, controlling Texas' shipping, banks, insurance companies, and the vast cotton export business.

One man, by the power of his designs, left a heritage for Galveston and Texas that all the power brokers combined could not equal. Nicholas J. Clayton arrived in Galveston in 1872, and changed the face of the booming cultural and business metropolis of Texas. Although he arrived without friends or business contacts, his position as supervising architect for a Cincinnati firm constructing the First Presbyterian Church and the Tremont Hotel caught the eye of Galveston notables.

A faithful Catholic, who attended mass most every day, Clayton began his connection with Galveston's movers and shakers by walking, as soon as he arrived in the city, to St. Mary's Church (now St. Mary's Cathedral) and discussing with the bishop improvements to Galveston's oldest church built in 1846. Clayton soon designed the central tower and later a new bell tower and the statue of Mary, Star of the Sea.

The bishop may have been influential the next year in Clayton receiving the contract to design Saint Mary's Church (now Saint Mary's Cathedral) in Austin, which served at that time as part of the Galveston Diocese. Clayton's residential, commercial, and church designs won respect for their exuberance of shape, color, texture, and detail. He was so involved in his work that he often continued sketching church buildings, windows, altars, and steeples, even while carrying on a conversation. He worked every day except Sunday and Christmas and expected near perfection from those he employed. His family claimed his most abusive term was "muttonhead" for those who did not meet his expectations.

He designed, built, added to, or remodeled eleven churches in Galveston and other churches all over the South and Mexico. In a time of slower communication, Clayton traveled extensively and made use of the telephone, telegraph, and letters.

Many of his designs have never been duplicated, such as the intricate brickwork on Old Red (1891), the first building for the University of Texas Medical Branch in Galveston. The carpentry has never been matched in the Beach Hotel (1883–1898) and the Electric Pavilion (1881–1883), both destroyed by fires. The flamboyant octagonal Garten Verein (1876–), an inspired work in wood, served as a social center for Galveston's German community.

Clayton worked quickly and new ideas appeared to come easily. Mrs. Clayton claimed that the idea for the design of the octagonal-shaped Garten Verein came to Clayton instantly, and he finished the plans in a single night.

His most spectacular residential design, the Walter Gresham House (1887–1892), known today as Bishop's Palace, rises three stories over a raised basement and boasts fourteen-foot ceilings. Among the grand details is a forty-foot-tall octagonal mahogany stairwell with stained glass on five sides lit by a large skylight. Listed on the National Register of Historic Places, the Gresham House is one of the most significant Victorian residences in the country.

Despite his prolific production and vigorous work ethic, Clayton's son acknowledged that his father wasn't a very good businessman. His insistence on perfection often caused him to go over budget for a project, and he would continue working at his own expense. He mostly left financial arrangements to others. His concern centered on creating outstanding buildings. Eventually his relaxed business practices and dependence on a partner to follow through on a contract while Clayton was out of town caused him to forfeit a bond that eventually resulted in bankruptcy. As the legal battle dragged on for ten years, many clients turned their backs on him and refused to pay. Devastated by the loss of his integrity and prestige, the final blow to him came when the 1900 storm severely damaged or destroyed many of his finest designs.

He continued to get small projects such as the design and reconstruction of the main building of St. Edward's University in Austin after a fire damaged the original structure. He built the new Incarnate Word Academy in Houston, but he could never get a bond for a large contract.

In November 1916, as he repaired a crack in his chimney, the candle he held ignited his undershirt. Severely burned, he developed pneumonia and died on December 9, 1916.

Mrs. Clayton grieved to her husband's dear friend, Rabbi Henry Cohen, that she did not have money for a proper monument. Rabbi Cohen replied,

Oh, you don't need one, my dear Mary Lorena. He's got them all over town. Just go around and read some cornerstones."

Today, eight buildings of Nicholas J. Clayton design survive on the Strand, thirty-four remain all over the country, and eighty-six have been razed. His legacy continues in the beauty and style he brought to his beloved Galveston, known as "The Texas Victorian Oasis."

Ezekiel Airship

Residents in the East Texas town of Pittsburg house in the local museum a full-size replica of the Ezekiel Airship, which many old timers declare flew almost a year before the Wright brothers' claim to fame at Kitty Hawk, North Carolina.

Burrell Cannon, a mechanical genius and part-time Baptist preacher, inspired by the first and tenth chapters of Ezekiel in which the prophet writes of angelic vehicles composed of wheels within wheels, worked over twenty years building models and improving his design for a flying machine. In 1901, Cannon convinced Pittsburg businessmen to establish the Ezekiel Airship Manufacturing Company and issue stock for twenty thousand dollars to underwrite the project.

Employees of the Pittsburg Foundry and Machine Company built the airship between March and October 1902. Its engine turned four sets of paddles, which powered large, fabric-covered wings—incorporating a compulsion force similar to a helicopter.

Local residents claim seeing the airship fly for about 160 feet at a height of ten to twelve feet. A former machine shop worker admitted that one Sunday, when Cannon and the other investors were out of town, the employees took the plane out to the field across from the shop and he flew it. All the conspirators, fearing the loss of their jobs, made a pact not to tell anyone. If the story is true, it explains why no newspaper coverage exists and why officials of the company denied the flight.

On December 17, 1903, the Wright brothers took their famous flight. The next year, investors loaded the Ezekiel on a flatbed railroad car for a trip to the St. Louis World's Fair. As the train neared Texarkana, a fierce storm blew the airship off the railcar and destroyed it.

The Reverend Cannon did not attempt another flight until 1913 in Chicago when his new craft flew only a few feet, hit a telephone pole, and received damage to the bottom of the ship. The Reverend, declaring God had not willed the airship to fly, promptly gave up the project.

A Texas Historical Marker, which sits beside the railroad tracks at Fulton and South Market streets in Pittsburg, tells the story of the Ezekiel Airship.

Elisabet Ney, Sculptor of Renown

In 1873, perhaps the most unusual and nonconforming couple in early Texas—German sculptor Elisabet Ney and her husband, philosopher and scientist Dr. Edmund Montgomery—bought a former slave plantation outside Hempstead.

"Miss Ney," as she was called even after her marriage to Dr. Montgomery, had always been beautiful, talented, and self-willed. She shocked her family by going to Munich at the age of nineteen to study art. She soon made a name for herself as a sculptor, but she continued to scorn convention by her open affair with young Montgomery. She undertook many important commissions, even moving into a studio at the royal palace in Munich to execute a full-length statue of Ludwig II, the mad king who almost financially ruined Bavaria before he was assassinated.

After Miss Ney and Dr. Montgomery married, it is said that her relations with him and her political activities caused the couple to decide that the United States offered a better environment for them. They lived about two years in a German colony in Georgia before moving to Texas and purchasing Liendo Plantation.

During the nineteen years she lived at Liendo, she devoted her life to rearing her two sons and trying to help the neighborhood freedmen. Neither venture was very successful. The blacks ridiculed her, one son died, and the story spread that fear of cholera prompted Miss Ney to cremate the child—a practice viewed with horror at the time. Lorne, her other son, separated himself from his mother, possibly because of her strict rules and the embarrassment he felt over the community talk generated by her lifestyle and behavior.

Miss Ney received a commission to execute the statues of Stephen F. Austin and Sam Houston for the Texas Exhibit at the 1893 World's Fair. (Both statues stand today in the state capitol in Austin. A copy of Austin is in the U.S. capitol Hall of Columns and Houston in the National Statuary

Hall.) She moved to Austin, built her studio Formosa, and completed busts of notable Texas politicians and a depiction of Shakespeare's Lady Macbeth (the marble is displayed in the Smithsonian's National Museum of American Art). She also assembled her works of European notables—King Ludwig II of Bavaria, Otto von Bismarck, and Jacob Grimm—she had created as a young artist in Europe.

Although she lived at Formosa until her death in 1907, she and Dr. Montgomery continued to visit, and she was buried at Liendo among the oak trees they had planted. Sometime after her death, friends organized the Texas Fine Arts Association, purchased her Austin studio and developed it into a museum of her work. Dr. Montgomery became a leading local citizen in Hempstead, serving as a county commissioner and helping to found nearby Prairie View College (present-day Prairie View A&M University).

The Cattle Baron's Daughter

An elegant 1930s Greek revival temple in Victoria, the Royston Nave Museum, has a story to tell of vast wealth, cultural challenge, creative genius, and high living as broad as the Texas landscape. In 2012 the Nave Museum held a month-long exhibit titled "The Cattle Baron's Daughter and the Artists Who Loved Her—James Ferdinand McCan (1869–1925) and Royston Nave (1886–1931)."

The cattle baron's daughter was Emily McFaddin, a beautiful, artistic young woman born in 1876 on a giant cattle ranch outside Victoria. The cattle baron was James Alfred McFaddin, son and brother of the Beaumont McFaddins, owners of vast stretches of ranch land, including Big Hill that became Spindletop in 1901.

James McFaddin moved to Refugio County and began ranching in 1858 with 130 head of cattle from his father's herd. After serving in the Civil War, he returned to Refugio, became a one-man bank, loaning money to his neighbors and started buying land where the San Antonio and Guadalupe rivers converge. As his holdings increased, McFaddin built a three-story mansion in Victoria with an art studio for Emily in the tower above the center of the home.

The first artist in this story was the lively James Ferdinand McCan from County Kerry, Ireland, who arrived in the United States at age seventeen. He settled in San Antonio and opened an art studio. An exhibition of his work caught the eye of Henrietta King. She moved McCan to the King Ranch where he served as artist-in-residence for two years. During that time his reputation blossomed, and Al McFaddin, Emily's brother, commissioned McCan in 1896 to paint a portrait of his and Emily's parents, James and Margaret McFaddin. Emily and McCan married the following year and moved happily into Victoria's social whirl, entertaining in the home her parents gave them as a wedding gift. Their son, Claude Kerry McCan, was born in 1899.

The second artist in the saga was Royston Nave who was born in LaGrange, Texas, and began his studies under his mother Lou Scott Royston, a well-known Texas painter. He studied with several New York artists, and his renown grew as his portraits were featured in many one-man exhibits.

After serving in World War I, Nave moved to Victoria to study art with James McCan. The two artists became such good friends that Nave painted a self-portrait that he gave to McCan with the inscription, "To my friend, J.F.M." and signed "Royston Nave." The portrait hangs today in the front hall of the home built for Emily when she married McCan.

Emily and McCan divorced in 1916, and McCan moved to Boerne where he continued to paint the Hill Country scenes he loved until his death in 1925.

A year after her divorce, Emily and Nave were married. The couple began a whirlwind life of worldwide travel with her brother Al and his wife. They finally settled for two years in New York where Nave enjoyed continued success with portraiture. In the late 1920s they returned to Victoria where Nave painted in his studio, and they enjoyed the social and cultural life of the city until Nave died unexpectedly of a heart attack at age forty-four.

The family was devastated, and after a year of mourning Emily commissioned the father/son architectural team of Atlee and Robert Ayers to design a fitting memorial for Royston Nave. The Greek revival temple opened in October 1932 as the Royston Nave Museum to house the work of Royston Nave and the library of the Bronte Study Club. Nave's portraits and his landscapes hung above the stacks of books until 1976 when the city of Victoria constructed a new library.

Emily continued her cultural and community interests until her death in 1943, even hosting Eleanor Roosevelt in 1940 when the first lady visited Victoria.

After Victoria built its new library, Emily's heirs deeded the Nave Museum to the city to be used as a regional art museum, and in 2003 it became the property of the Victoria Regional Museum Association. Noted for six to eight compelling exhibits each year that range from classical to modern, the McFaddin and McCan descendants agreed to sponsor an exhibit of the works of both artists, which had never been shown under the same roof. Family and friends generously loaned their private works from both artists to create the delightful exhibit known as "The Cattle Baron's Daughter and the Artists Who Loved Her—James Ferdinand McCan (1869–1925) and Royston Nave (1886–1931)."

15

Trouble Makers, Law and Order

Texas Troubles

*N*ewspapers around the country called it "the Texas Troubles" in 1860 when rumors—fanned by letters to Texas newspapers written by Charles R. Pryor, editor of the *Dallas Herald*—claimed that a mysterious fire on Sunday, July 8 that burned the newspaper office and all the buildings on the Dallas town square except the brick courthouse, was an abolitionist plot "to devastate, with fire and assassination the whole of Northern Texas...." On that same day other fires destroyed half of the square in Denton and burned down a store in Pilot Point. Fires also burned in Honey Grove, Jefferson, and Austin. The city leaders of Dallas (population 775) first blamed the extreme heat—105 to 113 degrees in the area on the day of the fires—on the new volatile phosphorous matches causing spontaneous combustion in a box of wood shavings at a drug store. They believed the fire quickly consumed the entire building before spreading over the downtown. The citizens in Denton, after experiencing other problems with "prairie matches," concluded that spontaneous combustion was the cause of their fire.

In Dallas, however, white leaders stirred by the prospect of Abraham Lincoln's election and encouraged by Pryor's claims, decided on a sinister slave plot hatched up by two white abolitionist preachers from Iowa. The preachers were jailed, publicly whipped, and sent out of the county. A committee of fifty-two men organized to mete out justice to the slaves in the county. At first the vigilante committee favored hanging every one of the almost one hundred Negro slaves in the county, but cooler heads prevailed and they decided to hang only three. Two days later the men were hanged on the banks of the Trinity River near the present Triple Overpass. The remaining slaves, out of consideration of their property value, were given a good flogging. Later, a judge who had been part of the vigilante committee said that the three slaves were probably innocent, but because of the "inflamed state of the public mind, someone had to be hanged."

The "troubles" were not over. By the end of July, towns throughout North and Central Texas organized vigilance committees to find and punish the conspirators. The committees terrorized the slave community. Interrogations focused on white itinerant preachers who were cited as insurrection leaders. Despite fears of a slave rebellion that lasted until after the Civil War, there was never an organized group of slaves in Texas that shed white blood. Vigilantes often obtained "confessions" and evidence points to white leaders spreading the rumors to garner public support for secession.

Estimates vary from thirty to one hundred Negroes and whites that died before the panic subsided. One historian described the times as "the drama of the imagination."

John Wesley Hardin, Son of a Preacher

Handsome and gentlemanly John Wesley Hardin, named for the founder of the Methodist Church, was the son of a Methodist minister and circuit rider. Perhaps his proper upbringing caused "Wes" to view himself as a pillar of society who claimed he never killed a man who didn't need killing. The numbers of dead differ, as do the stories about his escapades, but John Wesley Hardin managed in his forty-two years to kill at least thirty men. Some accounts claim forty.

Born in Bonham, Texas, in 1853, Hardin at age fourteen stabbed a fellow student in a schoolyard fight. He might have been expelled for the incident except his father founded and ran the school. Like many young men too young to fight in the Civil War, Hardin became the product of the hatred generated by the war. The restrictive policies of the Reconstruction government fueled anger, which encouraged citizens, especially impressionable young men, to lash out at freed slaves and the Union army overseeing Reconstruction. A year after the stabbing, Hardin met a black man, got into an argument, and shot the man dead.

His father, sure Wes could not receive a fair trial from the Reconstruction government, encouraged his son to flee, which began a pattern of relatives and friends hiding Hardin from law officers. Hearing that three Union

213

soldiers were headed for his hideout at his brother's house, Wes later wrote, "I waylaid them, as I had no mercy on men whom I knew only wanted to get my body to torture and kill. It was war to the knife for me, and I brought it on by opening the fight with a double-barreled shotgun and ended it with a cap and ball six-shooter. Thus it was by the fall of 1868 I had killed four men and was myself wounded in the arm."

Some accounts say within a year he killed another soldier. All stories agree that Wes Hardin served at age 17 as trail boss on a cattle drive up the Chisholm Trail. One account says he got into an argument with Mexican cowboys who tried cutting their herd in front of his. All the stories of the cattle drive agree John Wesley Hardin killed six or seven men on that trip to Abilene, Kansas.

Some say Hardin became friends with city marshal Wild Bill Hickok whom he admired. Others say he forced Hickok to stand down. Whatever really happened, Hardin left Abilene in a hurry. He wrote regarding the episode, "They tell lots of lies about me. They said I killed six or seven men for snoring. Well, it ain't true, I only killed one man for snoring." The gentleman to whom he refers was sleeping in the next hotel room and Hardin shot through the wall to stop the noise.

Hardin returned to Central Texas and married Jane Bowen, a beautiful, cultured girl from a respectable family who had been his childhood sweetheart. He did not, however, settle down. Despite constant absences as he ran from the law, Jane remained loyal. After being arrested, breaking out of jail, and taking sides in a major Central Texas feud, Hardin finally killed a deputy sheriff. Finding himself under constant pursuit, Hardin fled with Jane and their three children to Florida where they lived for two years under an alias. Some accounts claim he killed as many as six men while he was on the run.

Finally caught in 1877, Hardin stood trial in Austin, Texas, and was sentenced to twenty-five years in prison for killing the deputy. While in prison, he made repeated escape attempts, read theology, served as superintendent of the prison Sunday school, wrote his autobiography, and studied law. He received a pardon from the governor in 1894 and was admitted to the state bar.

Jane had raised their three children and died shortly before Hardin got out of prison. Upon his release, he headed to El Paso where he opened a law practice, became involved with a client's wife, and hired several law enforcement officers to assassinate the husband. One of the hires, Constable John

Selman, possibly angry over not being paid for killing the husband, found Hardin in the Acme Saloon and shot him in the back of the head. Hardin died instantly. The career of one of Texas' most notorious killers came to an end on August 19, 1895, but the legends and legacy continue to stir imaginations.

Judge Roy Bean, Law West of the Pecos

As the railroad spread westward across Texas it was often said, "West of the Pecos there is no law; west of El Paso there is no God." The Texas Rangers were called in to quell the criminal element that followed the railroad crews through the desolate Chihuahuan Desert of southwest Texas. The rangers had been hauling prisoners to the county seat at Fort Stockton—a 400-mile round trip—and they needed a local justice of the peace in Vinegarroon, a town just west of the Pecos River. It was August 1882 and Roy Bean, who had left his wife and four children in San Antonio earlier that year, won the appointment. He kept the job with only two off years––when he lost elections––until 1902.

Bean's training in the law consisted of a talent for avoiding it. He was in his early twenties when he made a quick exit from the law in Chihuahua, Mexico. He made a jail break in San Diego and avoided being hanged in San Gabriel, California. He prospered for a time in the saloon business in Mesilla, New Mexico, with his older brother. After the Civil War he settled in a part of San Antonio that became known as Beanville. He married in 1866 and spent several years in various jobs—a firewood business until he was caught cutting his neighbor's timber, a dairy business until he began watering down the milk, and a butcher shop that sold meat from cattle rustled from nearby ranches. When he began operating a saloon, a rival saloonkeeper was so eager to see him out of the business that she bought out his entire operation for $900. He promptly left his family, headed west, and set up his own tent saloon along the new railroad construction in Vinegarroon.

When Bean became justice of the peace, he acquired an 1879 edition of the *Revised Statutes of Texas* and undertook his first action—he shot up the saloon shack of a Jewish competitor. His tent saloon served as a part-time courtroom where the jurors were selected from an array of his best bar customers. When an Irishman named O'Rourke killed a Chinese railroad laborer, a mob of O'Rourke supporters surrounded Bean's court and threatened to lynch him if he didn't free O'Rourke. After looking through his law book Bean said homicide was killing of a human being; however, he could find no law against killing a Chinaman. He dismissed the case.

As railroad construction moved westward, Bean followed the line to a town that became known as Langtry, which Bean claimed he named for the English actress Emilie Charlotte (Lillie) Langtry whom he fell in love with after seeing her picture in a newspaper. In truth, the town, sitting on a bluff above the Rio Grande, was named for George Langtry, an engineer and foreman who supervised the Chinese immigrants who constructed the railroad.

Apparently Bean's reputation preceded him because the landowner sold to the railroad on the condition that no part of the land could be sold or leased to Bean. O'Rourke, the gentlemen Bean acquitted, suggested Bean establish his saloon on the railroad right-of-way because that land was not covered in the railroad contract.

Bean built his saloon, which he named The Jersey Lilly in honor of Lillie Langtry who was born on Jersey, one of the islands in the English Channel. He claimed to know Miss Lillie and wrote to her several times inviting her to visit his town. When his saloon burned, he built a new home and called it an opera house where he insisted Miss Lillie would come to perform. She actually visited Langtry ten months after Bean's death.

Bean's creative court decisions in The Jersey Lilly included the time he fined a corpse $40 for carrying a concealed weapon. It just so happened that in addition to his gun, the dead man had $40 in his pocket, which paid for his burial and court costs. Bean was known as "the hanging judge," despite never hanging anybody. Whereas horse thieves were hanged in other jurisdictions, in Bean's court, they were let go if the horses were returned to their owners. Since there was no jail, all cases ended with fines, which Bean kept, refusing to send the money to the state. Usually the fine consisted of the amount of money found in the prisoner's pockets. Although a justice of the peace was not authorized to grant divorces, Bean did it anyway, charging $10 for the service. He charged $5 for performing a wedding and ended each ceremony with "and may God have mercy on your souls." Bean was noted for his colorful language such as, "It is the judgment of this court that you are hereby tried and convicted of illegally and unlawfully committing certain grave offenses against the peace and dignity of the State of Texas, particularly in my bailiwick," and then he added, "I fine you two dollars; then get the hell out of here and never show yourself in this court again. That's my rulin'." But he also maintained tight control of the language used in his courtroom, even threatening a lawyer with hanging for using "profane language" when the lawyer referred to the "habeas corpus" of his client.

When Bean heard that Jay Gould, the famed railroad tycoon, was on a train heading toward Langtry, Bean used a danger signal to flag down the train. Thinking the bridge over the Pecos River was out, the train stopped and Bean entertained Gould and his daughter at The Jersey Lilly during a two-hour visit. The delay sent tremors through the New York Stock Exchange when reports circulated that Gould had been killed in a train wreck.

While the trains stopped to take on water, passengers poured into The Jersey Lilly where Bean served them quickly and then became very slow giving them their change. When the warning whistle blew announcing the train's departure, the rush was on with passengers demanding their money and Bean eventually fining them the amount they were owed. His reputation grew as the passengers ran cursing back to the waiting train. Future travelers could not resist stopping to visit the ramshackle saloon and its famous proprietor.

Prizefighting became illegal in most of the Southwest and in Mexico, which prompted Bean to open a side business promoting fights on a sandbar in the middle of the Rio Grande. In 1898 when promoters could not find a place to hold the world championship title prizefight between Bob Fitzsimmons and Peter Maher, Bean welcomed the event to Langtry. An excursion train arrived with 200 spectators on February 22 and Bean entertained them for a time in The Jersey Lilly before leading them to a bridge he had constructed to reach the makeshift ring. The Texas Rangers watched helplessly from a bluff on the Texas side of the river while Fitzsimmons beat Maher in 95 seconds. The fans and sportswriters enjoyed a few more drinks at The Jersey Lilly before the train carried them to El Paso to spread the news throughout the United States.

Books, movies, TV shows, and Roy Bean himself spread the legend of Judge Roy Bean, "the law west of the Pecos," with tales true and tainted. Despite failing health, Bean went on a drinking binge in Del Rio in March 1903 and died in his bed the following morning. The Texas Department of Public Transportation has restored The Jersey Lilly Saloon in Langtry and created a Visitors Center just south of US Highway 90.

Diamond Bessie Murder Trial

Jefferson, a thriving inland port in deep East Texas, enjoyed a cosmopolitan air of success in 1877. Steamboats designed to carry a thousand bales of East Texas cotton on water as shallow as three feet left the port of Jefferson. They returned from New Orleans with the latest fashion in clothing and home design as well as immigrants heading for settlement in Northeast Texas, Dallas, and the Texas Panhandle.

The giant sternwheelers traveled the Mississippi River from New Orleans, steamed up the Red River and finally entered Big Cypress Creek for the journey to the head of navigation at Jefferson. Town residents did not blink at wealth or lavish living until January 19, 1877, when a handsome man and a beautiful young woman arrived on the train from nearby Marshall.

The woman, although tastefully dressed, wore enough diamonds to open her own jewelry store. Some accounts claim townspeople, upon hearing the man refer to her as "Bessie," began secretly calling her "Diamond Bessie."

After registering at the Brooks House under the name of "A. Monroe and wife," the couple spent two days walking about town apparently enjoying the interested eyes following their every move. Hotel guests in neighboring rooms later claimed hearing them fight all Saturday night. On Sunday morning, January 21, they purchased a picnic lunch and disappeared into the fog on the footbridge crossing Big Cypress Creek. Late that afternoon the gentlemen returned alone. To questions about his wife's whereabouts, he claimed she had decided to visit friends. He casually went about his affairs until the following Tuesday, when he boarded the early-morning train headed east carrying all the couples' luggage.

On February 5, after several days of sleet and snow, someone looking for firewood discovered the body of the well-dressed young woman, sans jewelry, lying under a tree amid the remains of a picnic lunch. The coroner ruled she died of a gunshot wound to the head and due to little decomposition appeared to have been dead only four or five days.

Charmed by the beauty of the mysterious woman, the town collected $150 for a proper burial in Oakwood Cemetery. Further investigation disclosed the couple registered as "A. Rothchild and wife of Cincinnati, Ohio," at a hotel in Marshall two days before arriving in Jefferson. Authorities discovered Abraham Rothchild worked as a traveling salesman for his father's

Cincinnati jewelry business, and met Bessie Moore a few years earlier at a brothel in Little Rock.

Fred Tarpley in *Jefferson: Riverport to the Southwest* writes that Bessie's real name was Annie Stone, daughter of a prosperous shoe dealer in Syracuse, New York. "Black hair, brilliant gray eyes, a flair for grooming, and a well-chosen wardrobe combined to make her an extraordinary beauty and to attract early attention from men." At age fifteen she became, for a short time, a young man's mistress. Then, working as a prostitute, she traveled from Cincinnati to New Orleans and Hot Springs where she met Rothchild.

Tarpley claims a "considerable inheritance from her father" and gifts from her many admirers led to her stunning collection of diamonds. The nation-wide publicity surrounding her death, and the romantic stories growing in the imagination of mythmakers, obscured the accounts of her life published in the nineteenth-century. In reality, Bessie and Rothchild were drunks, and over the two years of their association, he pimped for her when they needed money. No one ever found evidence they were legally married.

Jefferson residents raged against the murderer of the beautiful young woman as authorities headed to Cincinnati to arrest Rothchild. In the meantime, Rothchild, in a drunken state of apparent remorse, attempted to shoot himself in the head. He succeeded only in blinding himself in his right eye.

Rothchild's parents disowned him; however, the family provided the best legal defense, including a future governor of Texas and a U.S. senator. The state, embroiled in the most high profile case of its history, involved the best lawyers available. Legal wrangling delayed the trial until December 1878. After three weeks of testimony, Rothchild was found guilty and sentenced to death by hanging; however, the judge of the Seventh Texas Court of Appeals declared a mistrial. During the second trial, a witness claimed to have seen Bessie with a man, who was not Rothchild, on two occasions after Rothchild left Jefferson. Despite the prosecution's attack on the credibility of the witness, he planted enough doubt that the jury on December 30, 1880, found Rothchild not guilty.

The verdict did not put to rest the tales continuing to circulate like the one claiming twelve $1,000 bills appeared in the jury room during deliberations or the report in the 1880s of a handsome, elderly man wearing a patch on his right eye asking to visit the grave of Bessie Moore and placing roses on it.

The mystery of who killed Diamond Bessie continues to stir imaginations each spring when the Jefferson Historical Pilgrimage presents its annual production of the "Diamond Bessie Murder Trial."

William Cowper Brann, The Iconoclast

His supporters called him a visionary and a brilliant writer. Some even dubbed him the "Prairie Voltaire" and the "American Carlyle." His detractors called him the "Devil's Disciple." Even his biographer Charles Carver described him as "a mean Mark Twain." Upon his death, after a gun battle that also killed his assailant, those who hated him said, "At long last he's in hell where he belongs."

W.C. Brann acquired a third grade education, ran away at age thirteen in 1868 from the Illinois family who took him in after his mother's death, and bounced around the country until he found work as a printer's devil and cub reporter. He wrote for the *St. Louis Globe Democrat, Galveston Evening-Tribune, Austin Statesman, San Antonio Express,* and *Houston Post,* gaining a reputation as a brilliant though vitriolic editorialist.

Brann and his wife had two daughters and a son. After his thirteen-year-old daughter committed suicide in Houston in 1890, the family moved to Austin where Brann decided his editorial experience and the publication of three of his plays offered reason enough for him to use the limited family savings to begin publishing his "journal of personal protest," the *Iconoclast.* It quickly failed.

Brann sold the journal to William Sydney Porter, the Austin writer who later became famous as O. Henry. After several more moves Brann ended up in Waco in 1894 as chief editorialist for the *Waco Daily News.* The following year he acquired the journal from Porter and started publishing the *Iconoclast.* This time the savagery of his writing gained attention across the U.S. and in many foreign countries—growing the circulation in three years to almost 100,000.

His articulate criticisms, even cruel comments fascinated his readers. He raged against the status quo and insulted people and institutions he viewed as overly sanctimonious or hypocritical. He held Episcopalians and Baptist in equal disdain but his attacks on Baptists garnered even more sensation because he published the *Iconoclast* in Waco, home of Baylor University, Texas' premiere Baptist institution. He wrote that Baylor was "that great storm-center of misinformation." He is quoted in a local publication as saying, "I have nothing against Baptists. I just believe they were not held under long enough."

He wrote about a potential sex scandal involving the son-in-law of the president of Baylor University and he accused male faculty members of having sex with their female students saying Baylor was "a factory for the manufacture of ministers and Magdalene's."

Despite his screeds against fundamentalism and its preachers, he wrote very little about religion and did not attack theology. In one essay he deplored the commercialization of Christmas. In another he said, "Remember that God is everywhere—even in church." The subjects of his opinion pieces ranged from cats, to cows, to cold feet. He called politics an "unsavory stew of Macbeth's witches."

Brann's hatred included wealthy eastern socialites such as the Vanderbilts, anything having to do with Great Britain and its people, the New York social scene, and women. He reserved his most vicious remarks for African Americans, and after reading one of his essays it is hard to imagine his popularity even in a day when lynching was accepted in many communities.

Despite his many friends and supporters, the anger he stirred in Waco boiled over in October 1897 when a group of Baylor students kidnapped Brann and demanded he retract his statements about the university. A few days later a Baptist judge and two other men beat Brann. A year later a street fight between one of Brann's supporters and two Baylor loyalists resulted in the supporter losing his arm and both men in the Baylor faction being killed.

Finally, on April 1, 1898, Tom E. Davis, father of a female Baylor student, shot Brann in the back on one of Waco's downtown streets. Despite having taken a bullet, Brann turned and began firing at his assailant, emptying his borrowed revolver into the body of Davis, who while writhing in agony on the ground, continued firing until he emptied his gun. Both men died the following day.

The word TRUTH is engraved on Brann's monument in Waco's Oakwood Cemetery. Beneath the word is Brann's profile with a bullet hole in it. One source claims Brann's wife Carrie Belle moved the *Iconoclast* to Chicago and continued covering Texas issues.

Baylor University holds the William Cowper Brann Collection in its Texas Collection.

Bonnie Parker, Dead at Twenty-three

She was an honor student and loved poetry, but she dropped out of school, married Roy Thornton before her sixteenth birthday and had "Roy and Bonnie" tattooed on her right knee to celebrate the union. After a stormy two years, Thornton went to prison; Bonnie never divorced him and died five years later, still wearing Thornton's wedding ring. Those five years would make her a legend as the partner of another man.

Bonnie Elizabeth Parker was four in 1914 when her father died. Her mother moved her three children to "Cement City," an industrial area of West Dallas to be near relatives and to secure work as a seamstress. That rough and tumble area was where Bonnie met and married Thornton, and it was where the four-foot-ten inch, eighty-five pound Bonnie met Clyde Chestnut Barrow one year after Thornton went to prison.

Clyde Barrow had already made a name for himself with the Dallas police for a series of robberies. When he was arrested again, Bonnie wrote letters pleading with him to stay out of trouble, and then she smuggled a handgun to him that he used to escape. He was captured in a week and sent to Eastham Prison Farm in April 1930. One account says that to avoid hard labor on the prison's plantation, Barrow had a fellow inmate chop off two of Barrow's toes on his left foot. Another account says that before Barrow was paroled in February 1932, he beat another inmate to death for repeated sexual assaults. Whatever happened in that two-year prison experience, Clyde Barrow walked out a hardened criminal, bent on getting revenge for the treatment he had received.

Historians believe Bonnie stayed with Barrow and his gang, which had an ever-changing list of members, because she loved him. She willingly took part in the series of small robberies of stores and gas stations with the goal of eventually launching an attack to liberate Eastham prisoners. She was arrested with one of the gang members as they tried to steal guns from a hardware store. After a few months in jail, a grand jury failed to indict her, and she was released. While Bonnie was in jail, Barrow was accused of murder because he drove the car in a robbery in which a storeowner was shot and killed. A few months later, while Bonnie was visiting her mother in Dallas, Barrow and a couple of his cronies were at a dance in Oklahoma and ended up killing a deputy and wounding a sheriff—the first time the Barrow Gang killed a lawman. Before the reign ended, they had killed nine.

The crime spree continued. In the last six months of 1932 the gang killed five men, law officers and private citizens they were attempting to rob. The following March, Clyde Barrow's brother Buck was released from prison and the two couples—Bonnie and Clyde and Buck and his wife Blanche—moved into a garage apartment in Joplin, Missouri. Their loud drinking parties caused neighbors to grow suspicious and report them to authorities. On April 13, 1933, when five lawmen approached the apartment, the gang opened fire, killing a detective and fatally wounding a constable. As the gang ran for their car, Bonnie covered their escape by firing her M1918 Browning Automatic Rifle (their weapon of choice). They got away without any of their personal belongings, which included Buck's three-weeks-old parole papers, a large stash of weapons, one of Bonnie's poems, and a camera with several rolls of undeveloped film. Before the police gave the film to *The Joplin Globe*, Bonnie and Clyde were known primarily for their crimes in the Dallas area. But the pictures—swaggering attempts to look tough as they posed with their guns and Bonnie with a cigar in her mouth—made the Barrow Gang a front-page story across the nation.

For the next three months they made headlines, roaming from Texas to Minnesota, robbing banks and stealing cars, killing those who got in their way, and kidnapping both lawmen and robbery victims. Sometimes they released their hostages with enough money to get back home. While the public enjoyed following the increasingly violent behavior, the five members of the gang, forced to ride in one car, began to bicker, according to a prison account written years later by Blanche Barrow. There was no place to hide—restaurants and motels offered the threat of exposure—forcing them to cook on campfires and bathe in cold streams.

On June 10, 1933, Clyde missed a construction sign and flipped their car into a ravine. Bonnie received third-degree burns on her right leg, either from a fire or acid in the car's battery. While they waited in a tourist court near Fort Smith, Arkansas, for Bonnie's leg to heal, other gang members botched a robbery and killed the town marshal of Alma, Arkansas. Despite the serious condition of Bonnie's leg, they were forced to flee. It was July 18 when they checked into a tourist court near Kansas City, Missouri, and began a series of stunts that drew immediate attention. Blanche Barrow, while wearing jodhpur riding breeches—clothing unfamiliar to women in that area—registered for three guests, and five people openly stepped from the car. She paid with coins instead of bills for the lodging and for meals at the neighboring restaurant that was a favorite hangout for Missouri highway patrolmen. When Clyde went to a drugstore to purchase bandages and ointment for Bonnie's leg and crackers and cheese, the pharmacist became suspicious and notified authorities who were on the lookout for strangers shopping for such supplies.

Ironically, the ensuing gunfight resulted in a bullet hitting the horn on the lawmen's armored car, which caused them to think it was a cease-fire signal. Although they got away, both Blanche and Buck Barrow were severely injured. Clyde Barrow was so sure his brother would die from his injuries that Clyde dug his grave. Again, they drew attention to themselves by tossing out bloody bandages. When the authorities arrived, Bonnie and Clyde escaped on foot; Buck was shot and died later, and Blanche was taken into custody.

For six weeks the remaining three members of the gang moved from Colorado to Minnesota and south to Mississippi, committing small robberies and trying to replenish their arsenal. They returned in September to Dallas where their families tended to Bonnie's leg injuries, which never healed properly and caused her to spend the rest of her life hopping on one foot or being carried by Clyde. He stayed busy pulling off minor robberies until November 22, 1933, when the Dallas sheriff almost caught the pair as they headed to a family meeting. Clyde sensed that something was wrong and drove quickly away amid police machine gun fire that struck both he and Bonnie in the legs.

The next week, a Dallas grand jury indicted Bonnie and Clyde for the 1933 murder of the Tarrant County deputy—the first murder warrant issued for Bonnie Parker. On January 16, 1934, Clyde Barrow succeeded in reaching his goal of revenge on the Texas Department of Corrections by leading an escape of former gang members and other prisoners from the Eastham Prison. One of the escapees shot a prison officer, which focused the full power of state and federal authorities on the capture of Bonnie and Clyde.

Retired Texas Ranger Captain Frank A. Hamer was employed to get the Barrow Gang. A tenacious hunter, Hamer had the reputation for getting his man—during his career he suffered seventeen personal wounds and killed fifty-three criminals. For over two months Hamer stalked the gang, but he was always one or two towns behind. On April 1, 1934, Barrow and another gang member killed two Texas highway patrolmen. A witness, who was later discredited, claimed to have seen Bonnie laugh at the way the patrolman's "head bounced like a rubber ball." The story was picked up in the papers and

ueled the public outcry against Bonnie Parker. The Highway Patrol offered
$1,000 for "the dead bodies," and Governor Ma Ferguson put up another
$500 for each of the killers.

Bonnie closed the door on any possible claim for clemency a few days
ater when Clyde and another gang member killed a sixty-year-old Oklahoma
onstable and took the police chief as a hostage. Before they gave the chief
a clean shirt and let him go, Bonnie asked him to spread the word that she
did not smoke cigars (she chain-smoked Camels). The arrest warrant named
Clyde, a John Doe, and Bonnie as the killers of the constable.

Frank Hamer had been studying the movements of the gang. He
realized that they visited family, moving in a circle along the edge of five mid-
western states, enabling them to escape without law enforcement being able
to follow them across the state line. He estimated when it would be time to
visit a gang family member in Louisiana. Hamer amassed an armor-piercing
arsenal, a posse of four Texas and two Louisiana officers and lay in wait on
a rural road near Arcadia, Louisiana. The father of one of the former gang
members, who later claimed that he was forced to cooperate, flagged down
the speeding Ford carrying only Bonnie Parker and Clyde Barrow at 9:15 a.m.
on May 23, 1934. The posse opened fire, hitting the stolen vehicle with 167
bullets. Reports said that Bonnie's bullet-riddled body was found holding a
machine gun, a sandwich, and a pack of cigarettes. Clyde, whose body was
barely recognizable, was still clutching a revolver.

The death scene erupted in chaos with souvenir hunters scavenging
pieces of clothing, hair, and shell casings. They were not buried together as
they wished, but in separate Dallas cemeteries. Mobs descended on the Parker
home, and a throng of twenty thousand people made it almost impossible for
the family to reach the Dallas gravesite. Although thousands crowded both
funeral homes hoping to see the bodies, the Barrow family held a private
service and buried Clyde next to his brother Buck. They shared a simple
granite marker with their names and the words that had been selected by
Clyde: "Gone but not forgotten."

No one will ever know the real extent of Bonnie Parker's involvement in
the crimes of the Barrow Gang. Some gang members claimed that she never
killed anyone, but she was involved in eight murders, seven kidnappings,
less than a dozen bank heists, many armed robberies and car thefts, and a
major jailbreak. One account says that the largest haul of any of the robberies
netted only $1,500.

Flapper Bandit

Just before Christmas in 1926, Rebecca Bradley, a twenty-one-year old student at the University of Texas in Austin, decided to rob banks to pay her college tuition. First, she set fire to a vacant house near downtown Round Rock and rushed into the nearby bank thinking the employees would be distracted by the blaze. When that plan failed, she drove south of Austin to the Farmers National Bank in Buda and pretended to be a newspaper reporter as she made careful notes while interviewing local farmers about their crops and government policies. She secured permission to use the bank's typewriter inside the teller's cage. After a time, she pulled a .32 automatic, herded both employees into the walk-in safe and fled with $1,000 in five-dollar bills. Her Ford Model T coupe got stuck in the mud on the way back to Austin; the bank employees used a screwdriver to jiggle their way to freedom; and by the time she reached home she was arrested.

Newspapers across the country went wild reporting on the pretty little coed who they dubbed the "flapper bandit." Rebecca's story soon emerged. With the help of a student loan and part time jobs she had earned a bachelor's degree in history and was beginning a master's degree program when her mother became ill and moved to Austin to live with Rebecca. To further complicate matters, Rebecca had been secretly married for a year to her high school sweetheart Otis Rogers, who had just graduated from the UT law school and was working for a firm in Amarillo.

Justice ground forward as a witness in the arson trial testified to seeing Rebecca enter the vacant house and leave again just before the fire erupted. The jury could not agree on a verdict. The December 1927 trial for the bank robbery resulted in a conviction and maximum sentence of fourteen years. Finally, her husband Otis Rogers joined the defense team that won an appeal and after lengthy legal wrangling she was granted a new trial. While many professionals wondered at the sanity of a young woman who would rob a bank, her husband actually argued that she was insane at the time of the robbery. One account claims that he pleaded passionately for the court to "hang her high or send her to the electric chair" instead of allowing her to suffer in prison. Again, a hung jury failed to convict. Before it all ended in September 1929, Rebecca Bradley Rogers had been tried four times for either arson or armed robbery.

Later, the sheriff reported that as he and Rebecca drove through Buda she laughed and said, "I have a whole lot to live down, but not as much as hose men back there who let a little girl hold them up with an empty gun."

Rebecca Bradley Rogers became a free woman the day before she gave birth to their first child. She and Otis moved to Fort Worth where he became a successful criminal defense attorney with Rebecca serving as his legal secretary.

John R. Brinkley, Medical Charlatan

By the time John Romulus (changed to John Richard) Brinkley came to Texas in 1933, he had amassed a fortune and become famous for transplanting goat glands into his male patients. A natural salesman with a smooth voice and plenty of confidence, Brinkley had been performing his $750 "restorative" operation at his clinic in Milford, Kansas, and offering medical advice and selling his patent medicine over his Kansas radio station, KFKB. In addition to long lectures on rejuvenation and testimonials from satisfied patients, Brinkley's station featured country music (including The Carter Family), and fundamentalist preachers. Brinkley conducted a "Medical Question Box" that allowed him to diagnose ills and prescribe medicine over the radio. The program became so popular that many pharmacists cashed in on the deal by selling Brinkley's concoctions at inflated prices and returned an estimated $14,000 a week to Brinkley. Finally, Dr. Morris Fishbein, executive secretary of the American Medical Association (AMA) and editor of *The Journal of the American Medical Association* (JAMA), called Brinkley a quack. Brinkley countered, claiming the AMA was a "meat-cutters' union" and said its members were jealous of him because he was taking their business.

Brinkley had tried unsuccessfully for years to get a medical degree from one of the diploma mills, even traveling to Europe in 1925 in search of an institution that would give him an honorary degree. After several places turned him down, an Italian institution finally awarded him a degree, only to have it revoked by none other than Benito Mussolini at the urging of Brinkley's nemesis, Dr. Morris Fishbein.

Fishbein's accusations finally forced the Kansas State Medical Board to revoke Brinkley's medical license, and the Federal Radio Commission (FRC) refused to renew his broadcasting license. Undaunted, Brinkley decided to fix the problem by running for governor and replacing the Kansas Medical

Board. He barnstormed around the state in his private plane and promised Kansans free textbooks, lower taxes, a lake in every county, and more rainfall. Meanwhile he relocated his family and all his medical operation to Villa Acuña, Mexico, across the Rio Grande from Del Rio, Texas. He narrowly lost the governor's race because as a write-in candidate, many of his votes were disqualified for not being written "exactly right."

Using the powerful radio transmitter across the border in Mexico, Brinkley broadcast his message to listeners all over the Midwest. In his new enterprise he offered six small vials of colored water for $100, which apparently aided the libido. He performed fewer goat gland transplants, offering instead a "commercial glandular preparation." He began prostate operations (charging up to $1,000 per procedure) and started using a mercurochrome shot and pills to restore youthful vigor.

Brinkley sold air time to advertisers at $1,700 an hour, which encouraged new hucksters selling anything from life insurance to religious items such as autographed pictures of Jesus Christ. When mind readers and fortune-tellers were banned from U.S. radio by the FRC, they followed Brinkley's lead and began opening "border blasters" across the border in Mexico.

By 1936 Brinkley's lavish lifestyle included a Del Rio mansion sitting on sixteen acres, a dozen Cadillacs, a greenhouse, a garden with a foaming fountain surrounded by 8,000 bushes, and a pool with a ten-foot diving tower. It has been estimated that Brinkley earned $12 million from the time he moved to Del Rio in 1933 until 1938 when his empire began to crumble. A rival moved to town and began offering similar procedures at greatly reduced prices. When city officials refused to put his competitor out of business, Brinkley moved to Little Rock, Arkansas, and opened a hospital.

In 1938 Fishbein was back again, publishing a series called "Modern Medical Charlatans" that completely repudiated Brinkley's career and his medical credentials. Brinkley sued Fishbein for libel and lost, with the jury finding that Brinkley "should be considered a charlatan and a quack in the ordinary, well-understood meaning of those words." That verdict opened a series of lawsuits that reached a purported $3 million. The IRS began investigating Brinkley for tax fraud. In 1941 Brinkley declared bankruptcy; an agreement between the U.S. and Mexico resulted in Brinkley's Mexican radio station being shut down, and the U.S. Post Office opened an investigation for mail fraud.

The famed healer, known by some of his Kansas followers as "The Milford Messiah," the man who was credited with over 16,000 goat gland transplants, who wore a goatee and named his Milford baseball team the Brinkley Goats, developed a blood clot that required amputating one of his legs. Then he suffered a series of heart attacks. Before the mail fraud case went to trial Brinkley, penniless, died of heart failure in San Antonio on May 26, 1942.

In an article written by Dr. Joe Schwarcz, he claims that Brinkley's last words were: "If Dr. Fishbein goes to heaven, I want to go the other way."

16

Bells Are Ringing

Bell of Many Lives

St. Mark's Lutheran Church in Cuero boasts three bells in its arched façade. The small bronze bell, the one on the lower right, began life on the *Reliance*, a merchant ship sailing as part of the Morgan Steamship Line between New Orleans and the thriving port of Indianola. In 1856, Indianola residents were enjoying a party aboard the *Reliance* docked at the end of one of the port's long piers extending into Matagorda Bay when a fire broke out. All the partygoers escaped unharmed and as they watched the burning ship sink into the shallow water they heard the ringing of its tiny bell. The Lutherans needed a bell for their new church, and with Morgan Steamship Lines' permission, some of the members dove into the bay to retrieve the bell for the church steeple.

Nine years later, during the Civil War, Union troops occupied Indianola for three months. While confiscating everything of value to take with them, a group of Union soldiers climbed the Lutheran church steeple and tossed the little bell to the ground, intending to return for it as they loaded the other booty.

That night, some of the church members quietly retrieved the bell and buried it. During the next ten years Charles Morgan, the shipping tycoon, gave bells to most of the Indianola churches, which probably explains why the little bell remained buried and forgotten.

In 1875 a terrible hurricane wrecked Indianola, destroying most all the church buildings. Many residents moved inland to places like the new railhead town of Cuero. Then, another devastating storm and fire in 1886 turned Indianola into a ghost town, forcing its residents to give up and move inland.

230

Lutherans in Cuero, after holding services for several years in the German school, finally built their first church in 1889. As the building neared completion and talk centered on the need for a bell in the handsome steeple, one of the members remembered helping bury the little bronze bell almost twenty-five years earlier. He led a group to the site where the little bell waited, and they proudly mounted it in the steeple. For about five years the bell called the congregation to worship until a member donated a much larger bell.

Again, the little bronze bell took a new life summoning volunteers of the Cuero Fire Department. After several years, the volunteer firemen installed a modern alert system, and an observant church member discovered the little bell tossed in a trash heap. Upon completion of the present church in 1939, the little bell found its final home as one of three bells in the peal.

Serving as St. Mark's Prayer Bell, it rings when worshipers pray the Lord's Prayer and it tolls softly at the conclusion of funeral services as the casket is moved from the front of the church to the narthex.

St. Mark's Lutheran Church history claims the little bronze bell as a symbol for the calling of God's people—to continue serving as circumstances change, even after being buried and resurrected or thrown on a trash heap.

Bell Saved from Ghost Town

The bell sitting on a stand next to the Port Lavaca United Methodist church has a colorful past. Originally, it belonged to the Indianola Methodist Church, but a hurricane in 1875 destroyed much of the thriving seaport and most of the church buildings. Although Indianola continued as a port city, the Methodists never rebuilt. In 1886 another horrible storm and subsequent fire turned Indianola into a ghost town.

That 1886 storm also caused major damage forty miles inland to the Victoria Methodist Church. After the congregation completed repairs to their building, they sent a group of men down to Indianola to retrieve "the finest bell in Texas" off the wrecked Methodist Church.

Melinda Harris, a tiny black woman, the only surviving member of the destroyed church, met the men and told them the bell was hers and they couldn't have it. They returned to Victoria empty-handed.

Melinda Harris moved up the coast to Port Lavaca and when the Methodists built a new building, she gave the old Indianola bell to the congregation. Old timers remembered her as Aunt Malindy, owner of a white boarding house. She went about town wearing a starched white apron and sat on the back row at the Methodist church every Sunday morning.

The *Frontier Times* reprinted a story written in 1925 by Reverend M.A. Dunn in which he says when he arrived to serve the Port Lavaca church in 1901, a little black woman named Malinda Harris came to him wanting to pay to have the church painted. When the work was completed and he went to collect the payment, Aunt Malindy drew thirteen $10 bills from an old Bible. He said the money was so stiff that he thought of Noah's Ark. Then, he realized that those bills had been gathered from the floodwater of the Indianola storm and pressed because they stood up like cardboards. When Malinda Harris died in 1914 she left her property consisting of one-half lot worth $250 and personal property worth $25 to the church.

The Methodist congregation outgrew its site and moved in 1958 to a new location. The sales agreement for the old property called for the congregation to take the church bell. The new facility didn't have a sanctuary, only a fellowship hall and classrooms so the bell was forgotten. Almost.

L.E. Gross didn't forget. He said he was a country boy and never got to enjoy a church bell until he moved to Port Lavaca. He nagged his men's class until they raised the money to hire a crane and move the bell to the new church site where it was placed on the ground and covered with a tarpaulin. In 1975, the church built a sanctuary and L.E. Gross had not forgotten that bell. Again, he nagged his men's class until they raised the money to repair the old bell and mount it on a brick pedestal. L.E. Gross served for the rest of his life as "ringer-of-the-bell" before every worship service.

Reverend Dunn, in his article said: "Today, if you are in Port Lavaca, and hear the Methodist Church bell ring, you will hear the bell that survived the storms of Indianola both 1875 and 1886. It will tell you that the workmen are buried, but the Church of God still survives."

Readers Guide

1. Why did the author lay out the tales under chapter headings such as "Grand Treasures" and "Legends in Their Day?" Was that partitioning a satisfactory way for you to read history?

2. Did you find it easier to remember the Texas history presented in story-form, or did you miss the chronological format of most history books?

3. Would you have arranged these stories under different headings? If so, what headings would you suggest?

4. Do you have a better understanding of Texas early history after reading the tales in the chapter titled, "Texas in the Beginning?"

5. Do you think women received adequate coverage in "Power in a Skirt," or should their stories have been blended in with the other chapters?

6. Were you shocked or surprised by some of the revelations?

7. Did you want to visit some of the locales after learning of events that occurred there?

8. Were you aware that there were communes in Texas?

9. Were there stories that you wish had been included? What are they? Under what chapter would they have fit?

10. Would you have selected "Bells Are Ringing" for the final chapter?

CPSIA information can be obtained
at www.ICGtesting.com
Printed in the USA
LVOW11s0231250317
528446LV00007B/9/P